"GO DOWN, OLD HANNAH"

D0746046

NUMBER

25

Jack and Doris Smothers Series
in Texas History, Life, and Culture

"GO DOWN, OLD HANNAH"

The Living History of African American Texans

NAOMI MITCHELL CARRIER

FOREWORD BY John E. Fleming

UNIVERSITY OF TEXAS PRESS I AUSTIN

Publication of this work was made possible in part by support from the J. E. Smothers, Sr., Memorial Foundation and the National Endowment for the Humanities.

Copyright © 2010 by Naomi Mitchell Carrier
All rights reserved
Printed in the United States of America
First edition, 2010

Requests for permission to reproduce material
from this work should be sent to:
Permissions
University of Texas Press
P.O. Box 7819
Austin, TX 78713-7819
www.utexas.edu/utpress/about/bpermission.html

⊗ The paper used in this book meets the minimum
requirements of ANSI/NISO Z39.48-1992 (R1997)
(Permanence of Paper).

Library of Congress Cataloging-in-Publication Data
Carrier, Naomi Mitchell.
"Go down, Old Hannah" : the living history of
African American Texans / Naomi Mitchell Carrier ;
foreword by John E. Fleming. 1st ed.
p.   cm.
(Jack and Doris Smothers series
in Texas history, life, and culture ; no. 25)
Includes bibliographical references.
ISBN 978-0-292-72133-3 (cloth : alk. paper)
ISBN 978-0-292-72242-2 (pbk. : alk. paper)
1. African Americans—Texas—Drama.
2. Slavery—Texas—Drama.   I. Title.
PS3603.A77447G6   2010
812'.6—dc22   2009015672

TO LANGSTON AND ROBESON,

Their children,

And their children's children

They called the sun Old Hannah because it was hot and they just give it a name. That's what the boys called it when I was down in prison. I didn't hear it before I went down there. The boys were talking about Old Hannah—I kept looking and I didn't see no Hannah, but they looked up and said, "That's the sun."

HUDDIE "LEADBELLY" LEDBETTER,
composer and lyricist of "Go Down, Old Hannah"

CONTENTS

Foreword ix | *Acknowledgments* xi | *Introduction* xiii

PART I: CELEBRATIONS
Overview   3
Jumpin' Juba: Uncle Bubba and Mammy Bell Jump de Broom   8
Christmas at Varner-Hogg: Patton Plantation Memories   17

PART II: FAMILY BREAKUP
Overview   23
Arcy Makes Room for Judith Martin: The Breakup of a Slave Family   29
A Little Slave for Sale — Cheap!   38
Sweet By and By: Barrington Farm Chronicle   45

PART III: RUNNING AWAY
Overview   75
Arcy Attempts Escape   81
Fugitives of Passion: On the Texas Underground Railroad to Mexico   86

PART IV: BATTLES
Overview   101
Hell or High Water: Brit Bailey Heads Off Stephen F. Austin   104
Still Am A'Risin': The Battle of Velasco and the Vigil at Bolivar   110

PART V: CIVIL WAR
Overview   131
Plantation Liendo: Civil War Reenactment   139
Cane Cutter Country: The Saga of the Lake Jackson Plantation   149

PART VI: EMANCIPATION

Overview   185

Slav'ry Chain Done Broke at Las'   193

Porch Politics: Sam Houston Style   201

PART VII: RECONSTRUCTION

Overview   215

Social Politics in Victorian Texas: A Living History Interpretation of African Americans and Their Responsibilities   224

Juneteenth at the George Ranch   235

Conclusion   243

Appendix: Lesson Plans and Additional Resources   247

Crossword Puzzle Answer Keys   304

Notes   313

FOREWORD

Once in a while, one encounters an author whose talent for bringing history to life far exceeds what the average historian is able to accomplish in hundreds of pages of narrative. "*Go Down, Old Hannah*": *The Living History of African American Texans* contains fifteen original plays that are vibrant testimonials to over one hundred years of our past. The key to these exceptional narratives is that they were conceived as plays and performed at the historical sites for which they were written.

Naomi Carrier is the founder and director of Talking Back Living History Theatre, and actors have been presenting her plays since 1998. The plays in this book cover diverse subject matter, ranging from slave celebrations, family breakups, and running away to the Civil War, emancipation, and Reconstruction. Carrier's talent for bringing historical figures to life is exceptional. She places faces and names on individuals long forgotten. We are fortunate to have her preserve our cultural heritage, which includes spirituals, ballads, and dances that are often sad, sometimes jubilant, and always relevant.

The book's title is taken from the song "Go Down, Old Hannah," which was made popular by a volume of Leadbelly songs released by the Library of Congress in 1994. Hannah was a name for the sun, and "Go Down, Old Hannah" is a song about post-slavery convict labor, where "they was working women like they do the men." The first verse reads:

Why don't you go down old Hannah,
well, well, well,
Don't you rise no more, don't you rise no more,
Why don't you go down old Hannah,
Hannah, Don't you rise no more.

These plays about African American history in Texas are important because they are a reflection of African American history nationally. Carrier's expert research and skills as a teacher/performer have allowed her to interweave into her narratives the ways in which the black history of Texas is both unique and similar to that of the nation.

As a museum director, I am aware that exhibitions cannot, by themselves, tell the whole story of our past. Museum educators know that along with exhibitions, there must be both moving and still images, exhibition catalogues, and educational materials for students and teachers. Talking Back Theatre has added another dimension to museum interpretation by presenting performances at museums and historical sites.

"*Go Down, Old Hannah*" is well written and can serve a wide range of audiences. We are fortunate that people like Naomi Mitchell Carrier exist. She has provided us with an entertaining alternative way of learning history.

JOHN E. FLEMING, PHD
Director Emeritus, Cincinnati Museum Center
President of the Association for the Study of African American Life and History

ACKNOWLEDGMENTS

In the summer of 1989, *I Am Annie Mae* was the featured performance for the Texas Playwright's Festival at Stages Repertory Theatre in Houston, and it ran for thirty performances. You may ask, what does this have to do with living history? Well, Annie Mae Hunt recalled and reported some one hundred and forty years of her family's history in taped interviews with Ruthe Winegarten. These interviews comprise what historians call an oral history. Oral histories are considered a primary source for information, as opposed to a secondary source, such as a newspaper or magazine article about a person or event. All of the plays in this volume are a combination of information collected from primary and secondary resources.

Our many performances of *I Am Annie Mae* across the state of Texas and throughout other places in the country brought history alive for numerous audiences. The musical received much acclaim and some awards for its insight into the past. First published in 1983, the University of Texas Press published the book again in 1996. I owe many of my accomplishments as a playwright and actress to the recognition this work received. Most recently I have performed it as a one-woman show after years of performing as pianist and musical director for casts of up to fifteen persons. Although the original full production is ninety minutes, we have developed a one-hour show, several excerpts, and a children's version that premiered at the Houston Children's Museum in 1998. The history embodied in *I Am Annie Mae* is as important today as it was twenty years ago, if not more so.

I will be eternally indebted to my father who nourished my interest in American history, to my mother who taught me to read and to play the piano when I was four years old, to the late Ruthe Winegarten for her continued support, to the late Annie Mae Hunt for her infallible memory, to Dr. Delmer Rogers, my mentoring music professor who supported my lectures at the University of Texas, to my students who were so eager to learn history, and to their parents who consistently supported my desire to teach them by providing me with the supplies and materials I needed. I owe a special debt of posthumous gratitude to Eugene Carrier, my husband of almost thirty years, who carried me on his travels while he played keyboards with the B. B. King band, and to our two sons, Langston Fidel and Robeson Cabral, who kept me company in his absence and still are my favorite company keepers. I am also indebted to Allen Grundy, my former spouse and business partner and the director of some of these plays at the various historic sites, state parks, museums, and festivals where they were performed. Without his assistance and many hours of research, much of this work would have been impossible. There are a number of actors and actresses, technicians, directors, librarians, museum administrators, and presenters whose research, imagination, and support have made performances of these plays possible, particularly directors James Reed Faulkner, the late Larry Durbin, and Dallas Jones, and actors Alex Gardner, Norelia Reed, Devonae Servance, Charles Fordyce, Rick Burford, Paul Mathews, Dolores Walker, Jia Taylor, and Elliott Jordan. I am continually indebted to the late Rita Starpattern, the late Boyd Vance, Dr. Patrick Nolan, Bill Irwin, Mark Texel, Will Griffin, Barry Hutcheson, Jeff Hutchinson, Bob Handy, Jamie Murray, Bruce Taylor-Hille, Michael Moore, Betty Hodges, Kijana Wiseman-Fusilier, Patricia Smith Prather, the late Gwendolyn McDonald Jackson, Joan Few, Dr. Randolph Campbell, Alecya Gallaway, Eleanor Caldwell, Ken Hammond, Fayette Mitchell Harvin, Brenda Jarrett, Lori Amare, Bobbie Greer, Michael Bailey, Brenda Jarrett, and Larry and Jeanne Byrd Mitchell.

tinction as a slave state is often lost to the southwestern image of cowboy culture. Hence the history that illumines the *peculiar institution* in Texas is off the record. And consequently, the enslaved pioneers who contributed to clearing the fields, building the roads, and harvesting cotton and cane have had little or no significance. It is as if a whole chapter of African American triumph has gone largely unrecognized. Hopefully the plays in this book will shed light on some individuals whose personal stories offer a fresh glimpse into the period between 1821 and 1930. The plays are grouped together in seven chapters covering the broad subjects of celebrations, family breakup, running away, battles, the Civil War, emancipation, and Reconstruction, each with an overview and production notes. An appendix with lesson plans for each play is also included for teachers and students desiring further study.

Concurrent with the absence or scarcity of African American history from the textbooks, my own knowledge of that history was filled with doubt and wonder, with far too many missing links. As a young college student at the University of North Texas in the late sixties, the urgency of that time during the civil rights movement encouraged me to learn more about myself. Exactly who were my people? Why were they treated differently? Where had they come from and what had been their experiences? My parents, like others before them, simply did not talk too much about the past, except for some anecdotal stories about loved ones. Those painful stories of old were left in the past, while we grew up with fresh hopes for things to be different in the future, unburdened by slavery and Jim Crow. My research carried me further and further back, back to slavery, back to Africa, to the shores of Elmina from which many in chains embarked to the New World, and today, I look at the period of enslavement as an empowerment, a triumph over insurmountable obstacles by the strongest, by the bravest, by those most clever to survive.

I hope these stories will encourage other students of history, from every culture and circumstance, for these stories not only illumine the African Americans involved—the blacks, the Negroes and the coloreds—but the whites and the Mexicans, all of whose cultures were interwoven as they depended on each other to survive the conditions of wilderness, work, and war. The American Indians, though not written about at length on these pages, are involved also because it was they who the European settlers displaced. As all these cultural threads weave themselves in and around the era of colonization—the Texas War for Independence, the Civil War, and Reconstruction—relationships were the guiding force of human interaction, and the utilization of skills and human labor guided politics and economics. Both then and now relationships triumph over race and skills triumph over racism. The undeniable strength of African American ingenuity rises to the surface in each of these stories, and in the end, slavery is not to be scorned or ridiculed but revisited as an example of achievement and victory.

It all came together for me during three particular episodes in 2007: (1) my trip to the Gold Coast of Ghana, West Africa; (2) two trips to Belize, Central America; and (3) a tour of Nottoway Plantation on the Mississippi River in White Castle, Louisiana. Admittedly, I knew very little about Africa prior to going there. In addition, following my return from Africa, I was employed by the Houston International Festival to do research on African civilizations to 1900. After these experiences, gaps in my understanding of the African and African American experience came together in one continuum of historical experiences, exemplified in similarities between two fishing villages and two slave castles: the slave castle at Elmina, Ghana, a small fishing village; Ladyville, Belize, another small fishing village; and the Nottoway Plantation castle, just south of Baton Rouge at the edge of sugar cane fields, where the fifty-three-thousand-square-foot mansion, the largest plantation home in the South, stands overlooking the Mississippi River.

A culture transplanted? Many cultures transplanted, European and African. The combination of prevailing colonial influences, of domination, and of resistance has yielded a history that reflects the indomitable spirit that encouraged Africans in America to be free to control their own destiny. It is that spirit that is celebrated in each of the plays presented here.

Each of these plays represents a commission by a historic site to create a research-based vignette that shows the inclusiveness of African Americans to the history of Texas. What they invariably show is the interdependence of all cultures in the site portrayed: the relationships of master to the enslaved, of the enslaved to the landowners, of master to his family, of enslaved families to each other, of people to the land. All these themes are central to each play. At a time in our history where the economics of land ownership included owning humans, the dynamics of domination inevitably resulted in resistance. Slaves in Texas ran away to Mexico. They were often assisted by Mexicans, sometimes by Germans, and at times by American Indians. The close proximity of Mexico necessitated stricter controls for Texas plantation owners, especially in East and South Texas. The ex-slave narratives yield many stories about feeding runaways and crossing the Rio Grande. Today when stories of the Underground Railroad come up, I tell people about these heroic escapes to Mexico and they are unbelievably surprised; they've "never heard no such a'thang." This is representative of the many other things they never heard of, like the freedom colonies that surfaced following slavery and during the reconstruction of African American lives. Hopefully these plays will help dispel some of the myths associated with slavery and emancipation, particularly in Texas. I am even more hopeful that the characters herein will add some much-needed humanity to the enslaved as being intelligent and sensitive individuals who loved each other in the face of severe obstacles; who never lost sight of freedom even when forced to stay on with their masters following emancipation; and who transformed their African culture into a new culture, fully Afrocentric in nature, to create new celebrations and new music and a whole new literature that celebrates folk heroes.

Two significant events put African American history in the spotlight in the year 2009: the inauguration of Barack Obama and the bicentennial of Abraham Lincoln's birth. As Americans and Texans (who were so much in the spotlight during the Bush presidency) came to grips with the reality of the election of their first African American president, there was no end to the historical comparisons of Obama and Lincoln, particularly with regard to the troubled times during which each took office. Though some conservatives question the comparison, there are several undeniable similarities between the sixteenth and the forty-fourth presidents: both were tall lawyers from Illinois, though born in other states, both grew up with one parent absent, and both entered the office of the president with only eight years of experience in the legislature. All of this, plus the whistle-stop train trips they took to their respective inaugurations, highlighted the drama surrounding America's race relations prior to the Civil War — a war that President Lincoln opposed — and the importance of race relations prior to the election of the first African American president, Barack Obama — who was opposed to the war in Iraq. These events propelled America into a post-racial society and brought us closer to the revolutionary theme of the founding fathers that all men are created equal. They also prompted many of us to question the validity of American democracy in light of its institution of slavery. African Americans began to want to know more about their history, and they questioned how that history is taught in schools and universities, as well as how they are portrayed in the media.

(top left) **Maceo D. Mitchell;**
(top right) **Ruthe L. Winegarten;**
(left) **Naomi Carrier and Annie
Mae Hunt**

Texas is annually in the spotlight because of Juneteenth, the only holiday that is a reminder of emancipation. When we celebrate Juneteenth, a state holiday in Texas and many other states, we celebrate equality for ourselves and for our nation. On this day, we recognize the importance of the Emancipation Proclamation and freedom from slavery in a nation capable of overcoming the ideologies of racism. Wherever we go we carry Juneteenth with us, because it is a part of who we are. We are proud of what we have accomplished, and we are proud of the living history of African American Texans.

The names of most primary characters in these plays are real. Giving them faces, feelings, intelligence, and dignity makes the events that happened to them live again. It is my fond hope that these stories will inspire readers to dig deeper into the history of their communities, to research their families, to conduct interviews, to record oral histories, and to preserve more stories. In the words of an African proverb, "Until the lion writes his story, the tale of the hunt will forever glorify the hunter."

"GO DOWN, OLD HANNAH"

CELEBRATIONS

OVERVIEW

The enslaved used many mundane occasions as opportunities for celebration. The end of a harvest for any type of crop became an opportunity for celebration; thus, corn shuckings, cane cuttings, and cotton pickings were times for "getting out the fiddle and tight'ning up the bow; sweeping out de barn and dancing round de flo'."

Most Texas slaves lived on farms and plantations and worked long hours clearing land, cultivating crops, and taking care of innumerable chores. Many had Saturday afternoons free from labor, but only Sundays, the Fourth of July, and the week of Christmas were regarded virtually without exception as days off.[1]

Gill Ruffin, who lived in Houston County, said he "didn't know any more about a holiday than climbing up a tree backward," but most slaves were more fortunate. Bondsmen traditionally did not work during the week from Christmas to New Year's Day.[2]

Harre Quarles, quoted in the *The Texas Slave Narratives*, says that "Us got one day a week and Christmas Day, was all de holiday us ever heered of, and us couldn't go anywhere 'cept us have pass from our massa to 'nother." And according to Agatha Babino, slaves "had Sunday off. Christmas was off, too. Dey give us chicken and flour den. But most holidays de white folks has company. Dat mean more work for us."

Slave celebrations were dependent on what slave owners allowed, but the way slaves celebrated was in keeping with African traditions. African traditions consist of numerous celebrations, and emphasize harvests especially. Even today's Kwanzaa festival, celebrated in many African American households the week following Christmas, commemorates the fall harvest. As African cultural traditions were transformed in the New World, corn shuckings, log rollings, hog killings, cane cuttings, and weddings became the big events for plantation slaves. The most memorable celebrations for many slaves were corn shuckings. Genovese argues that "with the exception of the Christmas holiday—and not always that—former slaves recalled having looked forward to corn-shucking most of all."[3]

Food and music were the heart and soul of a corn shucking. Blassingame reports that "the corn shucking was a combination of labor and recreation," when slaves enjoyed meeting their friends and lovers "away from the quarters, drinking the cider or hard liquor, eating cakes and pies, telling tall stories, and singing hilarious songs." All forms of work produced songs, but "corn shucking produced more secular songs."[4]

Some slaves, while grateful for the respite, did not excuse their masters for their enslavement. Jenny Proctor reported, "We had some co'n shuckins sometimes but de white folks gits de fun and de nigger gits de work."[5] And the corn shuckings still amounted to work for the slaves. According to Robert Shepherd of Kentucky:

> Dem corn shuckings was sure 'nough big times. When us got all de corn gathered up and put in great long piles, den de getting ready started . . . Master would send us out to get the slaves from de farms round about dere. De place was all lit up with light-wood knot torches and bonfires and dere was 'citement aplenty when all niggers get to singin' and shoutin' as dey made the shucks fly.[6]

A log rolling was another occasion for communal work followed by a celebration. Growing plantations required more and more land, so cutting down trees and clearing logs and brush was a necessity. Eugene Genovese relates that it was customary for neighboring owners and their slaves to help when land needed clearing. A tall pile was made from the logs and brush and a huge fire built around which all gathered for food and drink provided by the host.

Everyone had a favorite celebration. Only "hog killing rivaled corn shucking," according to Joseph Holmes, because that was when "we useta have sho' nuff meat."[7]

The end of the cane harvest was likewise celebrated. Sometimes the tallest sugarcane would be left standing, and a blue ribbon would be tied around it. Celebrators would sing to and dance around this special stalk of cane before it was finally cut and a slave would hand it to the master as a present and receive a drink in return.[8]

A slave wedding was the epitome of celebrations because many slaves were not permitted to marry. When they had the permission of their masters to "jump the broom," then everyone, black and white, from the fields, the big house, and surrounding farms came to "jine in" the celebration. When and where marriage *was* allowed, writes Blassingame, "Unfortunately for most slaves, the master had the final word in regard to their marriage partners." He further states:

> The marriage ceremony in most cases consisted of the slaves simply getting the master's permission and moving into a cabin together. The masters of domestic servants either had the local white minister or the black plantation preacher perform the marriage ceremony. And then gave a sumptuous feast in their parlors for the slave guests. Afterwards the slaves had long dances in the quarters in honor of the couple.[9]

Many a humble preacher sealed the vows of holy matrimony with the words:

> Dark an' stormy may come de wedder;
> I jines dis he-male an' dis she-male togedder.
> Let none, but Him dat makes de thunder,
> Put dis he-male and dis she-male asunder.
> I darefor 'nounce you bofe de same.
> Be good, go 'long, an' keep up yo' name.

The most important celebrations echoed "Free at Las'!" and occurred following the announcement of emancipation. While part six of this book is dedicated entirely to emancipation and part seven contains a play on the subject (*Juneteenth at the George Ranch*, which is set in 1930 and focuses on the annual festivities that honor the Emancipation Proclamation of June 19, 1865), we cannot overstate its importance as a reason for celebrating. Juneteenth celebrations still occur, not only in Texas but all over the United States. Earlier than 1930, however, Juneteenth was more of an occasion for political awareness with celebration secondary to a united call for education, self-reliance, and independent land ownership. *Juneteenth at the George Ranch* is a reminder of those late-nineteenth- and early-twentieth-century celebrations and is intended to preserve the songs and the spirit of a one-room schoolhouse or church house celebration.

On the subject of emancipation, Felix Haywood, a Texas ex-slave, told interviewers at his San Antonio home,

Hallelujah broke out —
Abe Lincoln freed the nigger
With the gun and the trigger,
And I ain't going to get whipped no more.
I got my ticket,
Leaving the thicket,
And I'm heading for the Golden shore.

Everybody went wild. We all felt like heroes, and nobody had made us that way but ourselves. We were free . . . They seemed to want to get closer to freedom . . . like it was a place or a city.[10]

Susan Ross, who was born in Magnolia Springs, Texas, told her interviewers:

When my oldest brother heard we were free, he gave a whoop, ran, and jumped a high fence, and told mammy good-bye. Then he grabbed me up and hugged and kissed me and said, "Brother is gone, don't expect you'll ever see me anymore." I don't know where he went, but I never did see him again.[11]

The enslaved have all too often been portrayed as happy and contented because they had a great propensity for singing and dancing their troubles away. Celebrations are explored in this first section because in my early experiences with living-history portrayals, back in 1994, I found that a performance including a celebration was less intimidating to audiences not ready to confront slavery in Texas, and therefore was more likely to be accepted than the harsher realities of involuntary servitude. However, there has been a slight change in the attitude toward slavery and considerably more dialogue since then. Slavery *happened*; it's a part of history, however uncomfortable, and must be faced in our efforts to come to terms with racial reconciliation and solidarity as Texans, and as Americans.

Jumpin' Juba: Uncle Bubba and Mammy Bell Jump de Broom, set in 1824, continues to be the most popular play at the Talking Back Living History Theatre. It makes people feel warm and fuzzy, and audiences always enjoy dancing the juba. While the play has only four characters, the singing and dancing involves the entire audience.

Christmas at Varner-Hogg: Patton Plantation Memories, set in the 1840s, is a somber soliloquy of a young mother eagerly awaiting the visit of her husband. When married slaves lived on separate farms or plantations, they were apart during the week and saw each other only on weekends and special occasions.[12] *Christmas at Varner-Hogg* is one such annual visit.

JUMPIN' JUBA
Uncle Bubba and Mammy Bell Jump de Broom

Written for Second Annual Austin Town Festival, 1998, and
sponsored by the Brazoria County Historical Museum

CHARACTERS

UNCLE BUBBA: slave to Brit Bailey since he was a young boy; age c. 45–50
MAMMY BELL: Uncle Bubba's wife, age c. 35–40
BROTHUH SOLOMON: the preacher, age c. 50
SISTUH SARAH: wife to Solomon, age c. 25

SETTING

TIME: *Spring 1824*
PLACE: *Brazoria County, Texas. Uncle Bubba and Mammy Bell's cabin; the barn*

SYNOPSIS

The first scene in this vignette is an intimate portrait of the private lives of early Texas slaves. Slave families were often separated at the discretion of their masters for economic reasons. Although marriages were often prohibited or unrecognized, slaves desired to be bound to each other for life and had to get the permission of their masters to be married. Having been stripped of their freedom and community structure, customs had to be recreated— among them "jumping de broom," which symbolized matrimony.

The social customs among slaves and Anglo settlers were both intimate and separate. Any celebration, including music and food, was a celebration for all. Uncle Bubba was a master of many skills, among them, fiddling. His music provides a backdrop for the lively wedding presented here, as do the prayer and praise of Brothuh Solomon.

(Scene opens on BUBBA sitting outside his cabin, cleaning up his old fiddle, while BELL nervously searches the yard for flowers to make a bridal wreath that she refers to as a headpiece.)

BUBBA: *(Cleaning an old fiddle)* Sugar babe, you's as nervis as one o'dese mosquitoes afta a frush rain. What's got you so wukked up?

BELL: *(Nervously working on a headpiece of flowers and preparing for the wedding)* I guess I can't he'p it. Ever since dat Injun stole one o'massa's horses de othuh night, I keep wondrin what if'n dey wuzta come up behin' de cabin and botha dese chillun when I'm in de kitchen cookin. Dey don't seem to care 'bout nothin 'ceptin what dey wants, an' why I—

BUBBA: Now, now, you jes needs to git yo mind on sumpin else. Ain't you got enuf to think 'bout, plannin for de broom-jumpin dis ebenin? Where is de chillun now?

BELL: I sent 'em to sweep out de yard ovah by de barn so when de peoples comes, evahthang would be nice and clean.

BUBBA: Awright! We done set up de benches and put all de tools away. An' don't you look lak de sunshine? Ooo-wee! Come on ovah here, sugar babe. *(He makes room on the bench for her.)* What's dat you makin?

BELL: *(She smiles and sits beside BUBBA.)* Jes trying to make up a lil'o headpiece, Bubba, hun. Why, I'se a bride, and I can't *be* a bride widdout some kinda headpiece, now can I? *(BUBBA hugs her.)* I can't he'p wishin my mama was here to *see* us jump de broom . . . *(They are silent.)* Gittin married wuz sumpin we always talked about, her and me, but none o'de folks on de place where mama n'em lived wuz able to do dat . . . git married, I mean. They massa jes plum didn't 'low it.

BUBBA: I 'member ol' Massa Varner. He nevah let his nigras hab no fun, not eben at Christmas—they had a halfa day off and *still* ate grits!

(They both are silent for a few seconds.)

BELL: Let 'lone dis sort o'broom jumpin ain't lak gittin married by a real preacher lak de white folks does theirs'n.

BUBBA: I know, sugar babe. It ain't de same, but least I wuz able to 'sway Massa Brit dat if'n we made it to Texas an' I stuck by 'im, lak I done, he'd let us have our wish to fin'ly tie de knot. Afta all, 'tween us, we's got fo' chilluns and we been here damn near six years now . . . And you know what else, since I had you, I ain't nevah wanted nobody else. Afta I git thoo playing dis fiddle t'night, you'll *swear* dat it ain't eben *possible* for a nigger to hab as much fun and you n'me is, jes you wait n'see!

BELL: I nevah in dis worl' thought you and me'd be gittin rightly married—wid a real cer'mony an' all. Brothuh Solomon tol' Sistuh Sarah he wouldn't miss it fo' de worl'. Thank God I fin'ly got dis dress all finished. (*Stands, twirls, then sits again*)

BUBBA: Folks oughta be 'rrivin 'fo long. You ain't nevah looked sweeta dan de firs' time I took you ser'ous. Why'ont 'cha sang me dat song I loves so much.

(*BUBBA tunes his fiddle and begins to play.*)

BELL: Now you knows we ain't got time fuh none o'dat.

BUBBA: Course we do. Dis here's our broom-jumpin day, ain't it? (*He kisses her.*)

BELL: I can't b'lieve you settin here kissin me in de broad day ... (*Looks at him affectionately*) and 'specially wif so much lef' t'do.

BUBBA: Long as we's been togedder, we has all de time in de worl' (*They sit.*) Been close to ten years now, huh?

BELL: Sumpin lak dat. (*She kisses him on the cheek.*)

BUBBA: What's wit dis jaw bizness? C'mon, sang my song fo' me. (*Starts to fiddle*)

BELL: Bubba, dat has got t'be yo' fav'right song.

BUBBA: You knows it is. I heard you hummin it dis mawnin.

BELL: (*She stands to sing the black spiritual "Do Lawd, Do Remember Me." After getting so wrapped up in the song, she dances for him, beckoning the audience to join in the song after the first verse.*)

Do Lawd, oh do Lawd,
Do remember me (3×)
Looka way beyon' the blue.

(*They sing, dance, and improvise on this for a while.*)

I got a home in glory land that outshines the sun (3×)
Looka way beyon' the blue.

(When finished, she returns to the bench beside BUBBA.)

BUBBA: *(Stopping to wipe his brow and the fiddle)* Sugar babe, I loves you more now n'I evah did . . . wit yo lil roun' nose. *(He takes his finger and circles her nose. They laugh.)*

BELL: If you ain't the bigges' chile I'se got. Jes lak a lil'o boy haf de time, an' yit youse so fine and han'some. *(Leaning closer to him and fanning herself with her apron)*

BUBBA: Uh-huh. *(Sticks out his chest, enjoying her affection)*

BELL: Member when we wuz wukkin fuh Massa Brit and his firs' wife, Miz Nancy, whilst we wuz in Tennessee?

BUBBA: Yep, yep, 'fo we come here . . .

BELL: We hardly looked at one 'nuther til Miz Nancy gimme dat red dress o'hern one Christmas for de frolic in Joe Bailey's barn.

BUBBA: Oh, yes, dat red dress! *(Continuing)* Yep . . . an' I saw you settin up 'gainst de wall whilst I was jes fiddlin away.

BELL: You was de life o'de pahty, you an' yo' fiddle, all tall and slim, wearin a pair o'Massa's boots—an' a ves'! All de wimmens wanted ya.

BUBBA: But I had my eyes on you!

BELL: You's de bestis' thang dat evah happen to me. I'se pow'ful proud to be yo' wife.

BUBBA: You meks me very happy, sugar babe. *(He listens.)* I think I hears the sound of wee voices.

BELL: Dat be's de chilluns awright. So much fuh sparkin' in de middle o' de day. Wonder is Massa Brit comin?

BUBBA: I was ovah at de cabin a lil while ago and guess what? He got on a suit o' frush clothes.

BELL: Say what?

BUBBA: Yes, yes, a suit o' frush clothes. An' you know, course he had to start talkin 'bout how we ain't aged and how we look so good, lak we ain't wukked a day. I had to tell'im, I started out younger'n you, but now I'se older'n you. *(Laughs)*

BELL: We's aged awright. We's aged jes thinkin 'bout how long we been togedder! *(Laughs)*

BUBBA: *(Laughs, rises, then speaks to imaginary kids)* Awright now, you chillun git on over there by the tree yonda an' quit yo' playing.

BELL: (*Rising and reinforcing BUBBA's directions*) Right here, in the shade.

BUBBA: (*Talking to children*) 'Member now, when all dis is ovah, we gone have a'plenny barbecue plus yo' mama done made one o' her special molasses cakes fuh y'all. So if'n I wuz y'all, I'd be good. (*Turns around and stares in the distance*) Look lak I see Brothuh Solomon and Sistuh Sarah coming.

BELL: (*Staring also, excited*) Me too.

(*Long pause as they anxiously watch them approach*)

(*BROTHUH SOLOMON and SISTUH SARAH arrive, slowly walking arm in arm, then breaking away to embrace the wedding couple.*)

SOLOMON: How do, Bubba and Bell!

SARAH: Bell, look atcha! Youse lookin mighty good!

BELL: Thank ya. I'm sho glad y'all could make it. Jes wouldn't be de same widdout 'cha.

SARAH: And Bubba? Youse still Bubba.

BUBBA: Don't know how t'be no othuh way. (*Points to bench*) Y'all come on over here and res' yo'sef. Y'all done walked close to six miles to git here so you mus' be tired. (*Shakes hands with SOLOMON, while SARAH hugs BELL*)

SOLOMON: We ain't thinkin bout bein tired yit, thank da Lawd! I'se jes tellin Sarah dat de Lawd's done awready blessed us wif de fines' wedder possible, plus two whole days off to enjoy de festivities.

SARAH: Hab mercy! We brung y'all a lil sumpin to warm yo' souls in de wintertime. (*Handing BELL a quilt as a wedding present*)

BELL: Lookie here, lookie here! (*Unfolding the quilt and examining it*) Sistuh Sarah, you done outdone yo'sef dis time. Dis is de pretties' quilt I evah seen, let alone owned. We's mighty grateful to you, ain't we, hun?

BUBBA: (*Admiring quilt*) My, my, we sho is. Thanks a'plenny, to bofe y'all.

SOLOMON: (*Handing BUBBA a jar*) An' Bubba, here's a lil sumpin I brung you. You know I cain't leave you out. Dis is jes fo' snake bites and back rubs, now.

BUBBA: Well, I best go on ovah here an' git myself bit by a snake. (*Laughs, then sets jar beside bench*) Well, let's git dis thang started. (*Turns to imaginary children*) Now you younguns set right here and min' yo' mannuhs. We's ready, Brothuh Solomon. (*Brushes off vest and removes hat*)

CEREMONY

*(All gather around BUBBA and BELL for the saying of the vows. BROTHUH
SOLOMON takes his place in front of them, slightly stage right; BUBBA and
BELL stand together in the center. SARAH helps BELL place the wreath on
her head, then moves to the left of the couple. Meanwhile, a broom is resting
behind the bench.)*

SOLOMON: Givin honah to Gawd, let us pray.

*(He kneels on one knee, all others kneel on both knees. SISTUH SARAH hums
and moans during this prayer.)*

Lawd, we come befo' your throne of grace, knee-bowed and body bent,
axing yo' tenda mercies 'pon yo' servants. We ax you to po' out a special
blessin for Bubba and Bell, two of yo' chillun who's come befo' you to jine
togedder in yo' name. You done brought us all f'om a mighty long ways and
we trustin you to tek us the res' o' de long ways home, til we's gathered
round yo' heabenly throne, togedder wit de angels. Amen. *(He rises, followed by all others.)* Bubba, take Bell by de han'.

*(The couple follow instructions and look each other in the eye sincerely, while
BROTHUH SOLOMON says the following.)*

Dark an' stormy may come de wedder;
I jines dis he-male an' dis she-male togedder.
Let none, but Him dat makes de thunder,
Put dis he-male and dis she-male asunder.
I darefor 'nounce you bofe de same.
Be good, go 'long, an' keep up yo' name.
Bubba, will you love huh til death do ye part?

BUBBA: I sho will.
SOLOMON: Bell, will you serve Bubba in sickness and healf til death do ye
part?
BELL: I will.
SOLOMON: Gimme de broom.

(SISTUH SARAH comes forth with the broom and holds it for them to jump.)

Now comes de time for y'all to jump f'om de ol' life, ovah into de new life!

(BUBBA and BELL jump over the broom, laughing. Everyone claps.)

SOLOMON: I now 'nounce you man 'n wife.
De broomstick's jumped, de world not wide.
She's now yo' own. Salute yo' bride!

(BUBBA and BELL shyly kiss. All the guests clap hands and shout congratulations.)

BUBBA: Now let the celebration begin! Hand me my fiddle.

(He breaks out into a lively "Jumpin' Juba" song. All guests begin to dance and celebrate. SISTUH SARAH teaches the audience the lyrics and how to do the Juba dance.)

Juba dis an' juba dat
Juba killed a yella cat.
Juba up an' juba down,
Juba dance yo' lady roun'.

Tek yo' dress and hol' it high,
Raise yo' hat up to de sky.
Juba right an' juba lef',
Juba all round yo'self.

Swang dat gal den let'er go,
Swang her all roun' de flo'.
Time done come t'laugh an' play,
We gonna jump de juba till de break o'day!

DANCE INSTRUCTIONS

("Patting Juba" was a form of music making for slaves. They patted different parts of their bodies to produce percussive sounds, in the absence of a drum. This patting provided a rhythmic accompaniment to their music.)

(SISTUH SARAH shows the audience how to "pat juba" to the music. She claps twice, crosses her arms in front of her chest and pats each shoulder twice, claps twice, pats knees twice. She repeats the sequence throughout the song, jumping on the handclaps.)

(SARAH then takes the lead in singing the lyrics in call-and-response until the audience catches on to the first verse.)

(Suddenly SOLOMON stops all the revelry to remind revelers of the seriousness of the occasion.)

BROTHUH SOLOMON'S CLOSING SPEECH

SOLOMON: Hear now, hear now! I got a revelation from my Gawd, dis ebenin. Altho' I may be de leas' o' his earthly servants, let us not fergit dat eben Mary's husband Joseph was a carpenter. The lowly Jesus was bo'n in a man-juh, but He riz up to be de king o' kings. I tell ya, brothus and sistuhs, dat we been dancing round here lak we wuz meant to be togedder. We come in de spirit of de Almighty to share in the richness of de Lawd's blessings. He maketh the sun to shine on de rich and po' alak. He gibs de rain so dat all us kin eat. Let us leab here today wit mo'n jes de music in our hearts, but wif de spirit to love one another as de Almighty has loved us. Travelin grace be yo's, in de name o' de heabenly father, Amen.

(Music resumes, cast bows)

(top) **Elliot Jordan and Naomi Carrier as Brothuh Solomon and Sistuh Sarah, arriving at Bubba and Bell's wedding;** (bottom) **Dallas Jones and Jia Taylor as Bubba and Bell jumpin' de broom**

CHRISTMAS AT VARNER-HOGG
Patton Plantation Memories

Written for and performed at the Varner-Hogg
Plantation State Historic Site, 1998

SETTING
TIME: *1840s*
PLACE: *Brazoria County, Texas*

SYNOPSIS
A young slave mother anticipates a visit from her husband, who lives on a neighboring plantation. She narrates the story to their newborn son of how his father was sold. Traditional Christmas songs complete this vignette.

(A young enslaved woman rocks her son while singing the following black spiritual.)

My Lord, what a morning,
My Lord, what a morning,
My Lord, what a morning,
When the stars begin to fall.

MOTHER: You don' know it, honey lamb, but dis time las' Christmas I wuz big wit you in my belly an' you wuz ackin lak you wuz gon' pop out any day, an' lo and behol' come New Years an' you still wuzn't here. On dat very day, de massa always summon all de slaves to de front o' de big house to give out a wuk and conduck repo't. All us goes, de mens, wimmens, and de chirren. *(Mocking the Massa)* "You too lazy, you too slow. You a hard wukker, a fine 'sample ub a good slave." Den Massa calls de names of dose who been sol' or hired out. Dat's when me and yo' pappy learnt he been sol' to ol' Doc Jones. An' no 'mount o' screamin an' hollerin I could do wuz gone stop'im. "Dat's it," he said. Two weeks afta dat, you came. Yo' pappy ain't nebber seed'ya.

(Readjusting the child, now almost a year old) Jake come from Doc Jones

today and marched right in to de big house kitchen wit the brightes' news I'se ebber heard. Yo' pappy got a pass to come see us tomorrow and spen' three whole days. Thank de Lawd! I gots a heap 'o tings t'get ready fo' den. Gone fin'ly be some joy roun' here. I got a shirt to make an' a possum to bake so you gots to sit here and stay outta trouble, you hear?

(*Giving the child a homemade toy and beginning to sing another black spiritual*)

Mary had a baby, my Lord,
Mary had a baby, my Lord,
Mary had a baby, Mary had a baby,
Mary had a baby, my Lord.[13]

(*She dances around, ties a red string on a piece of greenery, pins some dried herbs on a broom, and continues singing.*)

Where was he born, my Lord,
Where was he born, my Lord,
Where was he born, where was he born,
Where was he born my Lord.

(*Talks to child as she starts sewing*) Yo' pappy name is Esau and don't you ebber forgit it. He be's a med'cine man but dey meks him wuk at the sugar house and he'da nebber been made to leab here 'ceptin it caught fiah. Some no count worfless nigger went and blamed it on Esau and po' ol' Jim, who got nelly bu'nt up. Folks roun' here say it was done on purpose, 'count o' dat mean overseer what been wukkin so many hands to *deaf* on dis here place. Evuh'time we makes sugar sumpin go wrong, if'n it ain't no mo' dan two or three hands what dies on 'count o' us hab'n to wuk roun' de clock. Dat always 'fo de firs' fros' cause all de cane gotta be cut, boiled down, and sugar put in de barrels fo' any Christmas gon' be had. Anyway, afta dat fiah, Massa Kit start lookin to git rid o' yo' pappy. Nex' time Doc Jones come round here, Massa git de idea dat wit yo' pappy's knowing all 'bout herbs and stuff, maybe he make Doc a good hand, so he sol'im.

(*Changing her tone from disappointment to satisfaction*) Esau fin'ly comin home and you de firs' pusson he gone be lookin fuh. But when he sneak up on me and say, "Christmas gif',"[14] I gone hab dis shirt all ready fo'im.

(Stands up and holds out shirt for baby to see. She then performs "Pat the Juba" for the baby to keep him pacified. Clapping and stomping, she sings:)

Juba dis and juba dat,
Juba killed a yeller cat
Juba dis and juba dat,
Hold your partner where you at.[15]

Now I gon' cook a possum fuh yo' Pappy. I promised Jake a whole apple pie fo' dis possum. You is a good baby. Mek me wanna lub you mo' an' mo'.

(She takes a sack and places it upon a table. She gets her utensils, some sweet potatoes, etc., and begins cooking while repeating the following poem.)

De way to cook de possum nice
    Carve him to de heart
Firs' parboil him, stir him twice,
    Carve him to de heart
Den lay sweet taters in de pan,
    Carve him to de heart
Nuthin beats dat in de lan'
    Carve him to de heart.[16]

(As she continues preparing the possum, she gently hums, before breaking into the song.)

Go tell it on de mountain,
Ovah de hills an eb'rywhere
Go tell it on de mountain,
Dat Jesus Christ is born.[17]

(top) **Cooking a Christmas meal;** (bottom) **Judy cooking outdoors**

PART

II

FAMILY BREAKUP

sponsibility was entrusted to the mother than to the father. Slave fathers were an absentee phenomenon, not to mention white fathers, whether slave masters, friends of slave masters, or complete strangers who assaulted powerless victims and assumed no ownership for their mulatto children. The slave family was often perceived "as a woman and her children. However, when sale destroyed a slave family, wives lost husbands but husbands lost both wives and children."[4]

The sale of slaves had no sympathy for dividing families. Husbands were consistently separated from wives, mothers from children, and fathers from families. When sold separately slaves often brought higher prices. "The large number of single slaves on the market bears testimony to the ruthless separation of families that occurred during the slave period." The enslaved responded to these vicious "assaults on their familial relations by restructuring their social institutions into new forms." They resorted to African heritage, which resulted in the establishment of "distinctly African American relationships that preserved their families in the face of the most adverse conditions."[5]

By 1830 the settlers had made it clear to the Mexican government that they intended to keep their indentured servants and slaves for life. Settlement in Texas required slaves—an abundant supply of free labor. From the beginning of Jean Lafitte's profiteering off the coast of Galveston, the slave trade in Texas was a lucrative business. The Bowie brothers, James, John J., and Resin P., are among the long list of smugglers who made a living by buying and selling human flesh. The demand for slaves was so great that the early pioneers traded cattle in Cuba for African bondsmen. Many of the enslaved persons who populated the coastal counties—Brazoria, Matagorda, Waller, Fort Bend, Washington, Galveston, Chambers, and others—came directly from Africa, some via the Caribbean. Others walked to Texas from other southern states with their masters. In the 1830s in particular there was a mass migration to Texas due to the failure of many banks, a situation similar to the Great Depression in the 1930s or, more recently, the economic downturn that began in 2008 that forced populations to migrate or change their lifestyle due to high unemployment, rising prices in oil and food, and major bank failures throughout the industrialized world. One of the causes of the nineteenth-century Texan boom was that some planters, after wearing out their land with repeated crops of tobacco and cotton, just picked up stakes and left a "G.T.T." sign in the yard or tacked to the door. This stood for "Gone to Texas." Hopefully this bit of background will help you understand the climate of a desperate need for slaves as was the case in *Arcy Makes Room for Judith Martin: The Breakup of a Slave Family*.

There are three plays in this section that provide insight into what happened to a slave family when one member of the family was sold away or "hired out." For some it meant never seeing their loved one again. For others it was years before they were reunited. In either case the love for a family member proved to be a source of abiding strength to persevere with the hope that one day there would be a reunion.

Arcy Makes Room for Judith Martin is an interesting case study and provides some background on the effects of the Texas Revolution as it relates to the issues of slavery, manumission (emancipation from slavery), and the attitude that settlers had toward free blacks living in the Republic.

Here's the backstory. Peter and Judith Martin's family was separated prior to Texas independence and that continued for the better of part of their marriage. Although they were apart, writer Michael Moore found that they maintained "a stable union until his death in 1863." Further, "Peter was a trusted worker who managed the plantation and cattle herds of his master, Wyly Martin, and may have also assisted the stock raising efforts of Henry Jones."[6]

Moore, who cites Peter as a "Stockraiser of the Republic Period," makes it clear that Peter was "the first emancipated slave legally permitted to remain in Texas," following the death of his owner. He further explains how Peter assisted Wyly Martin just before the Revolution began in 1835 while Wyly was interim administrator of the colony at San Felipe. Peter used his own wagon and team to haul supplies to the Texian Army, managed the camp, and "hunted to keep Wyly's table supplied with game." In short, he "rendered material aid to the government by hauling military stores" from San Felipe to San Antonio and "was paid one hundred and eighty dollars for his services."[7]

Wyly Martin made a will dated September 3, 1833, to give Peter "his freedom in recognition of his faithful service and to ensure that he would not be treated poorly by a future owner." Manumission was promised to take effect upon Martin's death. After the Revolution, however, Martin began to take steps to free Peter. While he could manumit him at his own discretion, the Constitution of the Republic of Texas did not permit a "Free person of African descent . . . to reside permanently in the republic, without the consent of Congress."[8]

Peter was eventually granted his freedom, but not without considerable debate by the Texas legislature, following Wyly's petition in 1839. Randolph Campbell wrote that to free a slave was too much akin to the abolitionist notion that slaves were "capable of self government" and cites Senator E. H. Everett's opposition who called it "a bad precedent to allow a freed slave to stay in Texas." On the other hand, Campbell notes that Senator George W. Barnett favored rewarding Peter for his help, stating, "this boy gratuitously furnished supplies," however he should not be allowed to stay in Texas where he might "cooperate with abolitionists" which "would strike at the very root of our most useful domestic institutions." The arguments for and against Peter's manumission lasted several years, and he was finally granted freedom in 1842. Thereafter, he lived in the town of Richmond in Fort Bend County, where he made his living as a peddler and cook, "hiring his wife from her master so his family could be together."[9]

Following Peter's death, Judith suffered the additional grief of being evicted from their Richmond home, and the property was sold for Confederate money, which was practically worthless. This occurred partly because slave marriages were not recognized and partly because, as a slave, she had no legal rights to either inherit the property or sue in court. The proceeds from the sale were used to care for her and her children, but Judith was not satisfied. She continued to fight for her property, vowing that she would continue to "claim it while she had breath in her body."[10]

After the general emancipation in 1865, Judith was able to inherit Peter's property and she filed suit to reclaim it. Polly Ryon, daughter of Henry Jones, helped Judith finance the successful suit, which, after appeal to the Texas Supreme Court in 1873, upheld her rights to the property. She lived there until her death in 1890.[11]

This play centers on the beginning of Peter and Judith's separation and shows her initial attempts to cope with grief while trying to become accustomed to life hired away from her family.

As I think back to that first performance of *A Little Slave for Sale — Cheap!*, I remember that folks were so shocked that this was happening, they just stood there in their boots, mesmerized like they were in the *Twilight Zone*, too stupefied to move.

Before and after the eighteen-minute vignette, we talked to the audience so they would know what to expect. We explained the use of the word "nigger," and told them to stick around if they wanted to make comments or ask questions. More often than not they stayed until all was finished. For the most part they were sympathetic. Some guests cried, some just walked away. A couple of the children were made angry enough to throw rocks at the actor portraying the auctioneer. One audience member was so moved that he volunteered to buy the character to protect him from harm. One lady thanked us for teaching a valuable lesson to her children. All in all, it was a once-in-a-lifetime experience I will always remember and, no doubt, so will everyone else that was present. We have performed this piece at Sam Houston State University for many years with some folks coming back time and again to witness it. It has also been presented for schools, libraries, and museums around the state of Texas. The largest crowds witnessed this performance at the Houston International Festival in April 2008.

Sweet By and By: Barrington Farm Chronicle is a story about a family breakup, running away, and a subsequent murder. It takes place over a period of time from 1844–1850 and examines the events and attitudes that led to the annexation of Texas to the United States, especially the role of Anson Jones, the last president of the Texas Republic. This is the story of a smaller farm. Anson Jones only had a few slaves, so relationships were easy to define in this play, as were political and economic issues. *Sweet By and By* also examines the role of colonial women left in charge of a farm in the absence of their husbands, and includes source material from Jones's journal and biography, including a letter that he wrote to his wife Margaret.

Texas Parks and Wildlife widely publicized the debut of this play. All the important folks from the department would be there to cut the ribbon for the Barrington Farm inauguration and they were expecting somewhere in the neighborhood of eight to ten thousand visitors for the annual Independence Day celebration at Washington-on-the-Brazos State Park.

We assembled a cast of fourteen actors and actresses from the Houston company of Talking Back Living History Theatre and students from Sam Houston State University's theatre department. The logistics were extensive: arranging site visits for the combined casts, rehearsals, and sewing enough period-correct costumes for all the actors. I had a lot to learn and this project taught us more than any of the others. I still say this was our crowning achievement.

A diverse audience of over a thousand people enjoyed two days of performances. It was an epic moment in living interpretation of Texas history, and it longs to be repeated. The Texas Parks and Wildlife staff was immensely satisfied, maybe even shocked, with the power this type of interpretation could have in educating the public about slave history. *Sweet By and By* was everything we had hoped it would be.

Bryanna Leigh-Anne Marie O'Mara, in her 2007 thesis for Baylor University's Department of Museum Studies, covered the subject "Museums and Controversy: You Can't Have One without the Other." She included a study of our interpretation at the Barrington Farm. She wrote,

> In March 2001, on Texas Independence weekend, the Barrington Farm held a play entitled *Sweet By and By* written by Naomi Carrier Grundy. This play consisted of different scenes at various buildings and locations throughout the farm and revealed the day to day life of a slave . . . Despite the emotional subject matter, the event was very successful, and the staff received positive responses from those who saw it.[12]

ARCY MAKES ROOM FOR JUDITH MARTIN

The Breakup of a Slave Family

Written for living history interpretation at Jones Stock Farm, George Ranch Historical Park, and performed at the national conference of the Association for Living History, Farms and Museums, George Ranch Historical Park, May 23, 1996

CHARACTERS

HENRY JONES: born 1789, Richmond, Virginia. A successful farmer in Stephen F. Austin's colony whose stock farm provides the setting, age 41.

NANCY JONES: born 1805. Henry's wife, age 25. She moved from Virginia via Kentucky with her father, William, and settled in Miller County, Arkansas, where she met Henry in May 1819. They married on January 31, 1821.

ARCY: Henry and Nancy's first slave. Born in North Carolina around 1791, she is the mother of several children, now pregnant with another child. All live with the Joneses. She is approximately 39 years of age and came to Austin's colony with the Joneses from Miller County, Arkansas, in 1822.

WYLY MARTIN: Henry's neighbor, another successful colonist

JUDITH MARTIN: Peter Martin's wife, age 20. Both Peter and Judith belong to and traveled to Texas with Wyly Martin. They have several children.

SETTING

TIME: *1830*

PLACE: *Fort Bend County, Texas. The Jones Stock Farm*

SYNOPSIS

This vignette depicts what happens when a slave family is separated. When Henry and Nancy Jones came to Texas as part of Stephen F. Austin's Old Three Hundred — the original Texas colonists — they had only one slave, Arcy. Judith Martin was hired away from her family to help the Joneses and Arcy, and was thereby separated from her husband, Peter Martin, and their children.

(*As the scene opens, HENRY and NANCY sit on porch engaged in small talk while she spins at her spinning wheel and he cleans a rifle. ARCY is sitting near the other end of the porch on the ground, grinding corn and humming a lullaby to a child indoors.*)

ARCY: (*Screams and jumps up, wasting corn, and runs out from porch*) Massa Henry! It's a snake, come quick! (*She chases it under the cabin.*) It's gonna git away, Massa Henry, hurry!

HENRY: You hold on there, I'm coming! (*Grabs hoe, runs over and looks under the porch, chopping at snake*) Where is it?!

ARCY: It's done gone under d'cabin. S'pose it gits inside? My chile is in dere! Can't we do something?

HENRY: Hold on, now! Let me see if I can find it. Hey! Uh-oh! (*Making one big chop*) Here he is! By gosh, it's a big'un, ain't it?

NANCY: (*Has stopped her spinning and run over to see the commotion*) You think it come up here outta that creek? Probably from all that rain we had last week. (*Sees snake*) I declare, if it's not snakes, it's wild pigs. Thank God we don't have to put up with the Indians too much around here. Henry, what if that snake had gotten inside the cabin . . . or up on the porch and through the window and . . .

HENRY: Aw, Nancy, quit your fearing and worrying. (*Flinging snake away and turning around at the sound of someone coming*) Well, well, if it ain't Wyly. And I think he's got Judith with him.

NANCY: Henry, where are we gonna put her? In here with Arcy?

HENRY: And why not? I 'spect Arcy's just gonna have to make room for her cause we sure need the extra help. Now, maybe, I can git me another shirt made.

NANCY: I thought you was looking out for me by hiring Judith but now I see it's yourself you thinking of! Arcy, you gone have to make room for Judith in there.

ARCY: Yes'm. (*Continuing to grind*)

WYLY: Hello, Henry, Nancy. As promised, I brung you Judith. She's a bit tired, I'll wager. We were up half the night boiling cane and spooning down the syrup. Here you go, Nancy, I brought you a bucket of molasses. (*Handing her the bucket JUDITH was carrying*)

HENRY: Here, let me take your horse.

NANCY: Why, Wyly, you shouldn't've! Hello, Judith, we mighty glad to have you. Come now and make yourself at home. Arcy's gonna help you get settled.

WYLY: Alright Judith, come on. You ain't said a word the whole trip.

ARCY: Here, Judith, let's git you set up.

JUDITH: (*Looking sad, unwilling to talk*) Hey, Arcy. You's alright?

(*They go inside cabin kitchen.*)

NANCY:: Would you like a cool drink, Wyly? Won't be long 'fore we start dinner. You know you welcome to stay. (*Heads for inside house*)

WYLY: Much obliged, Nancy, but I got to get back and help Peter keep the cane mill going. The work goes faster when I'm around.

HENRY: We mighty glad you could bring Judith. My Nancy's about to work herself to death round here.

(*He and WYLY walk onto porch and sit down.*)

WYLY: I reckon you done heard about that new law the Mexican government passed on April 6. It's pretty clear they intend to regulate further immigration from the United States and, along with that, anymore importin of slaves.

HENRY: What?! How do they expect us to go on scratching some civilization out of this wilderness without slaves? Why, it's hard enough to hold on to what we've got, let alone expand. It's one thing they don't want us to bring in no more slaves, but no slaves, no settlers. Plus, it's a threat to the rest of us to even stay here if we can't get more support from Austin to put pressure on the Mexicans.

WYLY: I spoke with Austin just the other day when he was passing through here on his way to the Fort Bend settlement. He's planning to petition the Mexican government against it. I'm lucky I brought these few slaves I do have with me from the U.S. They're hard to get and they're not going cheap. You can't get anybody to sell nowadays.

HENRY: Course, I'm just telling you this, but I was hoping to purchase some of those African boys I hear tell was brought in from Cuba down roun' the Port of Velasco. Don't know as yet how I'd get 'em here 'cept make the trip myself. Maybe now that you brought Judith, she can help out around here while me and my brother, John, go pick 'em up. I could plant that whole bottom eighty acres if I had more hands. John's over there now with Arcy's two boys.

WYLY: That sure is some rich land you got down there. Gone plant cotton or corn?

(ARCY and JUDITH come back outside, off the porch, and continue grinding and talking among themselves.)

HENRY: Probably cotton and some corn up on the top half. *(Going in his pocket)* Here's the first payment on Judith, seven dollars a month, like we agreed. Thanks for hiring her out to us. Maybe in a year or two you'll let me buy her outright.

WYLY: Henry, I tell you, only problem with that is Peter. She and Peter are the same as married and when I brung 'em here, I made Peter a promise to never sell 'em apart. Seeing as how he practically runs my place for me, I just can't up and do it right now. Maybe, in the future. We'll see. I would've let you have Viney, but she ain't worth nearly as much as she used to be and she don't hear too well. Your Nancy will get a lot more work out of Judith.

HENRY: We're much obliged to you, Wyly. Take a look at this rifle I bought from this trader that came through here the other day.

(They rise and go around the side of house.)

NANCY: Here you go, Wyly, Henry. *(She hands them both a cup of water and carries one to JUDITH.)*

JUDITH: Thank you, ma'am.

NANCY: I can't tell you how pleased Mr. Henry and I are to have you here working along with Arcy and me. Did you get her all settled, Arcy?

ARCY: Yes'm, 'cept we gone have to make her a bed tick.

NANCY: Well, we can see to that after we finish dinner. I hear from Mr. Wyly that you can sew a right nice seam, Judith. Do you know how to spin?

JUDITH: No, ma'am. I never been roun' nobody that could.

NANCY: Then we'll teach you to spin in no time. Come see! You'll love my spinning wheel. It belonged to my mama and come here all the way from Kentucky. Come let me show it to you.

(*They go onto the porch to look at her wheel, where she demonstrates spinning. ARCY continues grinding.*)

ARCY: (*After they leave, she talks to herself.*) Umm-uh, Judith is hurtin' inside, having to leave her husban' and chirren. It's a wonder to me dat dey eben let her and Peter git married cause de law sho don't recognize it . . . eben Mr. Wyly don't recognize it . . . Po' chile is left to moan and cry almost as much as her chirren, who I know is missin' dey mama. Leastways Massa Henry and Miss Nancy lets me keep my chirren. (*Standing up and cradling her stomach, again with child. She looks up.*) Lord, if you's up dere, look on us, if you will . . . and hab a lil mercy.

NANCY: (*Hollers from porch*) Arcy, put some rosemary in the stew, will ya?

ARCY: Yes'm. (*Talking to herself as she goes first to the garden, then to the cooking pot*) I just hope Judith last through it without gettin de dreaded fever . . . I knows her pain, Lord, 'ceptin I'se never had a man to call my own. Dis chile I'se carryin may as well not hab no pappy, cause he ain't comin dis way no mo' . . . not since he run off wit the Mexicans to where he say he gone be free. Now Massa Henry talkin 'bout buyin some of dem Af'ican boys to come wuk here. Where dey gone stay? Here in dis same cabin wit us? Jes pack us all in dere togedder, I reckon . . . long as de wuk gits done. (*Begins to hum a sorrowful song*)

NANCY: You see Judith, ain't nothing to it . . . You just hold it out like this and keep turning the wheel. It spins almost by itself.

JUDITH: Yes, ma'am.

NANCY: We'll do more later. Let me see if you know how to card the way I like it done.

JUDITH: Yes, ma'am, I knows how to card. Like this, Miss Nancy? (*Starting to card cotton*)

NANCY: Sure, sure. Everything's gone work out just fine, you'll see. You can sit down right here and card away. You ever try to weave?

JUDITH: Once . . . long time ago. It alright, but I jes knows how to sew wit the needle, ma'am.

NANCY: I can see right now that you catch on quick. Just you keep carding.

Now, with you here, you can card, Arcy can spin, and I can weave. My Henry's been wanting me to make him a new shirt. Maybe, after I get a nice bit woven, you can help me sew one up, huh?

JUDITH: I made dat dere shirt Mr. Wyly got on . . . and his pants.

NANCY: I declare! You go right ahead. I'm gone help Arcy with the dinner. (*Leaving porch*) How you coming, Arcy?

ARCY: I added the rosemary. It near 'bout ready, now.

NANCY: I was figuring to have some of Mr. Wyly's molasses along with our cornbread. Something the matter, Arcy?

ARCY: No'm.

NANCY: Well, you looking awful sad. You should be rejoicing now that we finally got us some help round here.

ARCY: Oh, I'se glad for de he'p, ma'am, sho I is . . . jus po' Judith is missin' her younguns, is all.

NANCY: See here, you'll be good company for her, what with you and her been knowing each other for some time now. The Lord knows I'm gone need both of y'all. Do we have enough corn shucks to make another bed tick?

ARCY: I 'spect so, over yonder where we keep 'em.

NANCY: Soon as y'all eat, you and Judith can get to work on that bed tick. (*Complaining*) Huh, all this grinding for such a little meal. I don't know what I'd give to have some bread made from flour. Don't get me wrong, I love your cornbread. We just have to sacrifice so many of the nice things we had back in the states. Flour is just one of them.

WYLY: (*Coming from back of the house with HENRY*) Well, Henry, I best be getting on back 'fore sundown.

(*They walk over to where ARCY and NANCY are talking.*)

WYLY: (*He passes by JUDITH on porch, carding.*) Judith, I was just telling Mr. Jones here what a fine worker you are and how well you can cook and sew —

JUDITH: Mr. Wyly, you said Peter could come over every Sunday and see me and —

WYLY: I keeps my word! I mean to see to it that he does just that, if'n he don't —

JUDITH: You suppose he can use the cart to bring our chirren, too? I'm gonna miss my lil . . .

WYLY: Now, now, Judith, it ain't like you been sold. What d'ya say you jes—

JUDITH: (*Starting to cry*) But Mr. Wyly, you promised me and Peter. (*Coming down off porch, beginning to cry uncontrollably*)

WYLY: What I tol' you and Peter—

JUDITH: And what 'bout next Sunday being the day you—(*Cries uncontrollably*)

WYLY: I'll hear no more of this nonsense! (*Leaving for his horse*)

HENRY: Let me get your horse, Wyly.

WYLY: Now, Henry, I apologize for the way Judith's carrying on. I didn't expect her to take it this way.

NANCY: Arcy, take Judith in the cabin and set with her for a spell. I'll finish up here. Good day, Wyly.

(*ARCY rushes to console JUDITH.*)

WYLY: Good day, Nancy, Henry.

HENRY: Let me know if you hear anymore from Austin. Hopefully, he can talk some sense into 'em 'fore things get any worse. And, ah, Wyly, you been a true friend. (*Winking about JUDITH*)

(*Inside the cabin, JUDITH is heard praying and crying about her children with ARCY trying to comfort her.*)

HENRY: I don't know if this is gone work, and I done put out money on—

NANCY: Henry, I 'spect she'll go on like this for a while, til she gets used to the idea. We just have to give her some time to settle down. Go git that bag of shucks from the barn. We need it to make her a bed tick.

HENRY: You got any ticking for it?

NANCY: What about the wagon sheet?

HENRY: Wagon sheet? What about it?

NANCY: I'm not planning on moving anymore, Henry Jones. This wilderness and all its problems has got the best of me. I can't use my last few yards of muslin on a bed tick!

HENRY: Well, I guess that wagon sheet'll have to do. I'll say, Nancy, you always know just the way to work things out. A man's awful lucky to have a good woman like you on his side. (*Showing some affection*)

NANCY: Thank you, Henry . . . and thanks for Judith, too.

HENRY: You betcha. Let's bring those shucks around here.

(*They leave around the side of the cabin.*)

ARCY: (*Coming back onto porch*) Come Judith, sit on de steps wit de baby. It may make you feel better to hold her. Po' lil thang don't know what she gone hafta face in dis mean ol' worl'.

(*They coo and play with baby.*)

(top) **Arcy tries to console Judith. George Ranch Historical Park, National ALHFAM Conference, 1996;** (left) **Henry Jones, owner of Arcy, and Judith Martin. George Ranch Historical Park Jones Stock Farm**

A LITTLE SLAVE FOR SALE—CHEAP!

Premiered at the Sam Houston Folk Festival, 1999, on the grounds of the
Sam Houston Museum, at Sam Houston State University

CHARACTERS

JEFF HAMILTON: a thirteen-year-old slave; an emancipated adult; NARRATOR

JAMES MCKELL: Jeff Hamilton's former master

AUNT BIG KITTY: Jeff's mother

CROWD of onlookers

MR. MORELAND: top bidder for Jeff

Two **WHITE BOYS** who tease Jeff

Two **BIDDERS**

Two **COMMENTATORS**

GENERAL SAM HOUSTON: Jeff Hamilton's new master

Note: the **WHITE BOYS**, **BIDDERS**, and **COMMENTATORS** may come from the
audience.

SETTING

TIME: *October 1853*

PLACE: *Huntsville, Walker County, Texas. Slave block in front of the T.&S. Gibbs
general store*

NARRATOR: I guess y'all wondering why I'm here. Me, Jeff Hamilton, who was
first a slave and came to be one of General Houston's most trusted servants. Y'all see me now all dressed up and educated and you would never
guess how I got to be here.

(*Pointing to JAMES MCKELL*) That's ol' man McKell, a devil of a man
who could cuss and swear til you think hell was tumbling down on ya.

(*Pointing to the slave boy, JEFF HAMILTON*) And you see that boy yonder, that's me when I was just a thirteen-year-old lad.

(*Pointing to AUNT BIG KITTY*) And her, well, that's my Mammy as I remember her that fateful October day in 1853, when Mr. James McKell separated me from my dear Mammy—Aunt Big Kitty—and auctioned me off from the slave block to pay two past due whiskey bills. I tell you, folks, it was the longest day of my life of nearly one hundred years.

I had been nervous all day. Longin and hurtin for my mother had nearly drove me crazy. I didn't know what to expect and there I was standin on the slave block, a hungry little black slave boy, in front of the Gibbs' store in Huntsville.

MCKELL: Here's a little nigger for sale—cheap! (*Beckons to audience to pay attention*) Ever'body gather round here, take a look at 'im! (*Smacks JEFF on the shoulder with his cane*) Hey, you, all y'all! Step right up, gentlemen! (*Continues pantomiming the auctioning of thirteen-year-old JEFF*)

NARRATOR: Auctions of slaves were held most every day in those times. Yet and still they always brought together a lot o' people. Some folks took pleasure in seeing colored folk being sold, like it was some kinda show. And so, when I was being sold, a big crowd had gathered in front of the Gibbs' general store. I looked everywhere trying to find some friendly face, black or white. I was frightened—scared almos' to death. The sun beat down on my bare head without mercy.

(*JEFF pantomimes, wiping sweat from his head and whimpering.*)

I was hot, tired, thirsty, and hungry.

MCKELL: C'mon, somebody make me a bid on this little nigger. He's a strong and willing worker. He ain't but eight years old, but he's gone make somebody a husky field-hand!

NARRATOR: McKell prob'ly lied 'bout my age, knowin he never could sell a runty, small-fry boy like me, if the bidders knew I was already thirteen years old. Any buyer knowing my real age would know right away that I was never gonna grow into a big, strong slave.

I stood there on the slave block in the blazing sun for at least two hours.

(*JEFF [the boy] looks around to dodge something and flinches as if being hit by rocks. Two WHITE BOYS in the crowd tease him unmercifully.*)

BOY I: Look at that nappy hair! (*Pointing and laughing*)

BOY II: Ain't he black, though? (*Throws a rock at JEFF*)

BOY I: Like coal. And so skinny you could eat two of 'em for supper . . .

BOY II: . . . and still be hongry.

(*Both BOYS laugh. JEFF begins to hunch over and cry. Meanwhile, MCKELL continues to hawk the sale.*)

MCKELL: Step up, gentlemen and make me an offer. Do I hear a bid? Why wait? You can't lose on this one. He's young enough to give you a lifetime of service. Mold 'im any way you want 'im. Right here, a little nigger for sale — cheap! Do I hear a bid?

BIDDER I: Yeah. I'll give ya two bits for the runt.

BIDDER II: Why don't cha fatten 'im up and come back in a couple months. That boy can't even carry a cotton sack, let alone pick twenty pounds a day.

MCKELL: (*To BIDDERS*) Neither one of you fellers would know a deal if it bit you on the nose.

BIDDER I: That ain't a deal, it's a squeal!

(*Bursts of laughter. MCKELL ignores them and continues hawking the sale.*)

BIDDER II: Lil nappy head rascal! Yeah, I'll give ya a hunnurd dollars an' take 'im off yo' hands.

MCKELL: (*Ignoring the two fake BIDDERS*) Little nigger for sale — cheap! Take him home t'night and wake up with a new field hand.

NARRATOR: I don't know why Mr. McKell wanted to be his own auctioneer, unless he wanted to save the usual fees. The auction dragged on and on, and I couldn't help crying.

   If I should live a thousand years, I would never forget the fear in Mammy's face when McKell came to our cabin, pounding on the door, long before daylight, the morning of the auction. (*Pointing toward his mother*) We were all deathly afraid of Mr. McKell and we knew that he was drunk the night before.

(*AUNT BIG KITTY steps into the picture, stage right. MCKELL turns from his auctioning to face her.*)

MCKELL: (*He bangs on her door until AUNT BIG KITTY answers.*) Send Jeff over to the house right away! An' the rest of ya hurry up and git to your cotton pickin! Don' let de sun catch ya widdout dem hoes in yo' han' an' dem sacks on yo' back. Y'hear me?!

(*MCKELL freezes. AUNT BIG KITTY sobs, holding her apron to her face.*)

NARRATOR: I'm sho Mammy thought he was goin to whup me for sumpin he imagined I had done, or she may a'thought sumpin worse would happen.

(*AUNT BIG KITTY calls JEFF to her and gives him one last embrace. MCKELL returns to site of auction and freezes holding cane out to the audience.*)

As I was leaving the cabin, Mammy hugged me and kissed me goodbye.
AUNT BIG KITTY: (*Following embrace and looking JEFF in the eyes*) Jeff, whatever happens, don't you fergit yo fambly.

(*AUNT BIG KITTY pushes JEFF from herself, waving goodbye.*)

You hear me, Jeff? We's yo fambly! Don't you fergit us!

(*JEFF returns to the auction block as story resumes.*)

NARRATOR: When I was runnin toward the tumble-down barn, I turned my head for one las' look at my mother. She was standin in de cabin door, holdin her apron to her face and sobbin in a kinda hopeless way. I was not to see her again for a quarter of a century. She and the rest of the chirren were sol' apart f'om one another and scattered all across Texas.

It was so hot on that late October day, Mr. McKell was forced to take off his coat and vest.

(*McKell, coming back to life, removes his coat and vest.*)

It was long past noon. At last, he got a bid fo' me. It was made by a man by the name of Moreland, who offered five hundred dollars. After dickerin for a while, McKell accepted the offer.

MORELAND: (*Steps up to make bid, clearing his throat*) How old you say dat boy is?

MCKELL: Eight and a half and growing by the minute. Gone make somebody a strong field han' in a coupla years. C'mon now, you can't lose on 'im, no way you look at it!

MORELAND: (*Skeptical*) I'll give you four hunnurd fo'im.

BIDDER II: I'll make it four-fifty.

MCKELL: You fellers don't know the value of a good piece of property such as this . . .

MORELAND: Alright, alright, five hunnurd dollars and that's firm!

MCKELL: Do I hear five-fifty, five-fifty, you sir, is that a nod . . .

MORELAND: Five hundred cash dollars right now, McKell!

MCKELL: Five hundred, going once, five hundred going twice . . . (*Looking around*) Five hundred it is! Sold to the highest bidder.

MORELAND: (*Walks over to JEFF and pats him on the head. Then touches his mouth, motioning for him to show his teeth.*) I guess you'll just have to do. (*Turning to MCKELL*) I don't carry that kinda cash around, so you'll hafta wait here til I go git it. I don't live more'n two miles from here. (*Turns to leave*)

MCKELL: I ain't got all day. This deal will have to be closed in time for me to get back home 'fore night. (*He follows the man down the street with his eyes and a raised cane in his direction.*)

NARRATOR: No sooner had he lef' than a great big, important-lookin man drove up in a buckboard buggy, drawn by a fine black horse. My eyes opened wide.

(*JEFF stops whining to notice GENERAL SAM HOUSTON.*)

Never befo' had I seen such a buggy—nor such a man! Stepping down to the ground, the tall man tied his reins to a hitching post in front of the plank-walk. I saw that he was about six-foot, two-inches high.

(*GENERAL SAM HOUSTON approaches the slave block.*)

GENERAL SAM HOUSTON: What's all this excitement about?

COMMENTATOR I: Nothing at all, General. Just a little nigger boy being sold.

COMMENTATOR II: Yeah and for 'bout twice as much as he's worth, the little pipsqueak!

NARRATOR: Two keen, yet kindly, blue eyes looked at me. I was gazin for the firs' time at General Sam Houston, the hero of San Jacinto. My chance meetin wit' him was about to change the whole course o' my life, forever.

HOUSTON: (*Walking up to MCKELL*) My friend, don't you know it is against the law to block the plank-walk in this way? If you want to put on a show, why don't you move the slave block back to the courthouse square where it belongs?

MCKELL: (*Starts to say something, when the GENERAL cuts him short.*)

HOUSTON: This little Negro isn't old enough to have any sense, and these white boys are *scaring* him. What sort of offer have you had for the boy, anyway? Has he a father or mother?

MCKELL: I happen to be waiting on a Mr. Moreland to return with five hundred dollars to buy the boy before long. And for yo information, General, suh, he's got a mother, a brothuh and two sistuhs. What bizness is it of yo's, anyhow, if'n you don't mind my askin?

HOUSTON: Do you mean to tell me that you would take this half-starved child away from his mother and sell him to a yellow dog like Moreland?

MCKELL: Listen here, my creditors are gone close me out if I don't settle two whiskey bills by tomorrow noon. I'll sell this lil nigger to anybody who will pay me five hundred dollars, although he's worth mo'.

HOUSTON: (*Looking MCKELL straight in the face*) I wouldn't be guilty of separating the family. But rather than see this happen and let this little fellow fall into the hands of a slave driver like Moreland, I'll take him myself, if you will knock fifty dollars from the price, and sell me the rest of the family, too.

MCKELL: (*Thinking for a moment*) Well, General, it's a bargain. You pay me four-fifty in cash right now and I will also sell you the boy's ma, Aunt Big Kitty, and her other younguns at any price that Bolivar Sublett over at Trinity Ferry puts on 'em. You know he's the expert on the value of slaves.

HOUSTON: I know he considers Negroes as "property," just like a horse or a cow. That's what I know. I'll have Tom Gibbs draw up a bill of sale for four-fifty. Once you sign it, he'll pay you the money and charge it to my account.

(*MCKELL offers HOUSTON his hand to shake but HOUSTON refuses it.*)

Good day. (*He turns away, taking JEFF with him and talking to him kindly.*) You little squirrel. Come along with me. (*Takes him by the hand, leading him away. JEFF is relieved but so scared he can hardly move.*) You don't have to be scared and you don't have to cry anymore. (*Stopping to face JEFF and reassure him*) I have a son close to your age. You'll make a fine playmate for him, once Joshua cleans and fattens you up a bit. Let's stop in the store here and get you something to eat. Then I'll take you on home with me.

(*They exit from upper stage left.*)

NARRATOR: Then and only then came my deliverance from a cruel and inhuman master. Finally, I felt safe from the anguish and the terrors of the horrible nightmare of that morning. McKell didn't keep his word and the General never bought my family. I have to be thankful that he bought me.

I am reminded of Daniel in the lions' den. I felt like God Almighty had sent his angel all the way to Huntsville and shut the lion's mouth.

Just think of it! In less than ten years after the General saved me from the clutches of that "Simon Legree," McKell, I was the trusted right-hand servant of the governor of the great state of Texas. After he bought me that day at the auction, I learned to read and write, had plenty to eat and wear, and slept on a pallet beside the door of the room of one of the most famous men of our country! All because I had believed in my God, I saw with my own eyes some of the mos' excitin events that evah took place in any state capital of America. Me, Jeff Hamilton.

Rick Burford and Christopher Woodard. Sam Houston Festival, 1999

SWEET BY AND BY

Barrington Farm Chronicle

Written for the Texas Parks and Wildlife Independence Day Celebration and
the Inauguration of Barrington Living History Farm, 2000

CHARACTERS

NARRATOR: enslaved male, older and wiser than other slaves, age 50

JERRY: keeper of animals and field hand, age 37

WILLIS: field hand, age 45

MARY: field hand, age 20

JOSÉ LÓPEZ: poster (builder of fences), age 25

LUCY: housekeeper, age 22

CHARITY: cook, age 35

JAKE: field hand, age 22

MRS. MARGARET JONES: wife of President Jones, age 30

BOWEN: overseer, age 35

PRESIDENT ANSON JONES: president of Texas, age 51

ASHBEL SMITH: secretary of state of Texas, age 39

JAMES PINCKNEY HENDERSON: succeeded Stephen F. Austin as secretary of
state; ambassador for Republic of Texas; proponent for Texas annexation;
became first governor of Texas; age 36

T. J. ALLCORN: friend of President Jones, age 40

MALACHI: Jake's son, age 4

OKRY: age 6

SETTING

TIME: *August 1850*

PLACE: *Washington County, Texas. Barrington Farm*

SYNOPSIS

While Jake's murder didn't go unnoticed it was one of those slavery matters
of fact. In a story set at the farm of controversial figure Anson Jones, the last
president of Texas, this play chronicles the sad circumstances of Jake's death,
discusses the bravery and stamina of frontier women, and explores the economic and political importance of slaves in Texas.

SCENE 1

(As the audience enters the farm, the music of "Sweet By and By" is sung by all of the SLAVES who are in the process of having a funeral for JAKE. Visitors are greeted by the NARRATOR.)

NARRATOR: Howdy, folks. Welcome to Barrington Farm, the home of President Anson Jones, last president of the Texas Republic. The year is 1850 and I can tell by this sky *(looking up)* that it's gonna be one hot day in August. In 1850 ain't but a handful of free black folks in Texas. Freedom for the slaves didn't come til after the Civil War, in 1865. I suppose you can tell by the sound of that song that it ain't a happy time around here. Lucy and the rest of 'em is having a funeral for Jake. Let's go over and pay our respects.

SLAVES: *(Singing)*

In the sweet (in the sweet) by and by, (by and by)
We shall meet on that beautiful shore; (by and by)
In the sweet (in the sweet) by and by, (by and by)
We shall meet on that beautiful shore.

(The audience is encouraged to draw nearer, close enough to see a grave and a pine box. The slaves gather toward the back of the grave in a semicircle. Jerry assumes the role of preacher, as singing continues.)

There's a land that is fairer than day,
And by faith we can see it afar,
For the father waits over the way
To prepare us a dwelling place there.

(The slaves kneel and begin to hum the song's chorus while JERRY prays.)

JERRY: Father in heaben, we's gathered beneat' yo throne ub mercy for de homegoin ub our brudder, Jake. He libbed here 'mongst us, wukked in de fiel' 'mongst us, et wid us, and prayed wid us, Lawd Jesus. He was somebody chile, so bless his soul. Don't none o' us come here t'stay. An' don't none o' us come here to be shot down lak a dog in de dus'. But you knows de beginnin and de en', de alpha and de omega, de firs' and de las'. So ashes to ashes and dus' to dus', you is de only one dat we kin trus' to deliber us ober unto de breas' ob de udder shore, where dis pain and sufferin shall be no more. In de name o' Jesus, amen.

(*All rise; slaves continue singing chorus of "Sweet By and By" and slowly walk away from the scene. LUCY and JERRY are the last to leave. She leaves reluctantly, crying, while JERRY comforts her. They disappear behind the barn.*)

NARRATOR: (*Sympathetically*) Po' Lucy. (*Turning back to face the audience*) You are probably wondering who died and how? Well, that's just what we intend to show you. If you'll meet me over there by that woodpile (*Pointing*) in ten minutes, we'll roll back the clock to yesterday.

SCENE 2

(*The NARRATOR is standing in front of woodpile.*)

NARRATOR: Gather 'round folks. What happened here today caught us all by surprise. And Mrs. Jones, to say the least, wasn't sure how she was goin to explain this to her husband. Anyway, well, you can see for yo'sef. Lemme git out the way.

(*Slaves have returned to the field and kitchen where they are working when this incident occurs.*)

BOWEN: (*Coming out from behind the right side of barn, pointing his rifle and yelling*) Stop nigger, or I'll shoot!

(*JAKE runs out from behind Slave Cabin 1, in full view of BOWEN. BOWEN fires two shots and JAKE falls dead. Slaves run from the field, kitchen, and house to see what has happened. First to arrive on the scene, besides BOWEN, is LUCY, who has also come from behind Slave Cabin 1.*)

LUCY: (*Cradling JAKE in her arms, crying, she talks to BOWEN.*) Now see what you done gone and done? Kilt the only pusson whatever cared 'bout me. (*Looking down at JAKE*) Wake up, Jake . . . Come back please! (*Refusing to accept what has happened*) No, don't leab me here by myse'f. Jake? (*Shaking his body, hoping he's not dead*) Jake, look at me! I gots nobody and nuthin now . . . What I gone do? Jes be a slave here on dis plantation til I die?

BOWEN: Awright, gal, dat's enough, let go of 'im. Nigger ain't had no bizness coming back roun' here. If he'd a'heeded my warnin, he'd still be livin. Ain't done nothin but made a heap of trouble fo' me, anyway, runnin like dat!

(*LUCY cries loudly. BOWEN talks mostly to himself.*)

He shoulda stopped when I tol' 'im. President Jones sol' 'im to ol' man All-corn jes las week. Leave 'im be, gal. Git 'way f'om 'im, I say!

(*LUCY continues to hold onto JAKE's body. The slaves come running onto the scene. Last to arrive is MRS. JONES. CHARITY tries to calm LUCY and pull her away from JAKE's body. Some of the children start crying. WILLIS and JERRY look at each other, knowing their lives are worth no more than JAKE's.*)

JOSÉ: ¿Qué pasó? (*What happened?*) ¿Está muerto? (*Is he dead?*)

BOWEN: (*Continuing to supervise*) Go back to work, José. This don't concern you.

JOSÉ: Pero, señor, lo conocía. ¡Fue amigo! (*But, sir, I knew this man. He was my friend!*)

BOWEN: An' learn to speak English will ya. I can't git you to understand nuthin!

(*JOSÉ stands behind LUCY who is holding JAKE, and sadly ad-libs in Spanish.*)

Willis, you and Jerry pick 'im up and take 'im over yonder, out behind the slave cabin, yonder so ya kin do whatever y'all do to tek care o' him fo' burial.

(*They talk to each other softly, refusing to move when spoken to, confidently shaking their heads in sorrow.*)

MRS. JONES: (*Enters, coming from Farm House*) Mr. Bowen, what on earth made you do such a thing? I hope you realize that you will have to answer to my husband for this despicable destruction! (*Looking directly at BOWEN*)

BOWEN: Take it easy ma'am. This nigger refused—

MRS. JONES: Did you have to shoot him down in cold blood?

BOWEN: (*After a pause, and somewhat calmer*) It wasn't cold blood lak you thank, ma'am. He was runnin an' I tol' 'im to stop.

MRS. JONES: (*Astonished*) So you killed him? (*Looking back at JAKE, trying to figure what happened. Then she thinks of the children.*) Lord, have mercy! You children git back over to the yard. (*Pause*) Go on, go on, finish your work. Go with 'em, Mary. Charity, get Lucy over to y'all's cabin and tend to her.

CHARITY: (*Trying to coax LUCY up and away from JAKE*) Come on, chile. You gots t'be strong now. I knows how you feel, but you gots to git up now. I loss my man like dis, years ago . . . years ago.

LUCY: What 'bout his baby I'se carryin? He ain't never gone see his own chile. It ain't right, Lawd. It jes ain't right! (*Struggling to leave the scene*)

CHARITY: Come on, honey, uh-huh. By and by, it gone all be awright. (*Starts singing traditional song, "Down by the Riverside"*)

Gonna lay down my burden (down by)
Down by the riverside (down by)
Down by the riverside (down by)
Down by the riverside.
Gonna lay down my burden (down by)
Down by the riverside.
Study war no more.

I ain't gone study war no more
Ain't gone study war no more
Ain't gone study war no more-ore-ore
I ain't gone study war no more
Ain't gone study war no more
Ain't gone study war no more.

(*They disappear behind the barn back to Slave Cabin 1. While WILLIS and JERRY carry JAKE's body behind Slave Cabin 2, LENORA herds the children to the Farm House.*)

MRS. JONES: Mr. Bowen, I'll be needing to speak to you after you make some sense of all this. (*Shocked over what has happened, she returns to house.*) Uh, why, I never!

(*NARRATOR takes over at this point and directs audience to the next scene.*)

SCENE 3

NARRATOR: Well, I'm sure you couldn't help overhearing that President Jones had just sold Jake away from here last week. Which might make one wonder — if he was sold, how did he manage to break away from his new master? And after he broke away, why on earth would he return here and risk being caught? You and I both can sense that the overseer, John Bowen, had no great liking for Jake or any of the slaves for that matter. Why don't we go over by the Slave Cabins and roll back the clock.

(*The audience is relocated to a position behind the Slave Cabins where JAKE has just embraced LUCY and she is overcome with joy. They are standing behind Slave Cabin 1.*)

JAKE: I bet you thought you wuzn't gone see me no more, huh, gal?

LUCY: (*Covering her mouth to hide her excitement*) Oh, Jake, I'se so glad you come back. How long you gone stay?

JAKE: Now, you know well as I do, I can't stay. I jes had to see ya. How's dat lil one inside ya?

LUCY: (*Excited*) Gittin bigger ever day now. I didn't know what to do afta you lef'. I-I couldn't do nuthin, 'cept cry and, and wish you never lef' or dat you could at leas' tek me wid you . . . Please, Jake? Please tek me wid you! I can't stan' being widdout you, please —

JAKE: An' what gone happen to our othuh chile? You want tek him, too? An' us all git shot down in de dirt lak dogs? Naw. Uh-uh, honey, no way. I may be loose fom dat udduh man what bought me, but I ain't nelly free. S'pose I'll nevah be free. (*Abruptly stops to have a look around the cabin toward the big house*) Anybody see ya come here?

LUCY: Naw. Nobody know 'ceptin Big Mary an' you know how she is. She don't let off no secrets for nuthin nor nobody. Soon as she tol' me you wuz here, de Missus call me to suck her baby so dat's what hel' me up.

JAKE: (*Looks left, back around the other side of the cabin and toward the barn*) Look-a-here Lucy, I got sumpin fo' you. (*He pulls out two gold pieces and gives them to LUCY.*) Don't ax me where I got dese, honey, jes tek 'em. It's all I can offer ya, seeing as how I can't nevah marry ya or mek us any kinda home, lak real folks's got—

LUCY: Gold?! Is dese real gold, Jake? I ain't nebber seen no gold befo'! I wish we—

(*They are suddenly interrupted by the sound of BOWEN's voice in the distance.*)

BOWEN: Is dat you done come back, here, nigger? Come on out in the open, I know you back dere!

(*JAKE starts to breathing real hard and covers LUCY's mouth. He grabs her by the arm and they slowly move around the right side of Slave Cabin 1 away from view. BOWEN peers out from behind the barn. The audience is able to observe all this action from behind the Slave Cabin.*)

BOWEN: Don't try no tricks Jake, ya don stan' a chance! (*He doesn't see JAKE behind the cabins then moves back around the side of the barn.*)

JAKE: (*To LUCY*) I prob'ly won't see ya no mo', gal. Tek care o' my babies—an yo'sef. (*He kisses her goodbye quickly and runs in front of both cabins, then around the back of the barn.*)

BOWEN: (*Shouts*) Stop, nigger, or I'll shoot!

(*Two shots are heard.*)

SCENE 4

NARRATOR: You may be wondering why President Jones didn't appear on the scene of Jake's murder. Well, he's not here. Because he's a politician and a doctor he's often absent, leaving his wife Mary in charge. Let's understand one thing, women these days had to be rugged. In 1834, when Mary was 14, she came to Brazoria with her widowed mother and four siblings from Arkansas. She managed the house while her mother did a man's work in the fields. While she's rather quiet and modest, Mary Jones is quite capable of managing a farm. During the time Anson is away, Mary looks forward to receiving letters from him.

She thought she could get by this time without an overseer, but, well, suppose we hear it from her. Come over to the big house with me. Mary is reading a letter from her husband.

(MRS. JONES is sitting in her favorite rocker, reading a letter from President Jones.)

MRS. JONES: *(Reading aloud)* "My dear Mary, I trust you and the children are in good health and that the Negroes have not caused you too much grief. I am writing from Washington, where I will be for a few days before leaving for New York. Had dinner with Sam Jacinto last evening. The Congress is in an uproar over this business about fugitive slaves. Your letter troubled me. I regret poor Jake's unfortunate fate, but think Mr. Bowen was justified. This results in quite a loss in property for Allcorn. It is fortunate, however, that you had got nearly through harvesting the crops before Mr. Bowen left you. You may have to hire additional hands from some neighbors to finish the job. Bowen will probably return after court is over. From my view of the case I do not see how he could be hurt much, probably more scared than otherwise. I want the very best for you. Since Lucy is now pregnant, you do need a good honest servant. If you know of one you can get that will suit you, do make a purchase. You can always sell Lucy or turn her into the field. You might make an inquiry of Oliver Jones about the purchase of his two slaves, Frank and his wife.

Forgive me for having to be away from you at a time like this. I have depended on you so much through all these years, Mary. I have every confidence that you will make the right decisions. I wish that I could be at your side, this moment. Nonetheless, I will make haste to finish my business in New York, and return home. Give my love to the children. Tell the boys to be men until I return. And tell Jerry and all the servants that "Master" remembers them and sends them a "how-dy" now and whenever he writes a letter home. Your faithful husband, Anson."

(*Stands and reflects*) Dear, dear Anson, I miss you so much at a time like this. We all do. I wish I were half as smart and practical as you. I can't help but think back on when Texas was in the process of annexation . . . when you were president of the republic . . . and under daily pressure to conduct the affairs of state. You displayed so much courage.

CHARITY: Missus Jones, kin you come here to the kitchen, ma'am.

(*MRS. JONES exits*)

SCENE 5

NARRATOR: As you know, Anson Jones was the last president of the great Republic of Texas, from 1844 clear on up to the time Texas was annexed to the United States. But now, lemme tell ya, annexation was no piece of cake. And for all you little ones out there, to annex something means to add it to something bigger. Texas was added to the rest of the United States in December 1845.

Folks had been talking 'bout annexation all along. By and by, it was bound to happen. But Mexico didn't want to give up Texas. See, Texas had belonged to Mexico before the war in 1836. After Texas won the war and got its independence from Mexico, Mexico refused to recognize that independence. Mexico didn't want slavery, and refused to return any runaway slaves who crossed the border. All of this was part of the problem. In fact, Mexico was threatening to go to war again while Anson Jones was president. Those in favor of annexation thought Texas needed protection from the Mexicans. By making Texas part of the United States through annexation, the U.S. could continue its move westward—as far west as California, all the way to the Pacific Ocean. But there was the ever-present question: if Texas was admitted to the Union, would it be admitted as a slave state? Why, of course it would. Just what was Anson Jones's position in all this? Well, let's just roll back the clock to 1844 and see. Here he is now, and it looks like he's about to be visited by his secretary of state, Dr. Ashbel Smith.

(*ASHBEL SMITH enters porch from the crowd. He is very formal and diplomatic.*)

JONES: Good afternoon, Mr. Secretary, your visit is timely indeed. Rest yourself, sir.

SMITH: Mr. President, how does this lovely weather find you and yours?

JONES: As well as could be expected in the midst of so much controversy. I trust you have with you the answers to the annexation problem.

SMITH: I am happy to offer some optimism, yes. By the way, Mr. Henderson should be joining us shortly. I bumped into him in town just a while ago and he indicated that he was on his way here with some news.

JONES: Did he mention the nature of his news?

SMITH: I am afraid not, sir, only that it deserves your immediate attention.

JONES: *(Looking puzzled)* I see. And what about your negotiations with our European friends?

SMITH: Mr. President, through my prudence and skillful negotiation, I have succeeded in improving the republic's relations with France. Also, in yesterday's mail, I received ratification of a treaty of friendship and commerce between England and Texas. Of course if we succeed in getting certain powers within the Congress to recognize this treaty, they may well understand the necessity of acting quickly to annex Texas before it's too late.

JONES: What assurances do you have of this?

SMITH: Trust me, sir, the U.S. doesn't want to lose an opportunity to extend itself westward. Texas is a large piece of that pie. Until the annexation question is answered, the U.S. can move no further.

JONES: And what do you propose we do about Mexico? They would rather go to war than recognize our independence!

SMITH: It is my hope that they will yield when they learn that the major powers of Europe are willing to back us. Surely England and France are stronger than Mexico, whose government is still shaky. Wouldn't you agree?

JONES: I agree that our timing couldn't be better. The United States is more ready to act now than ever.

(JAMES PINCKNEY HENDERSON climbs onto the porch.)

Mr. Henderson, your timing is perfect. Welcome, sir.

HENDERSON: Mr. President, Secretary Smith.

JONES: May I offer you some water, or perhaps a stronger libation?

HENDERSON: Thank you, Mr. President—nothing for me.

JONES: Have you any news to share with us regarding the annexation of our great republic?

HENDERSON: I do, sir. I submit to you that the sentiment among the people of Texas is unanimous for annexation. I hasten to add that if the United States really desires Texas, she must act promptly.

JONES: I have instructed Mr. Van Zandt, our ambassador in Washington, to alarm Mr. Webster and the Congress that Texas is seeking alliances with Europe. I hope this will help them see the importance of taking immediate action. Once we receive the proper recognition from Britain and France, we may not need assistance from the United States.

SMITH: As I told the president, I have secured ratification of a treaty of friendship and commerce between England and Texas. And, I might add that I exhibited a modicum of prudence and skillful negotiation in improving our glorious republic's relations with France.

HENDERSON: Before you dislocate your shoulder patting yourself on the back, Dr. Smith, I must endeavor to remind you that neither England nor France is close enough to our sacred borders to guarantee a dang thang. (*With great conviction and self-importance*) My vote goes for annexation!

(*There is an uproar from the crowd.*)

SMITH: If you would allow me to finish my report, Henderson, I would be able to reassure you that friendly mediation by European powers is more than capable of stopping Mexican threats to reinvade Texas. As we stand here, they are encouraging immigration to Texas. And if you knew the positive attitudes of Russia, Prussia, and Austria toward Texas, perhaps you wouldn't be so shortsighted.

HENDERSON: I humbly beg your pardon, lest you forget that in 1837, I, myself, was appointed Texas Minister to England and France, with the charter to secure recognition and treaties of amity and commerce. It was largely through my efforts, not yours, that either one of these countries has ultimately recognized our independence. You simply cannot trust the Mexican government to stay south of the Rio Grande, Smith. You may call me shortsighted, but I am not blind. I say we need to declare war on them as soon as we have sufficient power to do so. And, furthermore, to pursue that war by any means necessary to secure our borders!

JONES: (*Clearing his throat emphatically*) Colonel Henderson, while your comments and opinions are understandable, I hereby admonish you to —

HENDERSON: Admonish me all you want! But if you admonish the people of Texas against annexation, sir, we'll see how long you'll remain their president!

(*He exits angrily. The crowd rumbles again.*)

JONES: I wonder who put a burr under his saddle? Well, Dr. Smith, have you anything more to report?

SMITH: If the president doesn't mind my saying so, I think we've heard enough reporting for one day. I'd best be on my way back to town. Good day, sir.

SCENE 6

NARRATOR: S'pose we take a look back at what happened back when things were a bit more normal around here. You see, Anson Jones built this place from scratch. Let's take a closer look at it. The big house, built in 1844, is the handiwork of Mr. J. Campbell, two of Jones's own Negroes, and four others hired from neighbors. This plantation is comprised of eleven hundred acres. It is worked by six slaves and several hired hands. It is a model of neatness and efficiency. Corn, cotton, and tobacco are the main crops grown here, as well as many vegetables, fruits, flowers, and shrubs.

About a week ago, Jones sold Jake to a friend of his, T. J. Allcorn. The year is 1850 and Congress has just passed the Fugitive Slave Law. This law requires states to return all runaway slaves. Of course runaways could also be killed if caught, as was the case for Jake. Bowen was never punished for killing him, and eventually came back to work for the Joneses.

People in both the North and the South began to wonder if there was going to be a war over the crisis of slavery. Oh, here comes Mr. Allcorn now. He's the man Anson Jones sold Jake to.

(*T. J. ALLCORN climbs onto the porch. JONES and MRS. JONES are on the porch. JONES is wearing a glove on his left hand and holds his left arm limply.*)

T. J. ALLCORN: Howdy, Mr. President.

JONES: Ah, glad you could come out, Allcorn. Quite a coincidence meeting you over in town the other day, wouldn't ya say?

ALLCORN: Indeed. And fortuitous too, seeing as how we can be of mutual benefit to each other.

MRS. JONES: (*Coming onto the porch*) How d'you do, Mr. Allcorn. How's your missus, sir?

ALLCORN: Very well, thank you. She sends her regards to you and the children.

MRS. JONES: Our cook has just prepared a fine meal. Won't you have a bite while you're here?

ALLCORN: Thanks, but no thanks, ma'am. I've got to be getting back to town 'fore nightfall.

JONES: What d'ya say we get down to business, Allcorn?

(*He motions to MRS. JONES, who touches his shoulder and returns inside house.*)

ALLCORN: This Negro of yours, just how old is the boy?

JONES: Not over twenty-five. Still got plenty of good years left in him. I've nothing against keeping him except I need the money to make a trip to New York.

ALLCORN: I see. Political business, huh?

JONES: Not exactly, although I will stop in Washington City while away. Pay a visit to Senator Rusk and ol' Sam Jacinto. This trip is primarily to do research on my family's history. As you see, I am a descendant of Sir Thomas Cromwell and I'm intending to document my genealogy—

ALLCORN: Uh-huh. (*Not the least bit interested*) I'm prepared to offer six-fifty for the boy.

JONES: I'm sure after you take a look at him, you'll agree that he's worth at least a thousand dollars.

ALLCORN: Surely you don't think I rode all the way ovah here to spend that kind of money, now do you?

JONES: Slaves are a man's wisest investment these days . . . especially since there's been an end to importation from Africa and this ain't Virginia, you know. Slaves are worth a lot more here in Texas.

(ALLCORN doesn't appear to be ready to back down.)

What about nine hundred? A—

ALLCORN: Suppose we settle on eight hundred. And I'm afraid that is as high as I can go—friend or no friend. (*He chuckles.*)

JOSÉ: (*Enters from right of big house*) *Perdóname, señor. Es la hora para salir.*

JONES: *Un momento,* José. Go tell Jake to come here, *inmediatamente. ¡Vamos, pronto!*

JOSÉ: *Sí, señor.* (*Keeps busy in the background—unnoticed by JONES and ALLCORN*)

ALLCORN: Ain't that one o' the López boys from 'roun Seguin?

JONES: Right. How did you know?

ALLCORN: His father built a fence for me once, 'fore he moved his family back to Seguin. Some runaways were discovered down there last I heard. Claim the Meskins are helpin em git 'cross the border into Mexico.

JONES: I doubt López and his boys would have anything to do with that.

ALLCORN: There's a good bit of our money hanging round that border, ya know that well as I do. Callahan and a few others is planning a expedition to go brang dem niggras back.

JONES: Ranger Captain James Callahan?

ALLCORN: Yep, that's him, alright. Texas ain't no different from any other slave state. Our way of life is gone stay our way of life. Wouldn't you say so, Mr. President?

JONES: Let's get back to our business. I expect Jake might put up a fight. Are you prepared for that?

ALLCORN: Long as you tell 'im that you're hiring 'im out t'me, there ought not be no fight.

JONES: As you like. Just have your draft in my bank by end of the week.

(They shake hands; JAKE enters.)

Ah, Jake, my boy, you're going with Mr. Allcorn here. He needs some work done over at his place in Independence.

JAKE: You hiring me out, suh?

JONES: That's right, Jake. (*He's lying.*) Mr. Allcorn will be leaving shortly. Best go get something to eat and some to take with you.

(In the background, we hear a male voice singing "We'll Understand It Better By and By.")

JAKE: How long I'm-a be gone, Massa Jones?

JONES: *(Pauses)* You'll be home before you know it. Run along, now.

(JAKE exits reluctantly—JONES calls after him.)

And you take care to mind Mr. Allcorn, ya here?

(JONES and ALLCORN exit to barn, ad-libbing—JAKE watches them leave and looks sad.)

JAKE: *(To himself)* Why you done that to me, Massa Jones? Why you done that?

(Sound cue 1: slaves sing "We'll Understand It Better By and By.")

(Chorus)
By and by when the morning comes,
When the saints of God are gathered home,
We'll tell the story how we've overcome;
For we'll understand it better by and by.

(Verse I)
We are often tossed and driv'n
On the restless sea of time,
Somber skies and howling tempests
Oft succeed a bright sunshine
In that land of perfect day,
When the mists have rolled away
We will understand it better by and by (by and by).

JOSÉ: *(Enters)* ¿Adónde vas, mi amigo?

JAKE: *(Angry)* To get some food to take with me. I'm leavin.

JOSÉ: *(Making sure they are unnoticed)* Yo sé, pero—¡espérate! *(I know, but—wait!)* Tienes razón estar enojado. *(You have reason to be angry.)*

(Motions JAKE to side of house. NARRATOR motions for the crowd to follow.)

¿Podemos hablar? (Can we talk?)

JAKE: *No tengo tiempo—* *(I don't have time—)*

JOSÉ: Señor Jones, he— *(Pauses and looks around again, cautiously)*

JAKE: Yeah, what de hell is it, José?

JOSÉ: Señor Jones—he sold you to that man, to him. *(Pointing to ALLCORN)*

JAKE: *(Anger rising, ready to fight)* He done what?

JOSÉ: I want you know so you can say *adiós* to your people . . . and Lucy. Don't say who tol' you. Remember, I have a family, too!

JAKE: *(Trying to contain his anger as he looks at JONES)* ¡Yo deteste él! *(I hate him!)*

JOSÉ: I must go now. *Vaya con Dios, mi amigo. (Go with God, my friend.)*

JAKE: *Gracias, mi hermano. (Thank you, my brother.)*

(They embrace; JOSÉ exits.)

(Sound cue 2: reprise of "We'll Understand It Better By and By")

SCENE 7

(JAKE crosses to the backyard—NARRATOR motions to the audience to follow. JAKE tries to get LUCY's attention. LUCY sees him but is called by MRS. JONES.)

MRS. JONES: Lucy, come feed Lil Anson—see if you can quiet him down. I want to write a letter to Mr. Jones.

LUCY: Ma'am, I just started baking bread.

MRS. JONES: Well, where is Lenora?

LUCY: She gone to the corncrib and I gots to be baking the bread. *(Starts to exit but is stopped by Mrs. Jones)*

MRS. JONES: Don't you walk away from me, gal. I am sick and tired of you always thinking what you doin's more important than what I want you t'do! And when you do what I ask, you're slow as molasses in January! Now you do what I say, gal. You come feed Anson, right now! *(She starts inside, but stops when LUCY speaks.)*

LUCY: *(She adjusts headrag and apron.)* Ma'am, I has tried to feed him three times already dis mawnin, but he ain't hongry. I think he sick, ma'am.

MRS. JONES: Are you sassing me, gal? After all I've done for you — keeping you around the house 'stead of out to the fields — because of your condition. I will not be talked to like that by any of you. Is that understood?

(Lenora enters.)

Oh, thank God, here comes Lenora! Mary, you come on over here, too.

(LENORA crosses to LUCY.)

Master Jones is going to be away for a spell and I'm runnin things until he gets back. That means Mr. Bowen, the field hands, and the two of you are gonna have t'do what I say. Am I making myself clear? If I tell Master Jones that I'm having the least bit of trouble out of you all — that Lucy sassed me in my own yard, he'll sell the lot of you faster than dew evaporating on a July mornin. And he'll replace you with slaves who'll be happy to do what they're tol'. Now do I have to tell Mr. Bowen to get his whip?

LENORA: Miz Jones, don't pay Lucy no never mind, she gone do what all you say. *(Gives LUCY an angry glance)*

LUCY: I'm powerful sorry, Miz Jones. I go feed Lil Anson right now. He prob'ly hongry.

(LUCY and LENORA exit into the house, followed by MRS. JONES. JONES and ALLCORN enter, looking for JAKE.)

JONES: Jake! Jake, time to go!

(JAKE enters from kitchen with a package wrapped in cheese cloth.)

ALLCORN: Come along, boy. You workin for me, now.

JAKE: *(MALACHI enters running.)* Malachi, yo' daddy's going away for a spell. You take good care yo' mama, ya hear?

MALACHI: How long you gone be gone?

JAKE: *(Looks at JONES and ALLCORN, then to MALACHI)* Don't rightly know, son. You tek care of you Mama an' the baby for me, ya hear?

MALACHI: Yessuh, Pappy, I will.

(MALACHI exits, running. JAKE crosses to JONES.)

JONES: Now, I told Allcorn here that you are as dependable as the sun and will do the work of two hands. Don't disappoint me. I 'spect we'll see you back here by Christmas.

ALLCORN: *(Hand on his pistol)* I ain't gone have no trouble wit ya, am I boy?

JAKE: *(Eyes lowered)* Naw, suh. No trouble, suh.

ALLCORN: *(Still staring at Jake)* No — I 'spect not. *(To Jones)* I'll be reportin back 'bout Jake — see if he's all you say. *(Shakes hands with Jones)* Well, Mr. President, I'm much obliged. *(Turns and exits)*

JONES: Allcorn. You give my best to your missus. *(With a little sadness)* Jake, you mind Mr. Allcorn and take care of yourself.

(Sound cue 3: instrumental version of "In the Sweet By and By")

SCENE 8

NARRATOR: Well, Jake's been gone for a spell. Lucy's made some adjustment to his leaving. Thinking about her new baby a'commin and all. Soon after Jake left with Allcorn, Master Jones left for New York to study up on his genealogy — that's all about his family tree, his ancestors and all. Who begat who, like in the Bible. Mr. Jones says he and his people been begat by famous historical people. Say he gonna find out about all of 'em. Anyway, he's been gone a while. He left Mrs. Jones to run the farm, with Mr. Bowen's help. This was a quiet, peaceful day — like the God Lord was sayin, "Y'all take it easy for awhile." Leastways, it all started out like that. The children are playing in the backyard and carryin on when Lucy came out of the house and headed for the smokehouse for some preserves. But all that peace was about to change.

LUCY: *(One of the children bumps into her.)* You chirren watch out! 'Bout knocked me down.

LENORA: *(Enters yard from house with a stack of plates)* Y'all settle down. An' cut out all dat foolishness! Come on sit yo'sefs ovah here so's you kin eat.

(They sit on the bench.)

Okry, come pass out de plates.

(OKRY does as she is told.)

LUCY: *(Quieting the still rowdy children)* If y'all don't settle down, we gone give all yo' grits to de hogs.

(They laugh.)

I ain't foolin—we feed y'all to the hogs, too.

(Some children scream in fear—others laugh.)

Them hogs just love little chirren—specially little black chirren.

(More screams and laughter as LUCY crosses toward the house. Before she gets there, LENORA's loud scream is heard from inside the house.)

LENORA: Oh, Lawdy, have mercy! I'm dyin fo' sho.

(JERRY runs past an immobile LUCY into the house.)

He'p me, Jesus!

JERRY: *(In the house)* Girl, what you done did to yo'sef?

LENORA: *(In the house)* I done dropped that butcha knife—went clean into my foot! Oh, Lawd, I'm dyin!

JERRY: *(In the house)* Girl, you ain't dyin. Just a flesh woun'. But if you track blood all over Mrs. Jones's floors, she gone skin you alive. *(Pause)* Now, hol' yo'sef still. I gots to pull it out. You better bite down on this rag, girl. This is likely to smart a bit. *(Pause)*

LENORA: *(In the house)* *(Screams)* Oh, Lawdy, please! I'm dyin fo' sho! Take me, Jesus, take me home!

JERRY: *(In the house)* Stop that caterwaulin fore Mrs. Jones hears ya. This rag'll stop the bleedin from gittin on de flo'. Mrs. Jones be thinkin we butcherin hogs here in de kitchen. She skin us all. Lean on my shoulder, gal.

(They enter from house—LENORA hopping, bandaged foot in the air.)

You jes sit here on the steps and let me tend to yo' foot.

(The children crowd around trying to see LENORA's foot. Two of them bump heads bending toward her foot and one of them drops a plate on her foot—she screams.)

LENORA: Oh he'p me, Jesus! I dyin fo' sho! I'm bound for glory!
JERRY: You bound for a good taste of Mr. Bowen's whip, you keep shoutin lak that. Hush up, girl. *(To the children)* Y'all git away from here, right now!
CHILD 1: We wanna see!
CHILD 2: Her toe cut off? Can we have it?
JERRY: No, but you can have my belt, if you don't git!

(They run away squealing. LUCY comes to look at LENORA's foot. She bends downs and bumps JERRY's head as he bends down, too—they ad-lib, "Ouch." LUCY drops a plate on LENORA's good foot.)

LENORA: *(Screams louder than before)* Oh, sweet Jesus! I'm dyin fo' sho! Mama, yo little girl is comin to be with you in heaben!
JERRY: You ain't dyin, Lenora. But you don't hush up, Mrs. Jones gonna shoot you an' you wind up in that other place. *(Hands plate to LUCY)* Dammit, Lucy, you worse'n the chirren! Go clean up that mess in the kitchen. Mrs. Jones have Bowen whip us all—see that mess in dare.
LUCY: How come I gotta clean up dat mess? Wuzn't me what dropped a butcha knife on my foot.

(Exits to the house, muttering, as MRS. JONES enters)

Why I gots ta clean it?
MRS. JONES: What's all this hollerin about? *(Sees LENORA's foot)* What on earth have y'all done, now?
JERRY: A little accident, Mrs. Jones—nothin to worry on.
LENORA: Whatcha mean, nothin to worry on? I 'bout loss my toe.
CHILDREN 1 AND 2: *(Running to the porch)* Can we have it?

JERRY: (*Chasing them away*) Y'all get out of here, 'fore I feed yo' toes to the hogs!

(*They run away, squealing gleefully.*)

MRS. JONES: (*Crossing to LENORA*) Let's have a look at this. You're gonna have to be more careful. (*To LUCY in the house*) Lucy, bring some water and clean rags.

LUCY: (*In the house*) Yes'm.

MRS. JONES: (*Looks at LENORA's foot—LENORA screams in pain.*) Hush up, gal. If you'd been payin more attention, 'stead of studyin on that buck of yourn, this wouldn't a'happened. Hold still. (*To LUCY*) Where's them rags, Lucy?!

LUCY: (*In the house*) Comin, ma'am.

MRS. JONES: (*To herself*) Girl's slower than molasses in a snowstorm. (*To JERRY*) Go get Mr. Jones's doctoring bag.

(*He exits quickly—she shouts to JERRY.*)

And mind you, don't go trackin dirt in Mr. Jones's study.

(*LUCY is exiting the house with a pan of water and some rags and collides with JERRY as he tries to enter. The rags go flying and the pan hits LUCY on the foot. She cries out in pain.*)

Will y'all please watch what you're doing 'fore ever danged one of ya is laid up and none fit for work!

(*LUCY stands looking at her injured foot. JERRY exits to the house.*)

Don't just stand there, Lucy. Pick up the rags and get some more water.

(*LUCY bends down, pregnant as she is, to pick up the rags—her head is to the left of the door but her behind is in the doorway. When JERRY comes out of the doorway, he bumps into her behind and knocks her down. He runs to MRS. JONES with the medical bag [or wooden box]. MRS. JONES shakes her head in disbelief.*)

JERRY: Here's Mr. Jones's doctorin stuff, ma'am.

MRS. JONES: Thank you, Jerry. Help git Lenora to the cabins. Take this and dress Lenora's wound. When you're done, go help with the plowing. I'll be by later to check on Lenora.

(*BOWEN enters hurriedly.*)

BOWEN: What's happened here? What's these darkies done now? (*Crossing to JERRY, menacingly*) Answer me, boy!

MRS. JONES: Mr. Bowen (*Stopping BOWEN with her voice*), I think that I have the situation well in hand, if you please.

BOWEN: Well, I don't know, ma'am. Mr. Jones asked to look after you and—

MRS. JONES: Well, Mrs. Jones is telling you that everything is being taken care of. I suggest that you take care to git your work done and leave me to mine. I expect the plowing to be finished, 'fore sundown. Now, run along and see to it.

(*He wants to say something, but thinks better of it. He exits, his anger apparent. LUCY enters from the house with a pan of water and some rags—she is limping. She and JERRY help LENORA to Slave Cabin 1. MRS. JONES watches them leave and shakes her head again.*)

NARRATOR: Well, so much for that peaceful day Mrs. Jones was planning on. But the worst was over. Now she had time to read the letter from her husband that she'd picked up in town that morning. She missed her husband a lot and was saving the letter until she had the time to read it carefully and savor each word.

SCENE 9

MRS. JONES: (*She opens letter slowly, with great anticipation, then speaks to herself before she reads the letter.*) My dear Anson, how I wish you were here to tend to things. It is so trying, especially now that I'm pregnant. However, there was no way for either of us to know before you left. I guess it's just fate. (*She reads silently as JONES's voiceover is heard.*)

JONES: (*Voiceover*) My dear Mary, it is my fondest hope that you and the children are in good health and spirits. I so hope that the business of running our small farm has not caused you to carry too much weight. It thrills me to know that we are expecting our fourth child, which is weight enough for you to carry.

(*MRS. JONES smiles and caresses her stomach.*)

JONES: (*Voiceover*) With the completion of my ancestral record, I will have reached another milestone in my life. I hope my public service as secretary of state and president of the Republic of Texas has rendered honor to the Cromwell lineage. I thank God that I have been blessed to serve my country and my family. Thomas Cromwell was born somewhere about the year of Our Lord, 1500. He was the Cromwell of Shakespeare and King Henry VIII. I presume that at some point in our lives we can see ourselves just a speck on the broad canvas that stretches between long ago and the future. Perhaps my grandest moment came when I had to surrender the presidency.

MRS. JONES: (*Remembering that time in her life also*) I can see him standing there, before the Congress and all those other high and mighty dignitaries . . . And he was never more tall, more stately, more confident. I was so proud of him.

(*JONES comes through the front door of the house, formally dressed. He speaks as if addressing Congress.*)

JONES: I, as president of the Republic, with my officers, am now present to surrender into the hands of those whom the people have chosen, the power and the authority which we have sometime held. This surrender is made with the most perfect cheerfulness . . . I lay down the honors and cares of the presidency with infinitely more personal gratification than I assumed them. The lone star of Texas has passed on and become fixed forever in that glorious constellation which all freemen must reverence — the American Union. May a gracious heaven smile upon this consummation of the wishes of the two republics. "May the Union be perpetual, and may it be the means of conferring benefits and blessings upon the people of all the States," is my ardent prayer. The final act in this great drama is now performed. The Republic of Texas is no more. Long live the great state of Texas![13]

(Sound cue 4: Fireworks are heard in the background.)

SCENE 10

(Sound cue 5: "Sweet By and By," sung by the slaves, is heard coming from behind the barn.)

NARRATOR: Well, on behalf of the Jones family and all their slaves, I'd like to thank you for listening to our story. Like Jake's short life, our story is over. We invite you to follow me to Jake's funeral.

(All cross to the funeral.)

SLAVES: *(Singing)*

In the sweet (in the sweet) by and by, (by and by)
We shall meet on that beautiful shore; (by and by)
In the sweet (in the sweet) by and by, (by and by)
We shall meet on that beautiful shore.

(The audience is encouraged to draw nearer, close enough to see a grave and a pine box. The slaves gather toward the back of the grave in a semicircle. Jerry assumes the role of preacher, as singing continues.)

JERRY: There's a land that is fairer than day,
    And by faith we can see it afar,
    For the father waits over the way
    To prepare us a dwelling place there.

(The slaves kneel and begin to hum the song's chorus while JERRY prays.)

JERRY: Father in heaben, we's gathered beneat' yo throne ub mercy for de homegoin ub our brudder, Jake. He libbed here 'mongst us, wukked in de fiel' 'mongst us, et wid us, and prayed wid us, Lawd Jesus. He was somebody chile, so bless his soul. Don't none o' us come here t'stay. An' don't none o' us come here to be shot down lak a dog in de dus'. But you knows de beginnin and de en', de alpha and de omega, de firs' and de las'. So ashes to ashes and dus' to dus', you is de only one dat we kin trus' to deliber us ober unto de breas' ob de udder shore, where dis pain and sufferin shall be no more. In de name o' Jesus, amen.

(All rise, continuing to sing chorus of "Sweet By and By." Now that JAKE has been buried, the slaves replace their hats, previously taken off for prayer, and begin slowly walking away in the direction of their cabins. The audience is led away from the scene and back to the road.)

(top) Naomi Carrier and Bill Dolman making plans for living history. Barrington Living History Farm, 1999; Jake waiting for a chance to tell Lucy goodbye. Barrington Living History Farm, 2000; (bottom) Overseer Charles "Kit" Fordyce looking for Jake. Barrington Living History Farm, 2000; James Reed Faulkner portrays Jake, a runaway slave. Barrington Living History Farm, 2000

(top) **Consoling Lucy over Jake's murder: Devonae Servance and Tiffany Williams. Barrington Living History Farm, 2000;** (bottom) **Carrying Jake's body away. Barrington Living History Farm, 2000**

Sweet By and By cast on steps of Anson Jones's Home. Barrington Living History Farm, Washington-on-the Brazos State Park, Independence Day Celebration and Inauguration, 2000

PART

III

RUNNING AWAY

OVERVIEW

No discussion of slavery is complete without emphasizing the importance of resistance to human bondage, including the Underground Railroad, abolitionists, and the legislation that helped underscore the separation between the North and the South. Chronicles of the slave revolt of Gabriel Prosser in 1800, the *Amistad* mutiny of the same year, the planned insurrection of Denmark Vesey in 1822, and Nat Turner's rebellion in 1831 are well known. Less known are the facts surrounding an Underground Railroad from Texas to Mexico.

Aaron Mahr Yáñez, supervisory historian at the Palo Alto Battlefield National Historic Site in Brownsville, Texas, in collaboration with the National Park Service, worked hand in hand with Talking Back Living History Theatre to coordinate "Blazing Trails: The Underground Railroad from Texas to Mexico," the first regional conference on the subject. The conference was held at the Sam Houston Memorial Museum in 1999 and engaged leading historians and scholars — including Randolph Campbell, Ronnie C. Tyler, Vincent Deforest, Alwyn Barr, and Bernadette Pruitt, to name a few — in a discussion of what appeared to be an overlooked moment in the history of African American Texans. The public was surprised at the phenomenon and hungry for the information, and two additional conferences were held in the following years: one in 2000 in Athens, Texas, and another in 2001 in Galveston, Texas. Mahr Yáñez introduced the idea in his report "The UGRR on the Rio Grande":

> Many of the features usually associated with the underground railroad, such as a clandestine network of abolitionist "stations," or heroic efforts by black leaders such as Harriet Tubman to guide the enslaved to freedom, are usually missing in the underground railroad story in Texas and Mexico — U.S. statehood in 1845 further guaranteed that slavery would continue in Texas and the institution spread and strengthened

through the next decade. As slavery expanded in the late 1840s and 1850s, so did the incidents of runaways to Mexico. Piedras Negras, Coahuila, opposite Eagle Pass, became one of the primary destinations for runaways. In addition, the expansion of cotton trails to the mouth of the Rio Grande caused by the federal blockade of Confederate ports brought many enslaved blacks to the Rio Grande as teamsters. Not a few crossed the river into freedom. This was particularly true in Matamoros, the outlet for much of cotton trade. Runaways found many spots along the Rio Grande where a hand-pulled skiff waited for them to pull their way to freedom. The National Park Service and its counterpart for cultural resources in Mexico, the National Institute of Anthropology and History (Instituto Nacional de Antropologia Historia) is working to identify resources associated with the underground railroad in Mexico and Texas, as this is virtually virgin territory.[1]

Runaways from the Texas Gulf coast escaping via oceangoing vessels is very plausible. According to Patricia and Fredrick McKissack in *Black Hands, White Sails*, "Opposition to slavery was immediate and strong and from sabotage to armed insurrections slaves used any opportunity to free themselves."[2] Southern slaves sought to cross the Ohio River and escape north, and when that became a problem following the Fugitive Slave Law of 1850, slaves in the northeast sought refuge in Canada. Slaves who lived in Tennessee and Kentucky escaped into the mountains; Louisiana slaves left their plantations and lived in the swamps; Florida slaves and others along the Atlantic seaboard found refuge on seagoing vessels, some fleeing as far north as Newfoundland or as far south as the West Indies. According to the McKissacks, "So many slaves were helped by seamen, one maritime historian noted that the Underground Railroad was virtually a ship."[3]

Uprisings, rebellions, and insurrections were a concern in Texas, too. According to Randolph Campbell there was an "insurrection scare" in Colorado County in 1856. Fear of an insurrection, suggested or otherwise, prompted this remark about "plotters" from the editor of the *Texas State Gazette*: he "would have no more qualms of conscience in hanging the white faced but black hearted fiend than in hanging a dog." Uprisings and insurrections were strictly not tolerated by Texans, who, in their opinion, had already lost too many slaves to Mexico. Officials of the law were poised to squelch that sort of activity at the drop of a hat and by any means necessary. Mexicans were warned not to assist runaways, resulting in some of them being expelled from Austin in October 1854. County representatives from as many as eight counties met and were on alert to counter any "threat posed by Mexicans to slavery."[4]

The official map and guide for the Underground Railroad distributed by the National Park Service, a division of the U.S. Department of the Interior, defines the Underground Railroad as "a movement in the United States from the early 19th century on to help bondspersons escape from slavery and reach freedom." Congress directed the National Park Service to conduct a study in 1990 that concluded, "The Underground Railroad was perhaps the most dramatic protest action against slavery in United States history." It characterized the activities as "a clandestine operation that began during the colonial period, later became part of organized abolitionist activity in the 19th century, and reached its peak in the period 1830–1865."[5]

The National Parks Conservation Association includes this statement that refers to routes:

> The Underground Railroad was the name given to the informal, early 19th century network of routes, safe houses, and allies, that helped guide enslaved Africans and African Americans during their escape from slavery to freedom. The Underground Railroad "ran" not just from the southern United States, north and into Canada, but west to Mexico and California, south into the Caribbean, and to a variety of international destinations that also held the promise of freedom.[6]

An additional definition may be found in the "Underground Railroad Resources in the United States Theme Study," published September 1998 by the National Historic Landmarks Survey.

These definitions give attention to the enslaved African Americans who escaped into Mexico. While some Texas historians disagree about whether there was an Underground Railroad in Texas, Ronnie C. Tyler wrote, "The loss of Negroes was not confined . . . to the traditional border states for the problem was even more vexing in Texas, where there was the luring possibility of escape across the unguarded international boundary into Mexico. Senator Sam Houston . . . often compared Texas to a border state such as Maryland or Kentucky. Mexico was nearer to Texas than Canada was to the slave states."[7] Tyler carefully points out that not only did "Mexico provide a haven for Negroes who risked their lives to run away," but "in fact, sheltered thousands of Negro fugitives by 1851."[8]

Tyler cited the specifics of the escaped slaves' exodus to Mexico at the Annual Meeting of the Texas State Historical Association, April 30, 1966, in Austin, Texas:

> John S. "Rip" Ford, long an advocate of reclaiming slave property from Mexico, had attempted to gain support for such action ever since purchasing the *Southwestern American* in 1851. Ford estimated in 1855 that there were approximately 4,000 fugitive Negroes in northern Mexico, valued at more than $3,200,000, and that the "evil . . . [was] augmenting daily." He warned, "Let men, goaded by frequent losses, once shoulder their rifles and make a forward movement in the direction of the Rio Grande, and nothing short of success will satisfy them." If the federal authorities continued to disregard the issue, they could "look for trouble on the Rio Grande frontier."[9]

Despite the threats, Mexicans and other abolitionists continued to help Southeast Texas slaves that escaped into Mexico. So many slaves had escaped from Texas plantations by 1855 that the loss to planters was great enough to prompt an expedition into Mexico for their capture. James Hughes Callahan, former military leader, early Texas Ranger, and soldier of Texas Revolution was the man to manage what became known as the Callahan Expedition.

This mission was shrouded in mystery and was promoted as a campaign to pursue the Lipan Indians, but was unsuccessful due to the lack of cooperation of the Mexican government in Coahuila. In the end, Callahan was forced to retreat when "a combined force of Mexicans, Indians, Seminoles, and Mascogos pursued Callahan's column to Piedras Negras." Callahan and his men were forced to retreat, but not before they "sacked and burned the town."[10]

Herbert C. Aptheker writes in *American Negro Slave Revolts*,

> In September, 1850, several hundred former Florida maroons fled from their abode in present Oklahoma to Mexico, and accomplished this by routing a body of Creek Indians sent to oppose them. Mass flights of slaves from Texas at about this same time seem to have reached the stage of rebellion . . . An item in *The Liberator* of April 18, 1851, declares: "Galveston dates to the 28th say that a large number of negroes in Colorado County have succeeded in escaping into Mexico; and the

late extensive plot was only partly frustrated." It was later reported that about fifteen hundred former American slaves were aiding the Comanche Indians of Mexico in their fighting, and it is a fact that Texan slaveholders, in the fifties, made several unsuccessful expeditions into Mexico in order to recover fugitive slaves, during which the Texans suffered several casualties.[11]

More than a few Texas ex-slave narratives relate stories about escapes to Mexico. Felix Haywood of San Antonio recounted that, "Sometime someone would come 'long and try to get us to run up North and be free. We used to laugh at that. There wasn't no reason to run up North. All we had to do was to walk, but walk South, as we'd be free as soon as we crossed the Rio Grande. In Mexico you could be free."[12] Another ex-slave, Jacob Branch from Double Bayou, Texas, said, "After war starts lots of slaves runned off to git to de Yankees. All dem in dis part heads for the Rio Grande River. De Mexicans rig up flat boats out in de middle de river . . . De white folks rid de 'merican side dat river all de time, but plenty slaves git through, anyway."[13] According to Ben Kinchlow of Wharton County, "We landed safely in Matamoros, Mexico, just me and my mother and older brother . . . We stayed there about twelve years. Then we moved back to Brownsville (Texas) and stayed there until after all Negroes were free."[14]

Arcy Attempts Escape, set in 1837, represents an earlier unsuccessful attempt to run away. Many attempts were thwarted because of weather conditions, inadequate food, poor health, or betrayed plans. Often runaways were inadequately prepared by not knowing enough about where they were trying to go, and assistance simply was not available for such secretive attempts.

Fugitives of Passion: On the Underground Railroad to Mexico is different from the other vignette in that it presupposes what I have conjectured and supported with facts known by historians about conditions that existed in 1845. Namely, some of the enslaved from East Texas no doubt escaped and hid in the Big Thicket on their way south to Mexico. The Big Thicket National Preserve has long been a favorite hiding place for fugitives of all kinds. Such enslaved fugitives were dependent on the fortune or misfortune of good-natured benefactors for food and shelter. While we have not yet documented such a network in East Texas, we cannot assume that sources for survival did not exist.

While the northeastern terms—like *engineer* (Harriet Tubman, for example), or *safe houses* and *stations,* which were operated by Quaker *station masters*— may be missing from the claims of an Underground Railroad in Texas, the evidence leads us to conclude that some revolts did occur, some successful and others unsuccessful. Free blacks, Mexicans, and, in later years, Germans were known to be benefactors to Texas slaves. We know that the conditions of slavery in Texas did not differ significantly from slavery elsewhere in the Deep South; the conditions for producing a cash crop, the terrain, size, and proximity of farms and plantations were all relative. Given *any* set of conditions, there was a resistance to the harsh realities of selling and owning human flesh, prohibiting the freedom to work for wages, and obliterating one's right to love and marry whom he or she chooses. The excuse that "old massa was a good massa" is no apology for his or her refusal to provide more than a menial subsistence for humans in exchange for free labor. These were the conditions of slavery in North America, and we used the setting of Montgomery County in 1845 to tell the story of Cudjo and Hannah.

We are deeply indebted to the writers of the film *Race to Freedom,* written by Diana Braithwaite and Nancy Trites Botkin, for ideas that helped form the content of *Fugitives of Passion.*

ARCY ATTEMPTS ESCAPE

Written for performance at Texian Market Days Festival
at the George Ranch Historical Park, 1995

CHARACTERS

ARCY: slave of Henry and Nancy Jones
FATHER MULDOON: Catholic priest
JACK: Arcy's son, age 14
HENRY JONES: owner of Stock Farm
NANCY JONES: Henry's wife
CROWD OF NEIGHBORS

SETTING

TIME: *1837*
PLACE: *The New Republic of Texas, Fort Bend County. Jones Stock Farm prior to the departure of Father Muldoon for Mexico*

SYNOPSIS

Around the Stock Farm there is tense debate for and against slavery in the newly formed Republic of Texas. The Mexican government is against it, but the proponents for slavery have won their cause. Slave imports are on the rise. Arcy tries to convince Father Muldoon, a Catholic priest, to help her and her son escape to Mexico.

SCENE 1

(At curtain rise, slavery in the new Republic of Texas is being vigorously debated. Some neighbors have gathered at the Jones' to herald a visit from Sam Houston, general of the Texas Army and now president of the republic. He has just departed from the area. The Mexican government was and still is against slavery. However, the proponents for slavery have won their cause. Since Texas won the Battle of San Jacinto and declared independence from Mexico, there has been an increase in the number of slaves imported to work the land, and HENRY JONES too has purchased more slaves. Now, ARCY, his first and oldest slave, wants to take her son, JACK, and escape to Mexico with the assistance of FATHER MULDOON, a Mexican priest, who she feels will be sympathetic to her cause. She waits to catch him alone.)

ARCY: *(Catching FATHER MULDOON unaware)* Father Muldoon, you a man of God, huh?

MULDOON: *(Compassionate at first)* Of course I am. You seem to be upset about something.

ARCY: *(Nervously looking around to see who may be watching her)* Yessuh, I is. S'cuse me if I ain't myse'f jes now, but I hear the way you talks to dese people roun' here and I know you and the Mexicans is 'gainst slav'ry. Dey's haulin us in f'om eb'rywhere. Eben Africa.

MULDOON: Well, we simply don't think it's right, but there is not a thing that can be —

ARCY: Since Texas done got innapendent, us slaves is bound to suffer more than we has already.

MULDOON: What is your name, child?

ARCY: *(Looking around fearfully, lest she be caught)* I'se Arcy, and this here is my boy, Jack. We want, suh —

MULDOON: *(Trying to distract her)* Buenos días, Jack. You are a strong, healthy boy. How old are you, boy?

ARCY: He's a slave, suh, like me, and we wants to git 'way f'om here. Can you he'p us, please?

MULDOON: You must be mistaken, child. There is no way I could possibly take the risk.

ARCY: I been prayin to the Lawd, suh, lak ya always tol' us to do when you used to come here and preach. I done asked almighty God to take me and dis boy 'way f'om here. You is our only chance, cain't you see?

MULDOON: *Señor y Señora* Jones are my friends. I couldn't possibly do such a thing.

ARCY: (*Intently*) Massa Henry and Miz Nancy is good white folk, if'n dere is such a thang, but dey done went and bought all dese othuh slaves, brung 'em wid no thought to how we gone all stay. Jes wuk is all dey know a slave good for. All us livin in de barn like pigs and chickens. I'm beggin you to please take us to Mexico wid you. We won't be no trouble—

NANCY: (*Calling to ARCY from across the yard, approaching her in disgust*) Arcy! Where in the world have you been? I've been looking all over for you to come nurse the baby. She's crying for you. Don't you hear, gal?

ARCY: Yes'm. I hears, ma'am. (*With pleading eyes*) Father? You heard me, Father?

NANCY: (*Somewhat suspicious*) What's going on here, Father Muldoon?

(*ARCY disappears into the house, with JACK behind her.*)

MULDOON: Oh, it's nothing, *señora*. Sometimes the slaves like to pray with me and I see it my duty to oblige them. Only prayers, *señora*, just prayers *con Dios*.

NANCY: (*Hesitating to approve*) I see. Well, Arcy is needed in the house now, she can scarce be hangin around prayin at a time like this.

MULDOON: As you wish, *señora*. (*Hastens to exit her presence*)

SCENE 2

(*ARCY looks out the window at the first opportunity, searching for FATHER MULDOON in the crowd. She tries not to speak too loud when he happens near the window.*)

ARCY: (*Whispering, somewhat*) Father Muldoon, Father Muldoon, you hear me?

MULDOON: (*Caught off guard, he looks toward the window, noticing ARCY, but immediately tries to ignore her by disappearing into the crowd. He hastens to find*

HENRY JONES so he can let him know that it is time for him to leave.) Oh, there you are, *Señor* Henry. It is about time I take leave of you for my long journey back to Mexico. My *compadres* are ready to travel.

HENRY: The best of luck to you, *Padre*. We hate to part company with you, but I suppose your work here is finished, wouldn't you say?

MULDOON: *Sí, amigo. Vaya con Dios.* (*Turns to leave*)

ARCY: (*Running out of the house*) Father, Father Muldoon! Please, I beg you, take us with you! Me and my boy won't be no trouble, I promise. I wants him to git some schoolin and maybe I can find me a husban'. We wants to live like people, not slaves, suh. I beg you, suh, please take us wid you!

MULDOON: *Mira,* somebody come get this child!

(*ARCY is determined not to let him leave. Now others have begun to take notice of what is becoming a scene.*)

Señor Henry, *por favor,* come get your girl!

HENRY: (*Not believing the trouble ARCY is causing*) I am utterly surprised at you, Arcy! Don't I treat you and the boy good enough? Where on earth did you get this kind of spunk? Nancy, take her to the barn, will ya, and see to it that she doesn't leave til I come out there. (*Apologizing to MULDOON*) The almighty gall of this wench is—nevermind. *Padre,* you have a trip to make, and I have to attend to this matter so—

ARCY: (*Ashamed of the scene she has caused, begging mercy*) I meant no harm, Massa Henry, Miz Nancy. I jes wants to be free!

(*NANCY takes her away as she sobs into her apron.*)

MULDOON: (*Anxious to take leave of the situation*) Good day, *señor.*

HENRY: *Padre.*

(*Both shake their heads at what they wish to dismiss as something that shouldn't have happened. HENRY follows in the direction of NANCY and ARCY to render punishment. He calls JACK.*)

Jack, come 'ere boy.

(*JACK comes reluctantly, afraid of what is about to happen.*)

Go yonda and brang me that cowhide. Be quick, boy!

(JACK obediently runs away. To restore his honor, HENRY turns to his guests.)

Sometimes dese niggers has to be taught a lesson. Am I right, boys?
CROWD: *(Cheering enthusiastically, speaking in alternating voices)* That black gal *need* to be taught a lesson.

Yeah, let me at 'er. I'll show 'er who's master and who's slave.

A slave has got to be kep' in his place or he spoils de rest of 'em!

Beat hell outta her, Henry. An' when you give out, I'll take ovah and finish de job!

(There is enthusiastic laughter, as was evident during many lynch mobs.)

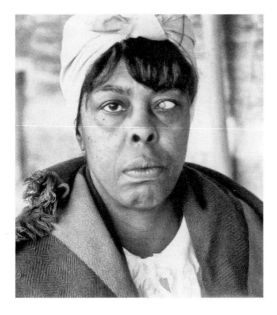

Naomi Carrier as Arcy. George Ranch Historical Park, 1997

FUGITIVES OF PASSION
On the Texas Underground Railroad to Mexico

Written for Sam Houston Museum Teacher Workshop on Texas History, 1999,
and performed at Fernland, a historical preserve in Montgomery County

CHARACTERS

CUDJO: age 28

HANNAH: Age 32

VINEY: a young slave woman whose lover was hung for attempted escape, age 20

PRINCE: mulatto child of Hannah and Jonathan Wood, age 5

MALONE: white banker, age 45

COLONEL JONATHAN WOOD: man who has never been a real colonel—it's just a nickname, age 40

PIERCE FONTAINE: Methodist abolitionist, age 35

WIDOW

MAN I: bounty hunter

MAN II: bounty hunter

WHITE FOLKS: Underground Railroad helpers and antagonists

SETTING

TIME: *1845*

PLACE: *East Texas, Montgomery County, Piney Woods*

SYNOPSIS

Cudjo and Hannah are slaves living on different plantations who desperately want to get married. Although the couple has made their wishes known, neither master will sell to the other. Furthermore, Cudjo's master has been overheard planning to sell him to settle a payment due on his mortgage. They decide to run away together, but dangerous matters complicate their decision because Hannah's master is the father of her young son.

SCENE 1

(Soft and moderately fast fiddle music plays. MALONE, a banker, and COLONEL JONATHAN WOOD, CUDJO's master, are wrapping up a conversation about a mortgage on which the bank is about to foreclose.)

MALONE: Sorry, Jonathan, you know if it was anything I could do, I would. But it ain't me, and I don't own the bank, as you well know. Best you sell one of your niggers and clear up the matter while you still got time. If you don't do something by Friday week, Wells is gone foreclose and that jes all there is to it. Soon as we 'come part of the Union, old Texas money ain't gone be no good. The bank's in no position to take a loss.

COLONEL JONATHAN WOOD: Yeah, yeah, I heard you the firs' time. Looking like this annexation's really gone become a reality, huh?

MALONE: Soon as them legislators boot Anson Jones from office as president, it's as good as a done deal.

WOOD: You look for me round noon next Monday. I'll have yo' money. *(Turns around and walks away, head down, exiting left)*

SCENE 2

(CUDJO and PIERCE FONTAINE, a Methodist abolitionist, enter from right, returning from a hunting trip. CUDJO is carrying a sack full of wild game. FONTAINE is holding a rifle in one hand, and has a gun in his belt.)

PIERCE FONTAINE: Cudjo, you ever heard about Mexico?

CUDJO: Heard what, suh?

FONTAINE: Mexico, it's a place where folks like yourself could be free to do as they please.

CUDJO: Free, suh? This plantation 'bout as much freedom as I gone ever have.

FONTAINE: *(Studies Cudjo for a while before making statement)* Well, you could perhaps be free, and this doesn't have to remain your home. *(Looks all around)* I'm here on more than one kind of business, Cudjo.

CUDJO: Most biznessmen like yourself, suh, firs' one kinda bizness or the other.

FONTAINE: Have you heard about the Underground Railroad?

CUDJO: Talking 'bout a train, suh? That's somethin I ain't never seen and prob'ly never will. A railroad?

FONTAINE: You'd think it was a train, but it's not exactly, even though it carries travelers—travelers to freedom. I'm what you might call a conductor, but I'm more like an abolitionist, someone who wants to abolish slavery. I desire to help anyone wishing to go to Mexico. I know of safe routes and how you can get some assistance.

CUDJO: I expect Colonel Wood, your friend and my massa, might not take to dat, suh.

FONTAINE: The colonel is not my friend. In fact, if he heard what I just said he would have me shot. Cudjo, you hardly know me. You—you will have to assume that you can trust me. Listen, your master offered you to me at a price few would decline for one such as yourself. You are aware of his intentions, are you not? He's planning to sell you!

CUDJO: (*He keeps his head down at first, then raises it to search for the truth in FONTAINE's face.*) Yessuh, I know.

FONTAINE: I will meet you right here, tonight, with plans. Be here. Will you do that?

CUDJO: (*Looks him in the eyes*) I better get back to the barn.

FONTAINE: Thanks for some fine hunting. (*CUDJO hands him the bag of game.*) No, no, give them to your cook. Let her cook up one for your Master, my host while I am here—where I do not expect to be any longer than necessary.

CUDJO: I will meet you tonight.

(*They exit, CUDJO going right and FONTAINE going left.*)

SCENE 3

(*HANNAH is in the field picking cotton, singing "Pick a Bale O' Cotton." [Optional: She interrupts the song to tell the audience about the importance of work songs—they keep the mind content while the body is allowed to work mechanically, to make the work go faster.] When she hears a love call from CUDJO, standing on the edge of the woods, she answers with a call of her own.*)

HANNAH: Jo, I can hardly b'lieve you here dis time o' day! What you wan'?

CUDJO: I'm leavin t'night. I want you t'go wid me.

HANNAH: You what?!

CUDJO: I say I'm leavin and I want you t'go wid me. I got plans t'go to Mexico f'om a bobolitionis'. I gots t'git back now. Meet me in de praise grove t'night when de moon comes up.

(He makes a quick exit, leaving HANNAH to question many things.)

HANNAH: Jo?! Wait, I—

(She is startled by his immediate departure, no questions answered. She begins to get her stuff together, singing "Wade in the Water," then leaves the scene.)

SCENE 4

(This scene takes place in the praise grove, an area deep in the woods where slaves were known to gather for religious services, a secret place unknown to the master or overseer.)

CUDJO: What took you so long, Hannah? We ain't got all night!

HANNAH: The missus is sick and I had to set up wit her all dis time, till she fell 'sleep.

CUDJO: *(Looking all around and through the bushes)* You by yo'sef?

HANNAH: I is now, but I tol' Viney to meet us here wit Prince so's I could say g'bye to 'im.

CUDJO: So you could *what*?!

HANNAH: I came straight here f'om the big house. Jo, I can't leave widdout sayin bye, can I? Why, dat's my chile!

CUDJO: Shh, you sound excited!

HANNAH: Course I'm excited! I been waitin all my life to be free an'—an' I can hardly b'lieve the time done fin'ly come. I'se jes happy dat's all—happy enough t'sang!

CUDJO: I is, too. Well? *(They sing the traditional song, "Woke Up Dis Mornin," in unison.)*

Well, I woke up dis mornin wid my min' stayed on freedom;
Woke up dis mornin wid my min' stayed on freedom.
Woke up dis mornin wid my min' stayed on freedom,
Hal-le-lu, (hal-le-lu)
Hal-le-lu, (hal-le-lu)
Hallelujah.

CUDJO: Hannah, we needs to pray. (*Praying, as HANNAH hums and softly moans in the background.*) Lawd, hear yo' humble servants, bowed befo' yo' throne of grace, and hab mercy on us, Lawd Jesus. We knows none but de righteous gone inherit yo' kingdom, and altho' we ain't done evahthang jes lak you want it, we has tried our bes' to please you, our Father, an' so we's askin you to fo'give us our debts as we fo'give our debtors. Send down yo' angel of mercy to guide us thoo de valley of de shadow of deaf. You an only you is de Almighty Gawd. An' it's you dat we's axin to carry us to de othuh side of de mountain. Fo' whilst it may be rainin on dis side, Lawd, we know dat ovah yonda dere's gonna be some sunshine an some res' fo' de weary. Dese an othuh blessins we ax in yo' son Jesus's name, amen and amen.

(*CUDJO rises from his knees and takes another lookout for VINEY and PRINCE's expected arrival. Satisfied that no one is near, he and HANNAH resume their praises and sing the traditional song "Oh, Freedom!"*)

Oh, freedom! Oh, freedom!
Oh, freedom over me!
An' befo' I'd be a slave,
I'll be buried in my grave,
An' go home to my Lord an' be free.

(*While repeating the chorus, they are interrupted by a noise, somewhere in the bushes.*)

CUDJO: Shh!

(*They all freeze. A child, PRINCE, walks into the clearing, rubbing the sleep out of his eyes.*)

Whew! It's jes lil Prince. Hey, boy, over here!

(PRINCE is followed out of the bushes into the clearing by VINEY, his nurse-maid. A soft ballad can be heard.)

HANNAH: Aw, c'mon, lil fella. Come to yo' Mama.

(PRINCE, a shy five-year-old mulatto child, runs into the clearing to hug his mother, somewhat sleepy and confused.)

Thanks, Viney, I'se gone always be beholdin t'ya fo' dis. What's de matter, baby?

PRINCE: I was scared, Mama.

HANNAH: Scared o' what, baby? Evahthang gone be awright.

PRINCE: *(Slowly, rubbing sleep from his eyes)* Aunt Viney woke me up and kep' tellin me t'hurry up. Why? Why you ovah here . . . *(Looking around)* when it ain't no church?

HANNAH: Now, you listen t'me . . . Mama gone hafta go 'way fo' awhile.

(He stares at her and starts to cry, but she shakes her head to let him know that it is not safe for him to make such noises.)

Viney here, she gone be yo' mama whilst I'm gone. Me and Cudjo, see Cudjo? You 'member him, don't you? Us got to leave here 'fore he git sol' away. Understan'?

PRINCE: Dis got anythang to do wit you gittin dat whuppin de othuh day?

HANNAH: Uh-hum . . . but I don't want you thinkin bout none o' dat, cause it ain't gone happen no mo' . . . not never.

PRINCE: Is I'm gone see you again?

HANNAH: Course you is, honey lamb, but it's liable to be a good while, cause we gone hafta go way far away . . .

(He grabs her neck and almost starts to cry again.)

Don't you worry chile, nobody roun' here gone let nothin happen to you . . . I hates to tell you dis but—but— *(She breaks down in silent tears.)* Oh, Prince, de massa? He be yo' pappy. *(She hugs him, crying softly.)* Dat's why

I could never tek you 'way . . . He be after me wit de dogs, til he hunt me down and brang me back.

PRINCE: Why you leabin, den?

HANNAH: It ain't cause I don't lub you, honey chile, I *gots* to git 'way. Me an' Cudjo jes can't stay here no mo', it ain't safe fo' us. (*There is silence. HANNAH looks all around, thinking.*) I was born here—been here all my life . . . an' now? Now, I got to leab evahthang I'se evah knowed, mos'ly I got to leab you, my onliest chile . . . But, now you hush up, don't you cry, uh-unh. Joy gone come one day when we meet again beyon' dat great river. You jes wait 'n see!

(*They embrace one last time. The slow ballad fades out.*)

VINEY: Come, Prince.

(*He bravely follows, but continues looking back, tears coming down his face. They exit into the woods, right. CUDJO, who has been watching out all this time, beckons for HANNAH to come into the woods, and both of them leave. Noises can be heard coming from the bushes and HANNAH runs back into the clearing, desperately sobbing, with CUDJO, close behind her, trying to get her to control herself.*)

HANNAH: You don't understan', I—I can't jes leave my onliest chile, I might not nevah see 'im no mo'. How come we gots to go clear to Mexico?!

CUDJO: If we don't go clear to Mexico, we liable t'git caught. You know well as I do, Hannah, dat any colored folk caught livin in Texas actin lak free folk, widdout no papers, is subjeck to be strung up, if not sol' to de firs' bidder. We has no choice—oh, I tek dat back, we can stay where we is! What you want, huh?

HANNAH: You done lost yo' min'?

CUDJO: You know yo' massa ain't nevah gone sell you to my massa so we can be togedder. He keepin you fo' hisse'f! And me? Massa's threatening to sell me any day now cause his mortgage done come due. How we gone be togedder wit him swearin he ain't got no othuh way out? I gots to run—an' I want you t'come wit me.

HANNAH: You'se axin me to gib up my onliest chile fo' you . . . uh-unh, I ain't goin.

CUDJO: You use t'say you wanted to marry me and hab my chile. Look, Hannah, I wants to go somewhere where I can be a man, where I can *do* for you—

HANNAH: Oh, Lord, why it hafta be so hard fo' us? Why can't we jes be happy wit what we got?

CUDJO: What we got?! What do we got? We ain't got nothin, nothin but what de massa give us. Now, we can't go on like dis. We gots t'try! Hannah, I means t'run. Now is you comin or ain't you? (*Long pause*) Hannah, I lubs you, gal. (*He embraces her.*)

HANNAH: (*Slowly looks up into CUDJO's face and begins to reconsider*) Okay. (*Wiping her tears*) Okay, I'll go.

CUDJO: Now git yo' thangs and let's go.

(*They disappear into the woods. Sound cue: play lowest E on a piano keyboard for suspense.*)

SCENE 5

(*Nature sounds can be heard. The next morning, CUDJO and HANNAH are awakened by sunlight coming through the trees. Lying next to each other, they are suddenly startled by a noise.*)

CUDJO: Wake up!

HANNAH: Uh-oh. Where are we?

CUDJO: In de middle o' nowhere. We got to git movin and quick.

HANNAH: Awright, awright. (*Adjusting her clothes and bundle*) We been truckin thoo dese woods nigh 'bout three days now and we gots no mo' food. You think dat bobolitionist know what he was talkin bout?

CUDJO: Well, either he didn't or we done messed up somewhere cause we still ain't seen none o' those safe houses he was talkin bout.

HANNAH: Maybe we should have stuck close to de river. (*Suddenly freezes*) Did you hear somethin?!

CUDJO: Uh-unh, where f'om?

HANNAH: I heard something coming from over there! Sound like dogs barking. Shh—listen!

CUDJO: (*Listening intently*) I don't hear nothin—you sho'?

(They stand still for a moment.)

You still hear it?

HANNAH: I—I . . . guess I'm jes hearin thangs. Scary is all.

CUDJO: *(Peering through the woods)* Hey, I sees a house up yonder.

HANNAH: *(Following close behind)* You do?!

CUDJO: *(Turning around to face her)* Hannah, we don't git some food, we ain't gone make it. *(Looking back in the direction of the house)* Look, look!

(They edge closer to what they discover is a small woodland house.)

Somebody is coming outside . . . Look like a ol' lady. Shh!

HANNAH: Don't let 'er see you! *(Getting scared again)*

(CUDJO can be seen peeping out of bushes, looking to see if it is safe to approach the house and ask for food. Just outside the house, an old WIDOW has stepped out to empty a dishpan. He is hoping she lives alone. After she goes back inside, CUDJO waits awhile, then cautiously runs to the house, leaving HANNAH behind, and rapidly knocks on door. Nature sound effects end.)

WIDOW: *(Stepping outside and cautiously looking around)* Anybody see you comin here?

CUDJO: No'm, nobody. Please, ma'am, could you spare some food? I'se lost an'—an'—

WIDOW: What happened to you? *(Looking him up and down, sorrowfully)* You alone, boy?

CUDJO: No' m, it's me and my missus. We won't be needing much, jes a lil food and some water, ma'am, and we'll be on our way.

WIDOW: Runnin, is ya? *(CUDJO starts to speak and she cuts him short.)* I ain't got much, but if you can take dat ax yonder and cut me some wood, I kin let you have a few biscuits . . . and a piece o'pork.

CUDJO: Kin I have two biscuits to start wif, ma'am? We ain't ate since yesterday mawnin, won't you please—

WIDOW: Okay, okay, wait here. But two biscuits is all you're gone git, til you cut that wood.

(She goes inside to get food. CUDJO beckons for HANNAH to come out of the woods. She does so warily.)

Now, y'all gone hafta go roun' yonder and eat 'em. I don't want *nobody* t'see ya.

(She points to the side of the house, where they take the food and run immediately, CUDJO stopping to pick up the ax first. Suspenseful music begins to play. Meanwhile, two bounty hunters [MAN I and MAN II] approach the WIDOW's house. So busy eating, CUDJO and HANNAH are caught unaware, and it is too late for them to run into the woods, so they freeze on the side of the house.)

MAN I: Miz Havlacek, you in there? Come on out here, ma'am.

WIDOW: *(Nervous and shaking)* Yessuh, what kin I do for ya, suh?

MAN II: You ain't seen a coupla runaway niggers sneaking roun' here, have ya?

WIDOW: *(Immediately)* Oh, no, why, nobody ever comes round here since Sebastian passed away. That's my husband. He had the yellow fever, ya know, an' folks hereabouts is plum scared to linger in places where someone died from it. Anyways, I'm kinda hard o' hearin and my eyesight ain't what it used t'be. Besides, even if—

MAN I: Yeah, yeah, nevermin', ma'am. Sorry t'bother ya.

(Sound cue: play lowest E on a piano keyboard for suspense.)

MAN II: Thanks anyway.

(All three of them are startled by a noise coming from around the side of the house.)

Uh-hum? *(Looks at WIDOW who begins nervously shaking)* Hard o' hearin, are ya?

(MAN I looks first at MAN II and then in the direction of the noise, and cocks his gun. If the bounty hunters are on horseback, they dismount. MAN I bolts around the side of the house on foot. CUDJO and HANNAH head for the forest again, but when MAN II fires a shot in their direction they are forced to stop

dead in their tracks. MAN I runs closer to the couple holding them hostage with his gun.)

MAN I: Hold it, I jes as soon shoot you as I would two rabbits! Yep, you's runnin alright.

MAN II: I say we string 'em up and take 'em back for dat reward, huh?

HANNAH: *(Terrified)* Oh, no!

(CUDJO, reacting to HANNAH's cries and to the ramifications of having to go back, abruptly turns to comfort her and speaks in a compassionate voice.)

CUDJO: Hannah—Han-nah. *(Unable to say more)*

(MAN I suspects his motive and immediately shoots him. CUDJO looks at HANNAH and falls slowly to the ground, dying. HANNAH is devastated and goes to his side, crying. The WIDOW, still nervously shaking in disbelief, slowly goes to comfort her.)

MAN II: *(Angry)* Aw, hell! Why'd you go do dat? Don't you know we can't make as much money off'n a dead nigger?

MAN I: *(Defensively)* He was comin at *me*, you saw 'im! You think I'm gone stan' up here an' let 'im attack me? No nigger is gonna attack me, you hear dat? Yeah, I shot 'im—and I'd shoot 'im again if I had to! Let's git him and that gal tied up on the horses and take 'em on back. *(He uses one hand to take a rope from his belt while still holding the gun on HANNAH.)* Don't you try nothin', gal! An' you, old woman, move on out the way. Remember, you ain't seen nothing. You hear me?!

MAN II: Yeah, nothing! Hush up that cryin' and git back in the house. *(Puts his gun back in holster and ties HANNAH's hands behind her back. She says nothing; just keeps staring at Cudjo.)*

(The WIDOW, looks at HANNAH with sorrow in her eyes, and slowly turns to go back inside. HANNAH is in shock. MAN I takes a rope and ties it around CUDJO. MAN II ties HANNAH's hands behind her back. The characters freeze and the quest for freedom ends.)

Cudjo convincing Hannah to run away to Mexico. Sam Houston Festival, 2000

PART

IV

BATTLES

OVERVIEW

Battles figure large in any history of any place, but especially so in Texas: the Battle of Goliad, the Battle of the Alamo, the San Jacinto Battle, and, slightly lesser known, the Battle of Velasco. All of these battles brought Texas from a colony to a republic in 1836, and eventually into statehood in 1845. In addition, the Mexican-American War and the last battle of the Civil War, at Palmetto Ranch, were both waged in South Texas. Battles have long been a decisive factor in the independence of peoples and the acquisition of land.

The two battles in the plays in this chapter are quite different in nature. One, in *Hell or High Water: Brit Bailey Heads Off Stephen F. Austin,* is more of a skirmish and disagreement over land holdings; the other, in *Still Am A'Risin': The Battle of Velasco and the Vigil at Bolivar,* is a battle that resulted from a dispute about runaway slaves from Louisiana who are attempting to go to Mexico via Texas.

James Britton Bailey, a main character in both these plays, was born in Kentucky in 1779 and fought in the War of 1812. His motto was "face west." He wore a coonskin cap. He always carried a gun with flintlock and ramrod, and was known to carry along a powder horn full of gunpowder. He and his wife Dorothy and six of their seven children migrated from Tennessee to Texas in 1818, three years before Austin's Colony. In addition to Bubba and Bell and their children (who are featured in their own play in Part One of this book), Brit brought "four additional slave men and such worldly goods as pots, pans, clothing, bedding supplies, one bed, one rocking chair, tools, seed, and two head of cattle."[1] Bailey argued and bickered with an agent of the Spanish government who "finally sold him a league and a labor of land, amounting to 4,587 acres."[2] This tract lay on the east bank of the Brazos River at the present site of Brazoria. According to Peggy Smith, "Bailey must have paid a goodly sum for the land, but was not given a deed." The area in which they settled was populated by the Karankawa Indians and was infested with mosquitoes."[3]

Dr. J. Mason Brewer, who has been called America's most noted black folklorist, gives the following account of Brit Bailey in his book, *Dog Ghosts and other Texas Negro Folk Tales:*

One of de ones what comed to be Nigguh rich rat heah in Brazoria County was Brit Bailey, what hab a great big plannuhtation what run jam up to Wes' Columbia. Brit comed to be a good liber by raisin' sugar cane on his plannuhtation, and habin' de knowledge to know how to sell hit an' meck money outen de deal. Dey call de paa't of de lan' he own Bailey's Prairie, an' dis heah de paa't what comed to be knowed by putty nigh evuhbody in dese paa'ts.

De why dat Bailey's Prairie done comed to be knowed by mos' de folks 'roun' dese paa'ts am dat many a one of 'em done seed Brit Bailey's ghos' ramblin' 'roun' dis prairie way late in de nighttime.

De why de ghos' meck his 'roun's am dat Brit Bailey's still watchin' ovuh his lan'. Whilst he was libin' he was knowed ez one of de bes' gunfighters in de county . . . he allus gittin' into shootin' scrapes. He allus toted a gun, and ca'ied a lantern wid 'im during of de nighttime, so when he died he lef' word in his will dat he wanted to be buried stannin' up wid his pistol in one han' an' his lantern in t'othuh one, an' a jug of whiskey at his feet. So his wife an' chiluns ca'ie out dis reques', an' dis jes' de way he buried. But t'warn't no time attuh he done been buried dat de reports was out dat folks passin' Bailey's Prairie way late in de nighttime seed ole Brit walkin' ovuh his prairie wid his pistol in one han' an' his lantern in t'othuh one . . . Ah knows lots of people 'roun' heah who's good Christuns who says dey done seed de Bailey Ghos' walkin' de priarie no longer'n de pas' mont' o' so.[4]

According to an article in the *Brazosport Facts,* dated June 6, 1976, Dr. Brewer was called "the best story teller of Negro folklore anywhere in America" by J. Frank Dobie, himself a distinguished folklorist. Brewer, who lived in Austin, died in Dallas in January 1975. Two of his other books provide additional interesting background material: *The Word on the Brazos: Negro Preacher Tales from the Brazos Bottoms of Texas* and *The Negro in Texas History.*

Catherine Munson Foster chronicled Brazoria County ghost stories for more than forty years for her book *Ghosts Along the Brazos.* According to Munson, Brit Bailey "was addicted to the bottle" and "he was supposed to have pulled a gun on Stephen F. Austin."

All these pieces of primary and secondary information were considered in the scripts for *Hell or High Water* and *Jumpin' Juba*, which can be found in part one of this book.

In 2002, when an opportunity presented itself to make our second appearance for the University of Texas Medical Branch at Galveston, we didn't want to repeat any plays we had previously performed. For this occasion I decided to employ the history that encompassed Galveston County. Knowing this was going to be an indoor production, I believed the element of dance was vital to its interpretation, as dance has its own intensity.

Three other elements were employed here for the first time. One, this play has a contemporary beginning that flashes back to colonial times. Two, the white characters pantomime while the enslaved characters speak their minds, giving the audience the benefit of two interpretations of the same situation. It was as though we could hear the intelligence of the enslaved in spite of their inability to tell their masters—they weren't supposed to think, just do. The third new element was the characters speaking to the audience and bonding with them in their monologues, as in Stephen F. Austin's and Jane Long's opening monologues.

HELL OR HIGH WATER
Brit Bailey Heads Off Stephen F. Austin

Written for Second Annual Austin Town Festival, 1998,
and sponsored by the Brazoria County Historical Museum

CHARACTERS

JAMES BRITTON "BRIT" BAILEY: an adventurous, gun-toting settler, age 42
UNCLE BUBBA: Bailey's trusted slave companion
STEPHEN F. AUSTIN: founder of first Texas Colony. He is educated, meticulous, small in stature, decorated, age 29.
AUSTIN'S SIDEKICK: white male, age 30–40

SETTING

TIME: *Spring 1822*
PLACE: *Bailey's homestead in Spanish territory, what is now Brazoria County, Texas*

SYNOPSIS

This vignette shows the hearty spirit and tenacious perseverance of the first Anglo settlers in Texas. It also reveals the colonists' attitude about the importance of slavery.

Brit was a gun-toting swashbuckler who refused to back down for any man, including the refined Stephen F. Austin. He arrived in Brazoria well ahead of Austin, and had carved out a home for himself on land that Austin claimed for his own. Brit held fast to his claim and Austin was bound to respect him for it.

The relationship of Brit Bailey to his trusted slave, Uncle Bubba, was more than that of master-servant. They were life-long comrades, depending on each other in life-and-death situations — one of which occurs in this vignette.

(At curtain rise, BUBBA is busy making a table from some wood he has chopped. BRIT is busy cleaning his muskets and taking inventory of his gunpowder.)

BRIT: Bubba, brang me my gunpowder, yonda, in that powder horn.

BUBBA: Yessuh. *(Some of his wood falls and he attempts to pick it up while another piece falls.)*

BRIT: Hurry up, would ya, Bubba?

BUBBA: Hold on, 'nare, Massa Brit. No sooner'n I git one thang finished, you tells me to do 'nother.

BRIT: Awright, awright! Let some o' dese Injuns git a hold of ya cause I ain't got these guns ready in case'n we needs 'em, and it'll be all yo' fault!

BUBBA: *(Handing him the gunpowder horn)* Here 'tis. Lawd knows I don' want no mo' trouble wit dese Injuns, not afta yestiddy. *(Going back to his woodwork)*

BRIT: That was what I call a close call.

BUBBA: You outslicked 'em tho, Massa, by offerin 'em dat firewater.

BRIT: Nevah seen one yet who wouldn't take a swig 'fore settling some disagreement. I always say, treat them right and they will usually treat you right, but treat them wrong and a nest of fiends will be loosed among you.

BUBBA: You think dis table I'se building gone suit Miz Dorothy?

BRIT: It's gone hafta suit 'er. This wilderness is hard on women folk. None of the thangs they craves is to be found out'chere.

BUBBA: My Bell had me up ha'f de night making beds for de younguns.

BRIT: What did y'all finally use?

BUBBA: Wit no more corn shucks around, we jes took some o' dat moss f'om dese oak trees and singed it a lil bit to git de bugs off'n it. Den we stuffed it inside a coupla ticks Bell sewed up wit a fish bone needle. I tell ya dat 'oman is some kinda clevah. She eben know how to make coffee outta roasted sweet potato hulls!

BRIT: Huh, you don't mean?! *(Filling one of his muskets with gunpowder and shining it with a piece of buckskin)*

BUBBA: Cross my heart and hope to die!

BRIT: To be hones', I dunno what we'd do widdout you and Mammy Bell. She's a heap o' company for Dot, and it's her cooking dat's keepin us alive. I'm hoping to go hunting and kill us a coupla deer. Bell sho knows how to smoke dat deer meat.

BUBBA: Yep, she sho do. Us mens has got the hard part o' skinnin dat rascal and cutting 'im up.

BRIT: I aim to do some tradin wit some o' dese Injuns 'round here, in a few days, when you and me take that trip up river to scout for some more land for Dot's folks who's planning to follow us. They oughta be arrivin this spring. I tried to git that brother of hers to come on wit us when we left fo' years ago but he decided to let me, as he calls it, blaze the trail.

BUBBA: Yessuh, we has sho nuf blazed de trail awright. Downright set it afire sometimes!

BRIT: Never a dull minute. You either keep peace wit these Injuns or they'll eat you for dinner. Know something, Bubba, this territory is like a virgin, jes ripe for near 'bout anythang we plant. Course we're still trying our luck to see what grows best. Last year we didn't do too bad. Least Dot and Bell was able to p'serve quite a bit of the vegetables we harvested . . . and we had plenty corn to last us through winter. With Bud, Speedy, Josiah, and Caleb working, and you overseeing 'em, I'll say we did right well.

BUBBA: I had Bud and Speedy clearin dat back lot jes beyon' y'alls cabin dis mawnin.

BRIT: Yep, when I left from back out there, they had already felled three trees. We need any lumber that's suitable for making furniture to be close to the cabin. Y'all bout to overwork that one mule to death.

BUBBA: Soon as we fell a few mo' trees, we're hoping to sow some corn, squash, and field peas. We plannin to plant a whole field o' corn back there, too.

BRIT: And don't forgit, we gotta plant that cane. It grows dern well in these parts. Out on the prairie, where y'all cutting grass for the horses, will be the best place for it.

BUBBA: Yessuh. You mentioned trading wit de Injuns. Don't you think we needs to take account firs'?

BRIT: Bubba, you is de smartest nigger I have ever known—even if you can't read nor write. To your recollection, what do we have that we might use for a trade?

BUBBA: We're bout out o' liquor, if that's what 'cha mean.

BRIT: Well, why don't you go check. And be sure an' ask Dot an' Mammy Bell.

BUBBA: Good 'nuf.

BRIT: Oh, yeah, brang me my ledger. I need t'do some figurin.

(BUBBA exits, stage left. BRIT talks to himself.)

I hafta say, my daddy really knew what he was doing when he gave me that nigger. Been wit me damn near all my life. Not only is he the best he'p I ever had, he's prob'ly my closest friend. Now him and Mammy Bell wanna git married. Like I say 'bout the Injuns, treat 'em right and they'll treat you right? Well, you treat niggers wit respect and the next thang you know, they wants the same thangs as decent white folk. Feature 'em wanting to git married? That's jes him knowing that I wouldn't never separate 'em . . . namely cause they's worth so much t'me. By golly, Bubba himself, why, I wouldn't let him go for a nickel less than twenty-five hundred dollars. He's the most valuable property I got.

(BUBBA returns, walking slowly and eyeing the ledger. BRIT doesn't see him because his back is turned the other way. He sits polishing a gun holster. BUBBA is taking more than a casual interest in the ledger.)

BUBBA: *(Reading)* "Maybe Speedy for two horses and a wagon?" *(Discreetly and mostly to audience)* I see here where Massa Brit was thinkin bout trading Speedy for them two horses and wagon he jes bought. I guess he figured a man was worth more to 'im. Jes lak dat! Speedy coulda been gone! I prays to de Lawd everday to keep me and my fambly togedder. An' I gots to git married to my wife. Dat's dat. I ain't lettin Massa Brit off'n de hook on it. *(Giving him the ledger)* Here you is, Massa. *(BUBBA continues)* I'm going on out behin' de house now, check on clearin dem trees. Might need to bu'n some brush dis ebenin . . . By th'way, you give anymo' thought to me and Bell jumpin de broom?

BRIT: I'm glad you mentioned that. Why don't we do it Sat'day week? We should be pretty far along wit the work by then and you and the others can take off next Sat'day afternoon.

BUBBA: Much obliged t'ya, suh. See ya.

(It turns out to be two more years before BUBBA and BELL get married.)

BRIT: (*Waits til BUBBA is out of earshot*) Reminds me of some of them frolics we use to have round my daddy's barn. Boy, dem niggers sho could cut up. Don't let 'em have a fiddler on the place, such as Bubba. They would cakewalk and quadrille till the break of day . . . (*Laughs*) trying to act like white folks.

BUBBA: (*Excited*) Massa Brit, Massa Brit!

BRIT: (*Turning around*) What the hell is it, Bubba?!

BUBBA: Some white mens is coming up on de place, looking kinda mean! (*Staring stage right, the direction from which they have been seen coming*)

BRIT: Gimme my rifle! See what I mean? That's why I keep this dang thang loaded at all times!

(*STEPHEN F. AUSTIN and a SIDEKICK ride up to where BRIT has been working. BUBBA stands at the ready, holding an ax in his hands.*)

BRIT: And just what can I do for you fellers? (*Pointing the rifle in their direction but aiming it more to the ground, since they appear to want to make peace.*)

AUSTIN: I see you've done quite a bit of work on a piece of land that's not yours . . .

BRIT: What the hell do you mean?! (*Raising rifle*)

AUSTIN: In case you don't know who I am, I . . . (*Dismounting, while SIDEKICK remains on horse. BUBBA holds them at bay with his ax and BRIT with the rifle.*) I happen to be Stephen F. Austin an'—

BRIT: I don't give a cat's meow who you are. I happen to own over four thousand acres 'round here and you standing on a piece—

AUSTIN: Show me your title, because I can prove that according to the Mexican govern—

BRIT: (*Pointing toward house with one hand and pointing the rifle with the other*) You see that house yonder? See them fields? I didn't jus git here, soldier boy—

AUSTIN: (*Removing papers from his upper coat pocket*) According to these papers, I own this land you built on—

BRIT: If you don't git back up on that horse and ride 'way f'om here fo' good, I'm gone blow you straight t'kingdom come! I ain't showing you nothing! The Spanish gov'ment sold me this property three years ago. I come to stay and if you know what's good for you, you'll leave here quick as I can pull this trigger! (*Aiming gun at his head*)

AUSTIN: *(Angrily getting back up on his horse)* You haven't heard the last of this. You'd better have a deed the next time we meet! I won't be alone!

(He and partner ride off swiftly, stage right, accompanied by sound effects of horses.)

BRIT: Saddle my horse, Bubba! And saddle one fo' yourself, too. I'm gone chase those rascals outta here fo' good and follow 'em far enough to see where they come from!

(He gathers up a couple of rifles and his gunpowder, puts on his holster, and gets ready to ride, all the time talking under his breath. BUBBA returns with a couple of horses.)

BUBBA: That must be some of dose folks dat Injun was tellin you 'bout yestiddy. 'Member he said they wasn't too far f'om here, f'om de way he wuz pointin.

BRIT: Yeah, yeah, I know it had to be somethin to what he was saying, all that sign language and crap. I just didn't take him serious. Can't trust nobody these days, and out'chere in this wilderness, one's liable to witness anything. Wit what all we been through to make this place into some kind o' home for our families, in spite of the Spanish an' the Mexi'can gov'ment, come hell or high water, I'll die 'fore I give up one acre! You hear me? Let's git after 'em!

(They mount and leave, riding off in same direction.)

STILL AM A'RISIN'
The Battle of Velasco and the Vigil at Bolivar

Premiered at Old Central Cultural Center in Galveston, Texas, February 2002

CHARACTERS

BOY: African American, age 6–12

GRANDPA: African American, age 50

AFRICAN KING: mature and wise-looking African American gentlemen

AFRICAN QUEEN: mature African American with poise and grace

DANCERS: six females and six males, used in all dance sequences as specified including CHAIN GANG

CHAIN GANG: five or more young males

SLAVE BOY: a young dancer, small in stature, dark (choreographer may be helpful)

OVERSEER: male, white, may wear a beard and have a heavy voice

SLAVE TRADER/AUCTIONEER: male, white, rough-looking

JAMES BRITTON "BRIT" BAILEY: tall, husky, and adventurous gun-toting settler, age 53

UNCLE BUBBA: Bailey's trusted slave companion, a tall, handsome fiddler, age 50

STEPHEN F. AUSTIN: founder of first Texas Colony. He is educated, meticulous, small in stature, and decorated.

KIAMATA LONG: Kiamata is her real name, but everyone calls her Kian. She is the property of Jane Long, age 24

JANE LONG: adventurous, exact, and charming, age 34. She was called the Mother of Texas because she gave birth to the first American child born in Texas.

(Dancers can portray the following characters.)

DOCTOR: male or female dressed as a doctor with stethoscope

CONSTRUCTION WORKER: male dressed as construction worker in a hard hat

BUSINESSWOMAN: female dressed as a businesswoman with a briefcase

SETTING

TIME: *June 1832*

PLACE: *Brazoria and Galveston Counties, Texas. Jane Long's Boarding House in Brazoria*

SYNOPSIS

Based on the history of Brazoria and Galveston counties, this play explores the significance of some of the first blacks who arrived in Texas in 1818–1832: a time when questions of the African slave trade in Texas, the Mexican laws against slavery, and the colonists' attitude that slavery was an economic necessity were all forces that governed the increase in the black population. These issues are examined from both points of view: the enslaved and the colonists.

Dance is used to dramatize the importance of Africa's royal kingdoms and to demonstrate that black people in America were not always "enslaved." *Still Am A'Risin'* also attempts to make slavery relevant for today's children, because African Americans still struggle to put a face to this controversial period in America's history.

INTRODUCTION

(A little boy is talking to his grandfather, leaning on his lap, down stage left.)

BOY: Grandpa, how come we call ourselves African Americans when we never been to Africa?

GRANDPA: We haven't been to Africa, but our grandpa's grandpa lived in Africa.

BOY: Well, why he leave? Africa is so pretty with all those beautiful birds and animals like we see at the zoo. If I could live in Africa, I would never leave.

(Their action freezes.)

DANCE: ROYAL KINGDOMS

(This dance features an AFRICAN KING and QUEEN on thrones wearing traditional robes, being entertained by a dancer, and being fanned with long

feathered plumes. At the end of the music, the dancer disappears and KING and QUEEN descend the throne and exit stage left, while a CHAIN GANG marches from center stage left [Africa] to stage right [America], followed by a SLAVE TRADER carrying a whip and a gun. Each member of the CHAIN GANG wears a loincloth. They have just arrived from Africa and look starved and frightened. They are chained together at the neck with their hands bound behind them. Black paper chains will suffice. All move slowly with slow dramatic music in the background. The SLAVE TRADER commands their every move with the gun and whip. Just before they exit stage right, the conversation between the BOY and GRANDPA resumes and the sounds of chains fades.)

BOY: So how did we get here, Grandpa?

GRANDPA: Well, son, that's a long story, or at least a long journey. You see that chain gang there? (*Pointing*)

BOY: Uh-hum.

GRANDPA: Well, that was the beginning of the Middle Passage, a trip across the Atlantic Ocean in the belly of a boat from Africa to America. The trip took two long months.

(Curtain begins to slowly close, or lights begin to go down.)

BOY: You mean we rode in a boat from Africa to Texas?

GRANDPA: That's just the beginning.

ARRIVAL OF SLAVES INTO THE PORT OF VELASCO

DANCE: ARRIVAL OF SLAVES INTO THE PORT OF VELASCO

(African drumming can be heard in the distance, and gradually gets louder. This dance represents the capture of a young slave. A young male dancer enters, running from stage left [Africa]. He is being chased by the SLAVE TRADER. Down center stage, he stops, not knowing which way to go, looking left and right. In his indecision, a net is thrown over him by the SLAVE TRADER who runs upon him from stage left. The captured slave writhes inside the net until he wears himself out. Behind this action, young boys and girls portraying another CHAIN GANG enter from stage left [Africa] and exit stage right [America]. The African drumming is slightly louder here. The action of

the CHAIN GANG happens in a silhouette behind the capture of the SLAVE BOY. Following the exit of the CHAIN GANG, the SLAVE BOY is left downstage, apparently "broken." The SLAVE TRADER removes the net, ties up his hands and places a rope around his neck. Using the gun he makes the boy get up onto a slave block. The SLAVE TRADER pantomimes the role of AUCTIONEER, beckoning for bidders to come forth while the actual auctioning is on a sound recording.)

SLAVE BOY: Where am I? What am I doing here?!

(An OVERSEER enters from stage right, examines the boy, opening his mouth and looking at his teeth, patting his shoulders, and checking for scars, and then purchases him. The OVERSEER carries him off stage right to his new home. BRIT and BUBBA enter from stage right laughing and talking. BRIT is wearing a pistol and carrying his jug of whiskey in one hand and a gun in the other. BUBBA is wearing a gunpowder horn and carrying his fiddle. BUBBA takes a seat on what was the auction block and begins polishing his fiddle. BRIT walks into the spotlight and takes a swig of liquor. He may sit or stand.)

BRIT: Bubba, come git my rifle and fill 'er up with gunpowder, in case dem Injuns show up round here. One shot'll prob'ly scare 'em to kingdom come. Look at all these folks out there. *(Talking to the audience)* Howdy. I'm James Britton Bailey, better known as Brit Bailey. I was born in North Carolina, August 1, 1779, to Kenneth Bailey, who was a descendant of William Wallace and Robert the Bruce from Scotland. And this is Bubba. My father, Ken, gave me Bubba when I was nine years old, and he's been my friend, my companion, and my slave all these years. Ain't you, Bubba? *(Drinks from jug)*

BUBBA: *(Nonchalantly)* We been together ever since, Massa. *(To himself, and looking the audience in the eye)* My name's Bubba, I was sold 'way f'om my mother, and my father is somebody I ain't nevah seen nor heard tell of, no way, no how. I can't tell you one thang 'bout Africa, 'cepting dat's where my folk is from. Lak Massa Brit say, I been wit him since he was nine and my age is anybody guess.

BRIT: We moved to Kentucky and that's where I married Edith Smith. We had six kids together, four boys and two girls, Betsy being the oldest. Where I went, Bubba went. Didn't you, Bubba?

BUBBA: Yessuh, we been together since you was nine years old and I wuz bout de same, although I don't know when I wuz bo'n, maybe it was —

BRIT: (*Ignoring BUBBA's concern with his birthday*) Well, anyway, then they had the War of 1812 and I was a Captain in the Navy, and Bubba went with me to New Orleans in 1814 when we took that little trip down there. And ever time since then, anytime any conversation came up and got long at all, we talked about going to Texas. Sure 'nough, first we moved on to Tennessee — that's where we were when Edith died. So I married her little sister, Dorothy, although all we called her was Dot. (*Laughs*) Well, we found that there was no way to make a living there with all these slaves and all these kids.

BUBBA: Yep, cause your Edith and my Bell was sho cranking out dem kids. Or leastwise, *we* wuz crankin 'em out, huh, Massa?

BRIT: Yep, we had six kids, and after that me and Dot had one on the way, plus all them younguns you and Bell had. We couldn't raise that many in Tennessee, so in March of 1818 we left to go to New Orleans to catch a boat to go to Texas.

BUBBA: Lak to never got 'em all packed up, wit de wimmen folks complaining and the chillun all whining.

BRIT: Let's see, when we left Tennessee, we had the six children, one on the way, Mammy Bell and you, Bubba, and all y'alls pickaninnies and four more slaves — each one of 'em drivin an ox-driven wagon, wit Bubba in the head wagon, after mine.

BUBBA: (*He speaks to the audience, but BRIT can't hear.*) It wouldn't have mattered whether I wanted to come to Texas or not, wasn't one thang I could do 'bout it. He could have taken me and left my fambly behind, an' I couldn't a'done nuthin 'bout dat neither. Us slaves ain't got no say 'bout nuthin. Yessuh and naw-suh and maybe-suh our way to heaven, is 'bout all. One thang y'all gots to remember, we ain't no slaves — not in the mind, we ain't. We's jes being made to do slave wuk fo' dese white folk. We can do dat, or run off to God knows where, leave our folks behind, and den what? One thang for sure, we ain't never going to Af'ica. (*Talking back to BRIT*) Uh-huh, I remembers tying down all the pots and pans to keep 'em f'om rattling long de way. An' we brought a coupla cows for milk, too, for de chillun.

BRIT: Sure 'nough we got here in the late spring and caught a boat immediately to Campeche, better known as Galveston. That was Lafitte's headquarters. That's where he had his red house on Galveston Island. Now the women and the slaves didn't wanna stay on Campeche so we took 'em on over to Anahuac and camped there while me and Jim Smith, Edith and Dot's brother who came with us, went to see the Spanish about some land. And that's where we got our league and our labor of land. Married men got leagues of land.

BUBBA: Yeah, but Jim was single.

BRIT: Jim *was* single so he got a labor of land, that's the way the Spanish was granting land out.

BUBBA: That's when we went all the way east of the Brazos River and you, me, and Jim laid out the land 'cording to our grant.

BRIT: When we got back, the people and slaves were in pretty good shape.

BUBBA: Except Mammy Bell said them mosquitoes was dern near big as mustang ponies.

BRIT: That first year I lost my son James in the flood.

BUBBA: And we lived in tents while we was waiting to cut the wood to build the cabins, the outbuildings.

BRIT: And fin'ly the slaves quarters. 'Member that Bubba? What a time we had.

BUBBA: How can I fergit it? We lak to wukked ourse'fs to death trying to make a home out dese woods. An' don't let it rain in dese parts.

BRIT: 'Member that night, Bubba, we heard that dog barking?

BUBBA: And dat alligator roaring? Mos' horrible sound you ever heard, huh, Massa? And sure 'nough we went runnin out dere.

BRIT: And dat fourteen-year-old slave girl had a twelve-foot alligator draggin her to the slew.

BUBBA: But the dog barked so much at the alligator, he let loose of her and she escaped. An after dat dose cabins got built a whole lot fas'er.

BRIT: I still can't git over losing my son James in the flood the first year we was here. Took us three years just to git started making a life and a living.

(STEPHEN F. AUSTIN slowly walks onto the stage from stage right, looking at a map, not really paying any attention to BRIT and BUBBA, and they don't particularly notice him either.)

BRIT: By then, all of a sudden this fellow, this man comes up and says he's Stephen F. Austin and tells me that I'm on his land—after I've already put

in two crops and lost a kid! I just have had a smoldering relationship with
him ever since he showed up here in 1821, when I been here since 1818.
(*Turning to spot STEPHEN F. AUSTIN*) That's him yonder.

STEPHEN F. AUSTIN: I see you've done quite a bit of work on a piece of land
that's not yours.

BRIT: What the hell do you mean?! (*Raisin rifle*)

AUSTIN: In case you don't know who I am, I happen to be Stephen F. Austin,
an'—

BRIT: I don't give a cat's meow who you are. I happen to own over four thousand acres round here and you standing on a piece . . . Bubba, git over here
wit that rifle.

(*BUBBA wastes no time obeying.*)

AUSTIN: Show me your title, because I can prove that according to the Mexican govern—

BRIT: (*Pointing toward house with one hand and pointing his rifle with the other*)
You see that house yonder? See them fields? I didn't jus git here, Empresario. I been here since 1818.

AUSTIN: I see you're becoming prosperous and I hear you're popular with the
Indians around here—

BRIT: And you got no right tryin to spoil my reputation by saying I'm a bad
guy and—

AUSTIN: And accusing you of being a wandering land-grabber, wild-Indian
tamer and trader, a wayward and undisciplined ne'er-do-well womanizer,
a whiskey maker and seller, plus a worrisome practical joker—

BRIT: Well, that would be a weaver of fun and frolic, a wrestler of man and
beast, and a persistent warrior in peace and in war.

AUSTIN: You must have spent some time in jail back in Kentucky, too.

BRIT: Well, that may be true but it was the time I spent in the Kentucky legislature that weighs heavy on my mind.

AUSTIN: However be it, next time I see you, I'll be asking to see the deed to
this land you're on. Good day!

BRIT: This is my land and I ain't goin nowheres! Hear that? Come on Bubba,
I don't have to stand up here and listen to some lil skinny paper-pusher.
Gimme that jug.

BUBBA: Yessuh! Just who do he think he is, anyway? Here you go, Massa.

(They exit stage right, talking and drinking and laughing, like old buddies.)

AUSTIN: *(Talking to the audience)* Like I said, I'm Stephen F. Austin, and I would not be here in *Tejas* ("Texas," to those of you that speak English) except for my father Moses, who was given a grant by the Spanish to bring in settlers to this beautiful and bountiful land. My father convinced me to join him in this venture, but due to his untimely death, I inherited the grant that is now under the government of Mexico. They have just gained their independence from Spain, you should know.

When I crossed the Sabine in 1821, there were no towns and few settlers. Any Mexicans here were located mostly around the missions. I chose the area of the Brazos and Colorado River Valleys south of the Spanish Trail to bring in three hundred colonists. It's an area where there were few Indians except for the small tribe of Karankawas, and their relatives, the Caddo, and a few wandering bands of Comanche.

It is now 1832, eleven years and several thousand settlers later, and I have just returned from Matamoros, Mexico. I went there to attend a session of the legislature. When I got back I learned that the state army had been ordered to sail up the coast to put down some trouble at Anahuac. That's another waterfront settlement here in Tejas. All this trouble with the Mexicans over slavery and trade with the United States is what resulted in the battle they just had at Fort Velasco. It all started over some runaway slaves who were granted asylum by Colonel Bradburn who runs the fort in Anahuac.

Look, folks, I know that slavery continues to be a real political problem for us because the Mexican authorities are totally against slavery and have continually tried to pass laws against having slaves in Tejas. Personally, I feel the same as they do. Slavery is that "curse of curses and worst of reproaches on civilized man; that unanswered and unanswerable inconsistency of free and liberal republicans."⁵ However, most of the colonists here have come from the southern states and brought their slaves with them. In order for our agricultural economy to continue, slavery is the only answer to our labor needs. We desire the increase of our productions, the increase of the comforts and wealth of all the colonists, and if slavery, or slave labor, or Negro apprentice labor ministers to that, then slavery we must have. Yes, slavery is indispensable to the prosperity of Tejas. It's an economic situation divorced from all its morality.

Well, I'd better get out to Mrs. Long's if I intend to make my presence at a ball she's giving in my honor.

(*AUSTIN exits stage left. JANE and KIAMATA enter from stage left, JANE carrying a basket of china, and KIAMATA carrying a table covered with a lace cloth, upon which JANE puts the basket. They peruse the china for chips and bruises.*)

JANE: I wish for the life of me I had ordered more of these cups from New Orleans. When I arranged for that last shipment I simply had no idea I would need more so soon. Things are so hard to get here in Brazoria, even if we are on the coast. Kian, let's check these very carefully to make sure they have no chips or bruises. This is my best china.

KIAMATA: Since opening this inn evahthing gone have to be prettier now, huh, Miz Jane?

JANE: And cleaner, and we going to have to work harder. Oh, yes, Kian, don't forget to wash all my linen tablecloths and matching napkins. I want this place to shine for the ball I'm having in Mister Stephen F. Austin's honor. It'll be a pleasure to welcome so many guests for the first time since we opened.

KIAMATA: Well, if I got that much washing to do I better get started. (*JANE goes on talking, her lips moving, while we hear KIAMATA thinking aloud, JANE paying her no mind.*) This here ball o' Miz Jane's ain't nothing but somethin that gone work me t'death. She need to get some more he'p round here, stead o' callin me fo' evahthang. (*Exits stage left*)

JANE: (*Looking at the audience*) All you folks are invited, too. Haven't you heard? I'm planning a welcome home party for Mr. Austin, who will be arriving shortly from Matamoros. Oh, I just had the sign for my new place here finished. Kian, bring me the new sign please.

KIAMATA: (*Runs onto stage with sign, anxious to get back to her work*) Here, Miz Jane.

JANE: (*Reading, then talking to audience, while continuing to adore the sign and check the china*) "Inn at Brazoria, Proprietress Jane Wilkinson Long." Folks keep trying to call me the Mother of Texas because my little Mary James was the first American child born in the new Republic of Texas. I've braved many a storm to get to where I am now. My husband General James Long and I landed on Galveston Island in the winter of 1820. And here I am in

1832—with a modest little inn and tavern I have recently purchased and opened here in Brazoria, so as to add a bit of culture to these parts. This is where Texas began—right here in Brazoria. And this inn will be a place of great historical significance. Before long, everybody will pass through those doors—Stephen F. Austin, Sam Houston, William Barret Travis, Ben Milam, Mirabeau Lamar—and it will be my job to see to it that they are made comfortable, and to entertain them. Frontier life needs a woman to add some color to it, some softness here and there. What a pleasure! A woman can tame most anything, you know, even the wilderness. Hopefully I can make enough money here to buy myself a modest plantation in Richmond. Kian? Oh, Kian? Where is that girl? (*Exits stage left*)

JULY 1832

(*Lights fade to black before coming back up on KIAMATA, stage left, who is busy sweeping the porch of Jane's inn in Brazoria.*)

KIAMATA: These white folks can carry on and on about their significance to history and hardly ever do they mention me. No one knows my name. There's Miz Jane and her old ball. Mister Austin and his mixing and mingling wit the Mexicans. This Battle at Velasco . . . Now how am I gone rise? Nobody even knows my name. They probably won't even mark my grave. They got me wearing Jane's last name as if I knew what mine really was. I be colored, I be what I want, and Jane loved me yet never freed me. Or did she? I wanna be able to leave that to this generation to decide. Was I free? See, I got separated from Jane and she had to buy me back. Was that her way of keeping me as best she could? Or was it for dual purposes, cause she was selfish, self-centered? But she kept me, because if I had left, what possibly could I have done? Once you were free, where were you going? Was I free? I leave that up to y'all to decide.

(*She looks up to spot guests approaching, STEPHEN F. AUSTIN and BRIT BAILEY. BUBBA, BRIT BAILEY's trusted slave, is with them.*)

KIAMATA: (*Excited*): Miz Jane, Mister Austin and Mister Bailey here to see ya!

JANE: (*Rushing outside*) Well, don't just stand there, get these gentlemen some chairs! And bring some water and towels for these men to wash up. Don't you know anything about what running an inn requires?

KIAMATA: (*Pulls together some chairs*) Yes'm! You gentlemens lemme get ya some seats so's you can rest yo'selves. Hi, Bubba. I see you brung your fiddle. (*Runs inside*)

JANE: I'm glad you two have arrived early so you can try on your suits I had my tailor make for you to wear to the ball. Well, well, Bubba, am I glad to see you! Thanks for bringing him, Brit. My ball will be the talk of the town with his fiddling.

BUBBA: My fiddling is what makes all the parties special 'round Brazoria. (*He sits down and begins cleaning his fiddle and tightening the strings.*)

BRIT: (*Exhausted from the trip*) You didn't have to go to no such trouble for me, Jane. I'm wearing the same thing I always do. My buckskins!

AUSTIN: Well, I need a new suit after that trip to Matamoros.

BRIT: I run into him on my way here and was just telling him what went on in the Battle at Fort Velasco!

JANE: Am I glad to see you both alive and well! We been on pins and needles waiting to hear how things turned out at Velasco. Must've been pretty bad, huh? Were there many wounded?

BRIT: (*Wiping his hands with a rag then checking his gun and pouches*) We licked 'em, darn Mexicans. You should have seen 'em scat.

AUSTIN: I see you made out okay. How 'bout the rest of our men?

BRIT: I'm the lucky one. Father Muldoon like to've got himself killed out there, trying to talk sense to Colonel Ugartechea. (*Mispronounced as "who-got-de-cha-ir"*)

JANE: (*To KIAMATA*) Kian, hurry, will you?

KIAMATA (*From inside*): I'se coming, Miz Jane! (*Running to the door*) De water got to boil firs' and dat takes time, ma'am, but I got de fire going.

JANE: Father Muldoon passed through here a few weeks ago on his way to the Velasco fort. (*Interrupting herself*) I wanna hear 'bout the battle itself! Tell me everything! Between the battle and this ball I'm planning, I can't tell you when life has been more exciting!

BRIT: (*Holding up his gun, looking at it closely. As he speaks, he stands in a stride and aims the pistol, making ready to shoot.*) You know that fort ain't but 'bout a hundred and fifty yards from the mouth of the Brazos River. But inside the walls of it is an embankment where musketeers can stand and shoot over without exposing anything but their heads. And did we shoot!

AUSTIN: It was John Austin who got the cannon and put it on the schooner at Brazoria. They were taking all this over to Anahuac.

BRIT: When the ship went by and they fired the cannon, ol Strap Buckner, my friend and a good ol free-loving guy, picks up this three-hundred-pound door and starts charging the walls of the fort.

JANE: (*Leaning closer to their conversation*) I wish I could've been there to see it!

AUSTIN: See, now Ugartechea had given orders not to let anybody come out of the harbor without them being cleared by the Mexican authorities. But John Austin wouldn't stop the ship at their orders, he just kept on going on his way to Anahuac . . . (*Pacing slowly back and forth on the porch*)

BRIT: Naw, let me tell it! You just talking, I was there. When Ugarte-whatever-his-name-is had his men fire on the ship, and Strap picked up that three-hundred-pound door to make a charge, my unit got up behind Strap and followed him up there, and just right before we got to the wall, an explosion hit that door and a splinter came off it and went right into Strap's brain at the temple! But because of his charge, we got over the walls and we conquered 'em. My son Gaines got wounded, but it was very few casualties considerin what they all went through.

JANE: That Strap Buckner is something else, isn't he?

BRIT: After Strap's charge, and we saw he had been wounded, Bubba went and laid ol Strap out on the door and drug that door off the battlefield with him on it!

JANE: They say Strap's the biggest white man 'round here.

AUSTIN: That's what I hear tell.

BRIT: Well, he ain't no bigger'n my Bubba, cause then Bubba, he went back and found my son, Gaines, who was pretty seriously wounded, and carried him off, too! Strap *was* the biggest white man in the colony, cause he could carry ponies. When the Indians gave him one of those mustang ponies he rode out of Brazoria and got all the way down to Jones Creek when the horse went lame. So he just picked it up and put it on his shoulder and went back to Brazoria. This guy was just one hell of a man. But my Uncle Bubba is about the same size. That's why me and Strap never got into any fights.

JANE: I'd have given anything to have seen some of that action!

BRIT: That's teaching 'em Mexicans not to mess with us colonis'! See, them Mexicans wants us to pay duties on ever'thing we bring in here—tools, iron, steel, even coarse bagging for cotton sacks. Plus, they don't want us bringing no more slaves into that port. Fact is, they don't want no slavery period. Well, you know that! That law they passed in 1830 outlaws it. Just who they think we gonna get to tread through these woods, cut down trees to plant crops, build cabins, kill deer, haul wood? Hell, we can't do all this work! We ain't got enough hands. (*Softly*) We gotta brang them Africans in here, or we're sunk. It's the way of improvement, like it or not.

JANE: Well, now, don't go getting yourself all upset. You men are to be congratulated. It takes brave, hardy men like yourselves to make this wilderness safe, especially with all these Indians still running around the country.

KIAMATA: (*Loaded down with a bucket of water and a big bowl of rags*) Here's the water and rags, ma'am.

BUBBA: Wait, lemme he'p ya wit dat heavy bowl.

KIAMATA: Thanks, Bubba. Jes set it right here on dis table.

JANE: Kian, go make these men some coffee. We'll have it inside the dining room. (*JANE gets up to assist her guests, except Bubba, with the ritual of hand washing.*)

KIAMATA: (*Turning to go back inside*) Yes'm, Miz Jane.

BUBBA: S'pose I go 'long wit ya.

AUSTIN: (*Suddenly remembering, pulls a small brown-paper-wrapped package out of his pocket*) Begging your pardon, Jane, here is a small present I had made for you in Mexico.

JANE: (*Blushing*) Stephen F. Austin, you are too generous. (*Carefully opening package*) Stephen F. Austin . . . I don't know when I've seen one prettier—a lace handkerchief with a "J" embroidered into it. Those Mexican women are so clever. (*Folding it carefully and putting it back into the wrapping paper*) Well, gentlemen, let's go inside and have some coffee.

KIAMATA: (*Coming outside*) I got it all set up for you on the dining room table.

JANE: Thanks, Kian. S'pose you and Bubba stay outside here and take in some fresh air. Gentlemen, let us celebrate winning our first battle for independence!

(*All exit, leaving KIAMATA and BUBBA on the porch.*)

KIAMATA: (*Uses a mosquito swatter to swat flies and mosquitoes as she talks*) All dey knows 'bout me is Kian, slave of Miz Jane Long. When I gone ever git to be a real person? My real name is Kiamata, a Indian name given me by my black mother. And my pappy was Indian.

BUBBA: Least you know dat much 'bout yo'sef. I hardly knew my mammy 'fore she got sol' away in Norf Ca'lina. An afta my firs' massa die, I got sol' and give to Massa Brit when he were nine year old. I wouldn't know my pappy if'n he walked right up to dis here porch.

KIAMATA: After my mammy died, I come to b'long to Miz Jane. I were bout twelve years old when me and her came to Texas.

BUBBA: I saw my mammy git a awful whuppin once. Ol Massa beat hear til she barely had any meat on her back. Worse'n dat, overseer mek everbody come out dey cabin and watch dis whuppin—teach us all how to ack, he say. Or how *not* to ack.

KIAMATA: What dey whup her for?

BUBBA: She refused to let the massa breed her. I found out later f'om anothuh slave woman after dey sold her.

KIAMATA: You ever think 'bout runnin?

BUBBA: I would nevah wanna leave Bell and my younguns. Dat's what keeps me here 'stead o' going to Mexico. Plus, Massa Brit pretty good ol massa when you come to think on it. But dat battle down at Velasco had a lot to do wit dem runaway slaves dat was being hid by Colonel Bradburn over in Anahuac.

KIAMATA: I heard 'bout dat Colonel Bradburn . . . heard dat he was working for the Meskins. And if dat wasn't bad enuf for a white man, to be working wit Meskins and 'gainst othuh white mens.

BUBBA: Yep. Say he up and arrested dat Travis man, William Barret Travis I think he's called, an' anothuh one called Patrick Jack who calls theyselves some kinda lawyers, long wit one dey call Monroe Edwards, a known slave trader right here in de Brazos district. Say Bradburn threw Travis and 'em all into jail for attacking some woman up in Anahuac. Dey arres' caused so much trouble dat a mob of colonis' tried to break 'em out Bradburn's prison.

KIAMATA: But 'cordin to what I hear Miz Jane n'em sayin, it was all on account o' Bradburn offering freedom to three runaway slaves from Louisiana dat was claiming his protection under the Meskin flag. I heared by accident dat a hunnurd men was planning to cross de Sabine River and take dem three Negroes by force. Anyway, all dis mess jes kept gittin stirred up worser and worser til fore we knowed it, it done gone f'om a molehill to a mountain!

BUBBA: Massa Brit love a fight anyway.

KIAMATA: Dere was mens coming in here lak flies, all of 'em carryin guns, muskets, knives, whatever weapons dey could git. Next thang I knowed, dat schooner Brazoria wuz trying to sail upriver to Anuhuac wit a cannon to teach Bradburn and de res' o' dem Meskins a lesson . . . den dis battle broke out at Velasco . . .

BUBBA: White folks says a plenty 'bout what happened, but it a heap dat dey don't say neither—that still happened.

JANE: (*Calling from inside*) Kian, Kian, you're needed in here!

KIAMATA: Ooh-wee! Dat heifa 'bout to run me ragged! See, what'd I tell ya. Dey works a niggra to deaf, den replace her wit another one. (*In a deliberately sweeter tone*) Here I come, Miz Jane!

BUBBA: I'm gone go 'round back here, myse'f.

(*KIAMATA exits inside, stage left. BUBBA exits stage right.*)

DANCE: RUNAWAY SLAVE SCENE

(*The music for this dance must be fast and fleeting as must be the dancer, who appears to have been running for some days and nights. He/she is ragged and worn with lots of ragged clothing so as to keep warm, and wears a hat and old shoes and carries a big stick and very small bundle. In the background can be heard the sound of barking dogs. Since this scene is intended to be a memory flash, it need not be longer than one minute.*)

JANE: (*Coming onto the porch with AUSTIN and BRIT. KIAMATA and BUBBA are sitting down in the background. He plays a slow spiritual for her on his fiddle.*) Kian, Mr. Austin and Mr. Bailey will be spending the night. Please see to it that everything is made ready. Place some clean night chambers in their rooms and don't forget the mosquito netting.

BRIT: Dese jotbone mosquitoes can eat through de toughest of hides. They even bite the dogs! (*Laughs*) Hey Jane, what's this I hear 'bout you having a dog named Galveston?

AUSTIN: Seems I heard that, too. Is it true?

JANE: Why yes, you heard right. Talking about my dog Galveston takes me back to that lonely vigil at Bolivar's Point. That was the winter of 1821.

BRIT: The winter of 1821 was the coldest ever known to this area. Even the Indians'll tell you that. (*Sitting down to listen*)

JANE: (*Shivering*) You're right, Brit. It was so-o cold, I still get the shivers just thinking about it.

AUSTIN: I doubt any *man* could have endured what you did, Jane. Talk about bravery!

BRIT: Cold-blooded courage, we soldiers like to say.

JANE: I woke up one morning to spot an enormous bear scuttling across the ice onto the island. Had not my dog Galveston barked so loudly, I might have missed seeing him altogether. Anyway, during the fierce storm the girls and I were forced to take shelter in a makeshift tent, but the snow fell so heavily, it barely held up. It was there in that tent, with the north wind screaming, that I gave birth to little Mary James. She and I were lying in a bed of snow and poor Kian was sick with a fever. (*Pauses, thinking*) I was twenty-three at the time. Young and too daring, no doubt.

BRIT: What about the Karankawas? Legend has it that they're cannibals.

JANE: Therein lies the most fearsome incident on the Point. James told me before leaving that they had eaten more than two hundred Americans already. One morning as I lay nursing little Mary, and while Kian was searching the beach, scavenging for food . . . (*Her voice dies out and KIAMATA enters to tell the story from her perspective. The wind and waves can be heard in the background.*)

KIAMATA: (*While JANE, AUSTIN, and BRIT continue talking without being heard, they get up and walk offstage while KIAMATA picks up this story to tell it from her perspective.*) So she say, but 'cordin' to what I knows, first, me and Miz Jane, we follow dat man, General Long, to dis place called Nacogdoches or somethin like dat. Right befo' we can settle the dust outs our mouth, why, he be ready to go cause he done upset them Spanish peoples talking bout Texas being a innapendent nation!

BUBBA: Why white folks thinks they's the only peoples that want to be free?

KIAMATA: Well, it ain't no surprise to me. So now we be at this place called Point Bolivar. General Long and about fifty-two other mens has left the fort headed for Copano Bay, I hears them saying, and there she go cryin again. Dat Miz Jane fo'ever cryin 'bout dat man. Mr. Long been gone a long time now. Everybody else what's there start talkin bout leavin. Miz Jane don't want to go. She wants to stay and wait for Mr. Long to come back. Miz Edgar pleaded with Miz Jane to change her mind. But with Miz Jane being stubborn, and bullhead strong, it looks like we be here by ourselves.

BUBBA: Bolivar, dat not too far f'om here den, huh?

KIAMATA: Not far at all. But 'fore long, they's all gone. Dr. and Miz Edgar and dat Miz Allen who kept telling Miz Jane she'd be all alone with only a chile and a slave to protect her! Well, I says to myself, "only a slave?" Who's the one who catches the fish for the Longs, gathers the wood for fire, and keeps up with Ann? Why, it's me, I say. Why I be the one who has always taken care of Miz Jane and Ann f'om de time Ann was born when I were six year old. Dat Mr. Long always moving from pillar to post talkin 'bout freedom. What do he know 'bout not being free? Seems to me he and his men be plenty free leaving they women and chilluns!

Well, seeing as how where we wuz had been a fort, we had some ammunition and a few muskets. We knew how to catch fish and Ann was helpful with the crabbing. Miz Jane and I did a lil huntin, and dat spring, we had our lil garden. Wasn't no soap, but ashes and water I put together made our clothes clean enuf.

(Sound effects of wind and waves get gradually louder.)

KIAMATA: Now after dat pirate Lafitte lef', we start seeing de Indians over across the island. We can see dey campfires at night. Miz Jane say they might come to where we wuz. She say they aren't friendly. So ever'day I watch for their footprints in the sand. One day I sees 'em. (*DANCER 1 portrays an Indian who appears in the background, bravely stalking some unseen intruders. He/she enters and exits from stage right.*) Ann and I go yelling for Miz Jane, "The Indians been here!"

BUBBA: Sound lak some o' de narrow escapes me and Massa Brit done had wit de Indians when we firs' come here.

KIAMATA: We wasn't sure when they would try and attack us, cause they kept going down to the beach. So we hung up Miz Jane's red petticoat on a flagpole to keep them at a distant. That made dem think it was a flag and a manned fort. (*DANCER 2 portrays a slave girl who enters from stage left* *carrying a pole with red petticoat across the stage, struggling against the fierce wind. She exits stage right.)*

'Fore long, them Indians, they come back. Miz Jane and I had to finally load the cannon the soldiers left behind. It was awful heavy but Miz Jane worked it. Loud? I can hear it still. This was to our good fortune. Cause we had to fire it twice before they leave us 'lone. To be sure, I would wear a uniform and guard the island at day, Miz Jane would guard the island at night. Miz Jane and I survived the coldest winter they say ever in Galveston.

1822

KIAMATA: Fin'ly, Miz Jane gets a letter from the Calvits, and with it comes one slave named Tom and two mules. It seems Miz Jane's sister thinks Miz Jane should get help from Tres Palacios.

In September, we set out for San Antonio. Miz Jane rode a horse and carried Mary James in her arms. Lil Ann rode the big pack mule that Tom had brought. Randall and James Jones shared a horse between them. Tom and I walked along after the party. It was a very hard trip.

(DANCERS 3 and 4 portray two tired slaves, walking barefoot to San Antonio.)

BUBBA: Lotsa Negroes walked to Texas f'om all over de South, some f'om far away as Virginia and Norf Ca'lina. Hear tell how plenty ol Negroes died on their way here. Dey jes stops on de side o' de road, dig a hole, and buries 'em right where dey lay. No fun'ral, no nothing. Jes a few quick prayers.

(BRIT calls Bubba from offstage.)

BUBBA: Well, I has a heap o' 'miration fo' what you has been thoo, Kiamata. Look lak we'll have to finish our talk some othuh time. Hand me my fiddle there by you please, ma'am. *(Exits stage right)*

KIAMATA: *(Solemn soliloquy, spoken to the audience)* On earth, freedom is fo' de white folks. Down here, ain't nothin but slavery fo' us. We gits no freedom til we gits to heaben. But us gone rise up one day, I tell ya. Lak a story I heard tell 'bout de people dat could fly. Got so tired of trouble and pain, dey jus sprouted wings, rose up ovah dis evil lan', and took off toward de sky. You might keep me down now, you might keep me down for another hunnurd years, but one day, I'se gonna rise up, I say, and keep on a'risin til I git to heaben. (*Music*) An' when I git to heaben, I'm gonna put on my robe and shout all over God's heaben, heaben, gonna shout so loud, gonna come back down and git my freedom crown.

DANCE: I'LL FLY AWAY

(*All the dancers make movements that express liberation, freedom, and flying away. Dancers move their arms like wings, step out in defiance, hold their heads high, and every movement should be esteemed and free. The lights fade out.*)

FINALE

(*Lights fade back in on the BOY and GRANDPA.*)

BOY: Grandpa, just how long ago was that, the Middle Passage, I mean?
GRANDPA: Oh, 'bout a hundred and fifty years.
BOY: That's equal to three whole lifetimes, huh?
GRANDPA: That's one way to look at it.
BOY: We still trying to get our rights back, huh?
GRANDPA: Yep, son, we still working on that. Still working and still am a'risin' . . .

DANCE: ROYAL KINGDOMS/RISE

(*Contemporary jazz music plays. This dance features the AFRICAN KING and QUEEN in a procession from stage right to stage left [from America back to Africa]. They are led by a DANCER and followed by three professional people: a DOCTOR, a CONSTRUCTION WORKER, and a BUSINESS WOMAN. Any remaining dancers may follow in contemporary dress representing other careers or industries.*)

PART
V

CIVIL WAR

OVERVIEW

In late October 1999, Talking Back Living History was approached to write a piece for the first annual Civil War Weekend, featuring a Confederate war re-enactment, scheduled for the last weekend in November at Plantation Liendo. Liendo is recognized as a Texas historic landmark and listed on the national register of historic places. Our recommendation came as a result of our performance at Fernland in Montgomery County where we premiered *Fugitives of Passion: On the Underground Railroad to Mexico* for the Sam Houston Memorial Museum. Contract negotiations began with less than four weeks to do a site visit, complete research, mobilize our cast, rehearse, and perform. So? So I got busy. This was a tall order challenge and I liked it. While we came in on time, budget constraints prohibited performance. To date this play has never had a premiere, but we are working on it.

Plantation Liendo is located in Waller (originally Austin) County, less than five miles from Prairie View A&M University, the alma mater of my grandmother, who graduated in 1911 (when it was Prairie View State Normal and Industrial College) and of my father, who graduated in 1951. I was four years old when my daddy graduated one hot day in August, and I suppose it was the first big celebration I witnessed—him in his black cap and gown, graduating magna cum laude, whatever that meant.

The site visit to Liendo was like a trip to the past—only I didn't know how far. Fortunately for me, there were tons of information on the property, its former owners, and the 1853 house built by slave labor that belonged to Leonard Groce. It was during this research that I was time-machined back to the beginning—the beginning of colonial slavery that came to be practiced in the Texas empire. Historic details helped me envision the 90–120-person slave coffle that marched alongside and assisted with the fifty-wagon entourage of Jared Groce, all coming from Alabama. I could see the women in their bright colored head ties and the children all piled into wagons on top of supplies, crammed in with the chickens and pigs. There were no white women in this group, just men who drove the wagons, some with oxen, while others rode horses. I imagined their music, perhaps happy in the morning and sad in the evening. I knew the children would have played games. The campfires at night might have been lively with stories, music, and such food as there was, including lots of game. Crossing the rivers had to be a challenge because they were much wider and deeper than they are now. According to some sources, the passing of Groce's entourage was like a circus parade, inviting the interest of all who witnessed it.[1]

Leonard Groce, born September 27, 1806, the builder of Plantation Liendo, was a young man when he took leave of his studies to accompany his father to Texas in 1821. After the move he went back to South Carolina to complete his studies. Upon his return in 1831, he married Courtney Ann Fulton, daughter of Alexander Fulton, an ex-congressman from Louisiana. The little town of Courtney in Grimes County was named in her honor.[2]

According to Mrs. Sarah Wharton Groce Berleth, the great granddaughter of Jared Ellison Groce II, her great grandfather migrated from Virginia to Lincoln County, Georgia, in 1787. In his new location, he became actively identified with political affairs, serving as a delegate to the convention that framed the state constitution of Georgia in 1798. From Georgia, Groce moved to Alabama in 1814 and settled on the Alabama River, where he established what came to be known as Fort Groce. In 1821, while in New Orleans, he became interested in the colonial scheme of Stephen F. Austin. Upon his return to Alabama, he disposed of his land and began preparation for the trip to Texas. The next few weeks were spent buying equipment, such as farming implements, tools, and seeds, and when they left Alabama, the procession was more like a caravan than anything else. Commenting on the trip to Texas, Mrs. Berleth says:

> Mr. Alfred Gee, the overseer who had served with [Groce] in Georgia, had charge of several hundred Negroes. [According to his application for land, Groce had only ninety slaves when he came to Texas.] There were fifty or more covered wagons in which the women and children traveled; the men, most of them on horseback; horses, mules, cows, sheep, hogs, came next; then came more wagons containing furniture, spinning wheels, looms, provisions, etc. Colonel Groce and his son, Leonard, then a lad of sixteen years, accompanied by their body servants, Edom

and Fielding, brought up the rear. Rivers and streams were crossed by pontoon bridges, which they carried with them.[3]

He arrived in Texas in the fall of 1821, established himself on the east bank of the Brazos River, in the vicinity of the present town of Hempstead. He was granted ten *sitios* of land by the Mexican government: five in Brazoria County, two in Waller County, and three in Grimes County, all patented July 29, 1824.[4] This large acreage was granted "on account of the property he has brought with him."

According to Randolph C. Campbell, "Groce, who arrived in January, 1822 . . . established a plantation called 'Bernardo'. He could not occupy all the land to which he was entitled (7,200 acres for his slaves alone)."[5] Stephen F. Austin had arranged with Antonio María Martínez, governor of Mexico, to offer land to three hundred settlers in quantities of 640 acres to the head of a family, 320 acres for his wife, 160 acres for each child, and eighty acres for each slave. These first settlers came to be known as the Old Three Hundred. Austin's compensation for service in obtaining land, duly surveyed and with title delivered at his expense, was to be at the rate of 12.5 cents an acre.[6] It was a tremendous boost to the economic status of any colonist to receive acreage for each slave in addition to the free labor of the slave and their offspring for life.

Groce's first cotton was planted in the spring of 1822, and it is said that this was the first cotton planted in Texas. Corn was also planted, and so scarce was food that it was necessary to maintain a watch over the fields at night to prevent the Negroes from scratching up the seed for food. Because of a protracted drought, very little corn was harvested from this crop. As the drought continued into 1823, the plantation was destitute. According to Mrs. Berleth, Groce established the first cotton gin at his retreat in 1828.[7] Others claimed Groce built his gin on the Brazos River as early as 1825.

Cotton was a money crop. Once the cotton was open, the tedious, back-breaking business of picking began. Slaves—men, women, and children—drawing long coarse sacks behind them, picked from morning until night, "weighing up" at the cotton house or the wagon each time the sack was filled. On occasion large baskets were used to hold the white fiber as it was picked from the tough, crisp brown burs. After the cotton was picked and weighed, it had to be loaded on the wagon, if it was not emptied into the wagon at the time of weighing. Next, it had to be hauled to the gin, ginned, and baled. It was then ready for market. Most large plantations, as in the instance of the Groce plantation gin mentioned earlier, provided their own gins.

There were no railroads until 1857, when the first and nearest came to Hockley, some fifteen miles east of Hempstead on Highway 290. Cotton, therefore, was hauled overland in oxcarts, or ox-wagons, to Houston, then to Galveston, and then by boat to New Orleans and all ports of the world. The trip to Houston with the loaded wagon usually required two days, one day each way with the night spent along the way or in a wagon yard around Houston.

By 1845 Austin County east of the Brazos (now a part of Waller County) had become a profitable plantation area, with over a thousand slaves employed by about two hundred people. All life, however, was not lived on plantations. The small farmers, trappers, traders, and the like carried on life in a manner quite different from that of the plantations.[8]

By the time Leonard Groce built his home at Plantation Liendo, his land holdings equaled some seventy-five thousand acres. It was Groce and other wealthy planters who financed the Confederacy in Texas. The prominence of Liendo established itself worthy of becoming a Civil War camp for recruitment of Confederate soldiers and imprisonment of Yankee soldiers. No battle ever occurred there. Nonetheless, the impending Civil War reenactment in which Talking Back Living History had been asked to participate was planned to honor the significance of this historical site and the role it had played in "de war."

In a *Houston Chronicle* article dated June 30, 2002, there appears a photo of the "House of History" with the caption, "The Liendo Plantation was completed in 1853." The two-story, fourteen-room house was built of longleaf yellow pine from Georgia. The chimneys and foundation were made of bricks from the clay of the Brazos River—these, as well as the magnificent stairwell, were made by slave hands, which also completed practically all the labor on this and other fine antebellum mansions.

At the height of its prosperity, Liendo had some 129 slaves[9] and was the site of the first bale of cotton produced in Texas. The Civil War brought an end to all that. After the fall of Galveston, a prisoner-of-war camp commanded by Custer was built at the gates of Liendo.[10]

Even with a war, there was always work to be done. There was always a calf being roasted. Leonard Groce armed his slaves and sent them to Mexico to sell his cotton during the war because the Union embargo at Galveston

Bay prevented trade along the Texas coast. Often the enslaved, from Texas to New York, escaped bondage to fight for their freedom alongside the Union soldiers. Others kept the home fires burning and the fields in production while the Confederates went to war to protect their way of life.

I wrote the play for Plantation Liendo during an interesting time in American history. There was considerable controversy over homage paid to Confederate monuments in the southern United States. Georgia had just redesigned their state flag to remove the prominent image of the Confederate battle flag and adopted one more representative of their diverse population. However, in nearby South Carolina, Alabama, and Mississippi, the Greys were not about to abandon their flag. That flag was an icon that showed respect for their loved ones lost in Civil War battles. The blacks, on the other hand, resented the overt reminder of slavery and its brutal past — one group's cherished memory was something the other group wished to forget. This bitter battle over the flag lingered through the holidays and culminated in one of Alabama's largest protest marches on the birthday of Dr. Martin Luther King, Jr.

It seems I had come full circle with my research when we went into production for *Cane Cutter Country*, which is set in Brazoria County where my living-history work began. I made my first trip to Brazoria in 1994 for the University of Houston–Clear Lake symposium on antebellum Brazos plantations. Some forty-five antebellum plantations are listed in the PhD dissertation "Educational, Social and Economic Characteristics of the Plantation Culture of Brazoria County, Texas," by Allen A. Platter of the University of Houston. This list and an accompanying map are included in the *Final Report of Research and Excavation at the Lake Jackson State Archeological Landmark*.[11]

At the symposium, I received a preliminary copy of the incomplete report and began to study it in earnest. I shared parts of it with my students of Texas history. I was overwhelmed and astounded by the facts revealed therein. I cannot remember when I first became aware that my people had been enslaved. I cannot even recall the impact it had on me, but I do remember crying when I read Arna Bontemps's *Chariot in the Sky: A Story of the Jubilee Singers*. I knew we had been made to labor against our will, for no pay, but just how much and how hard, I had no idea. I knew nothing of the sugar cane hellholes that had worked so many of our ancestors to death.

Abner Jackson, for whom the city of Lake Jackson is named, owned three sugar cane plantations: Lake Place, the Retrieve, and Darrington. The Re-

Table 5.1. **The Major Planters in Brazoria County in 1860**

300–500 Slaves Owned	
Mills, David G.	343
Low Wood Place[1]	192
Bynum Place	120
Palo Alto Place	31
200–300 Slaves Owned	
Jackson, Abner	285
Lake Place	84
Darrington Place	96
Retrieve Place	105
Bell, Josiah H.	213
100–200 Slaves Owned	
McNeel, James Greenville	176
Coffee, Aaron	157
Kennedy, William	144
Jordan, Senator Levy	134
Wharton, John A.	133
Mims, Alexander	103
Spencer, Joel	102

Source: Joan Few, Principal Investigator. *Final Report of Research and Excavation at the Lake Jackson State Archeological Landmark,* Lake Jackson, Texas, 41CO172, between 1991 and 1996 Under Antiquities Permit 1072. Table 2-2.

Note: *Additional research has yielded conflicting reports on the number of slaves held by these men. Slaves were property and, as such, were taxed, so more likely than not, the above numbers reported in the 1860 Slave Census Count are misrepresented. For example, the* New Handbook of Texas *online reports the David and Robert Mills estimate at around eight hundred; according to family oral history, Levy Jordan often boasted that he owned one slave for every day of the year; and according to Abner J. Strobel, Abner Jackson's count was believed to be in excess of three hundred.*

1. Low Wood was the largest sugar plantation in Texas and was owned by three brothers: David, Robert, and Andrew Mills, who also owned three cotton plantations.

trieve plantation, the first that he developed, opened between 1842 and 1845 and was four miles up Oyster Creek from the Lake Jackson plantation where he made his home. His first home was made of logs from the nearby forest. However, he soon converted every building—slave cabins, the sugar house, and his residence—into brick made on the plantation, and stuccoed with cement fully an inch thick, which made all the buildings look like they were made from solid rock. The residence was a twelve-room, two-story house in the shape of the letter I, with six galleries with immense brick pillars spanning their entire length. It was cool in summer and warm in winter with its large fireplaces. Built colonial style, the residence cost, excluding the slave labor, over twenty-five thousand dollars to complete. There was an artificial island made in the lake, visible to this day, said to have cost ten thousand dollars. Fine orchards and gardens with brick walks laid in them were also constructed on the plantation, and slaves were allowed to use them.

Major Jackson, up to the beginning of the War between the States, had the finest and most developed properties in the county, and owned three sugar plantations, seventy thousand acres of land, and over three hundred slaves. His stock of cattle branded annually over five thousand calves.[12]

Many planters grew both cotton and sugar in the Brazos River Valley. The amount of intensive labor required throughout the year for these crops required a large workforce.

For sugar cane, planting began in January and February. The fields required extensive drainage canals and ditches to prevent standing water in the fields, which would cause the roots to rot. Keeping the fields well drained was a year-round job because sugar cane in Texas "ratoons," or grows more than one crop from a single planting[13], and sometimes produces for three or four years. Sugar cane, when planted, was placed in high ridges that were about six feet apart. Planters had a variety of methods for placing the seed cane in the rows. Placed lengthwise in the ridge, the cane was cut separating the "joints" or "eyes" and then covered with dirt. The cane ridges were carefully hoed and tended for about three months, until the cane was high enough to prevent weeds from growing in the fields.

During the summer months the preparations for harvest were intense. Sugar was stored and transported in hogsheads. A hogshead is a large barrel or cask that, in the United States, contains between 63 and 140 gallons. For each hogshead of sugar produced, about three to five cords of wood were needed for fuel in the sugar mill.[14] The 1859 *Peach Point Farm Journal* of the Perry plantation states that over 950 cords of wood were cut that year for the mill.[15] Hogsheads and molasses barrels had to be made, the sugar mill prepared, and the boilers cleaned before the October harvest began. About the middle of October the cutting of the cane and the processing of sugar started. About 1,300 pounds of raw sugar cane would yield one hogshead of sugar and two to three barrels of molasses.[16] Most planters kept their mills

Table 5.2. **The Process of Making Sugar**
(Records of Sugar Production in Brazoria County by year, in hogsheads)

Plantation Owner	1852	1853	1854	1855
Mills, Robert & David G. (totals)	1,338	600	1,085	1,280
Low Wood Place	780	467	670	820
Bynun	558	133	415	460
Jackson, Abner (totals)	746	727	480	784
Lake Place	296	142	160	133
Retrieve	450	585	320	651
McNeel, James G.	368	250	325	312
McNeel, Sterling (Darrington)	235	430	405	450
McNeel, P. P.	210	95		
Patton, Christopher R.	210	130	120	
McNeel, Leander Harrison (Magnolia)	208	105	305	263
McNeel, Pleasant Duke (Pleasant Grove)	80	14		

Source: Few, *Final Report of Research and Excavation at the Lake Jackson State Archeological Landmark,* Tables 2.9–2.12.

going twenty-four hours a day until all the sugar cane was processed, during which time they could produce eight to ten hogsheads.[17]

There are some interesting parallels in these two plays and some differences. For further study and additional references, please review the lesson plans for each play.

PLANTATION LIENDO
Civil War Reenactment

CHARACTERS

COLONEL LEONARD GROCE: owner of a vast plantation, age 56. He was commissioned as a colonel in the Texas Army by Governor Henry Smith in 1835.

COURTNEY ANN FULTON GROCE: wife of Leonard Groce

GENERAL JOHN BANKHEAD MAGRUDER: Commander of Confederate forces in Texas

PRIVATE AVERY T. PARKER

FIELDING: an armed cowboy and trusted Negro who transported cotton to Mexico for sale, age 35 (*May double as JOSH*)

EDOM: another armed cowboy in his early thirties (*May double as JOSH*)

CAROLINA: Miz Courtney's servant who traveled with her family from North Carolina, age 40

AUNT LIDDY: cook for the Groce family, age 50. She is chiefly responsible for the feeding of the soldiers and slaves. (*May double as GEORGIA*)

ELI: body servant to Private A. T. Parker, age 17

GEORGIA: a washerwoman who was born in Georgia, age 25

MOSE: gardener, a mature black man

JOSH: a field hand doing yard work, age 25

SETTING

TIME: *1862*

PLACE: *Waller County, Texas*

SYNOPSIS

Plantation Liendo was the largest cotton plantation (67,000–75,000 acres) in Waller County and, as such, was the home of several hundred slaves — just how many depends on the year and source cited. Leonard Groce and his wife, Courtney Ann Fulton (niece of the inventor of the steamboat), entertained everyone from Sam Houston to General Custer in their gracious home, the social center of Southeast Texas.

Liendo was the site of considerable activity during the war. It went from a recruiting station for the Confederacy at the war's outset to a Union prisoner-of-war camp at the war's end. Colonel Leonard Groce, an excellent manager with a keen sense of humor, supplied the Confederate forces with manpower, raw materials, supplies, horses, and anything necessary to gain an advantage over the Union troops. Part of his contribution was financed by returns on selling his cotton, and at one point Groce armed some thirty Negroes and had them transport and sell his cotton in Mexico. In this play, numerous scenarios evolve that represent the wealth and prevalence of old South aristocracy during the war. The varied relationships between enlisted and civilian, free and enslaved, and white and colored demonstrate the extent of wartime interdependency.

SCENE 1

(It is early morning, but not too early for Army roll call. PRIVATE AVERY T. PARKER comes running across the front yard, late, not fully dressed, and anxious to get to the field. He severely reprimands his body servant, ELI, for not waking him in time. ELI, who is carrying PARKER's equipment, is so distracted that he fumbles and drops things, causing them to be further delayed.)

PARKER: Eli, you make me wish I had left you back on the plantation, you no-count, lazy rascal! How many times have I tol' you t'have me up 'fore daybreak? Huh? Ain't you lis'ning t'me!?

ELI: Massa Av'ry, t'wuz nelly sunup when we went to bed, 'hind dat fox hunt las' night, suh — *(Dropping the supply bag)*

PARKER: Boy, don't you d'spute me. *(Turning around emphatically, and raising his hand)* I oughta — now look whatcha done? Git dat stuff up f'om nere and hurry up will ya? I ain't got all mawnin. I'm subjeck to git a night in de stockade behin' yo' molasses slow behind . . . *(He continues mumbling under his breath while running off, still tucking in his shirt and buttoning his coat. He looks back one last time.)* Eli! Hurry up boy, if'n ya don't I'm gone sen' ya back to d'fiel', ya hear!?

ELI: (*Now really taking his time getting supplies back in the bag*) I'm sick and tired o' him talkin t'me lak I ain't worf nuttin. (*Answering PARKER*) I'se coming, Massa Av'ry! (*Somewhat softer voice*) If I wasn't worf nuttin, why didn't he *leab* me back in de fields where I could least pick two, three hunnurd pounds a day? An' if I ain't worf nuttin, why dey's fightin dis war ovuh some no-count, worfless niggras, when nuttin don't git done less'n we do it? I don' git it. Lawd knows I don'. (*Runs off to join PARKER on the battlefield*)

SCENE 2

(*COLONEL LEONARD GROCE, owner of Liendo, and GENERAL JOHN BANKHEAD MAGRUDER come out onto the front porch and stop at the top of the steps, whereby they are interrupted by EDOM and FIELDING, who are armed and ready to leave for Mexico to sell the Colonel's cotton.*)

COL. GROCE: (*To MAGRUDER*) You shore five horses will help you out any, General? I could have let you have more, 'cept what extra I got, my hands is using to take my cotton down to Mexico.

GEN. MAGRUDER: I s'pose that's the only way it's gone git sold, with that Union blockade in Galveston Bay. Who's runnin it for ya?

COL. GROCE: Fielding and Edom, coupla my right-hand boys when it come to branging home the bacon on dat cotton. They oughta be leaving shortly.

GEN. MAGRUDER: Right now, any horses you can spare us'll be a big help out on th'field. I tell you, me n' my troops is mighty grateful for yo' offer to feed us these past few days. An', why, that cook o' yours, I wish I had the money to buy her off ya.

COL. GROCE: *She* ain't for sale.

GEN. MAGRUDER: It's all cause o' de fine folk lak yo'sef, that we's beatin hell outta dem Yankees.

COL. GROCE: Oh, yeah? Well, as long as I got cotton in de field and Negroes to pick it, you can count on me to do my share, General.

FIELDING: Massa Groce, suh, me and Edom jes as soon leab 'fo it git much later. We's hoping to make it cross de Brazos by sundown.

COL. GROCE: How much cotton you figure we sellin this time?

EDOM: We loaded up 'leven wagons at ten bales a piece, so's it be right at a hunnurd bales, suh, long wit de supplies.

COL. GROCE: Y'all got enough ammunition?

GEN. MAGRUDER: (*Trying to be inconspicuous*) Now that's a sight fo' sore eyes —

(*COL. GROCE is at a loss what he's referring to, and backs away wondering for a minute.*)

Let's face it, *a nigger wit a rifle?* You shore dis is a good idea, Colonel?

COL. GROCE: A good idea?

GEN. MAGRUDER: Where I come from —

COL. GROCE: You ain't where you come f'om and don'cha forgit it. You may be the commanding General of the Confederate troops, but at Liendo, I run thangs here! And as long as you're dependent on my horses and my food to keep this operation goin, you'll have nothing to say 'bout how I plan to git that cotton sold! It's money from my cotton that my Negroes risk their lives to haul 'cross the Rio Grande that keeps an ox on the fire — for your men. Do you git my meanin?

GEN. MAGRUDER: I'm beginning to . . . suh.

COL. GROCE: (*Saluting and turning to walk away*) G'day . . . General, suh. Fielding, Edom, let's check on that wagon train. Now what is it about the ammunition?

FIELDING: We got thirty rifles and thirty men, suh, long wit a few pistols. Dat oughta hol' off any Injuns. Afta dat las' trip, I 'speck da word done got 'roun dat we's some rough ridin rubulators.

(*They laugh.*)

EDOM: What ain't scared o' alligators.

FIELDING: We Mexico-boun' an' 'ave cotton t'sell.

EDOM: Mess wit us and we'll 'ave yo' tail.

(*All roll with laughter and familiarity.*)

We needs you t'write up somethin so we kin stop in town and pick up mo' ammo — 'nough to las' til we git back.

COL. GROCE: An' how much might that be? (*Taking out a pencil and small book*)

BUD: Well, if we figga on bein' gone fo' roun' two months, lak las' time . . .

(*The conversation trails off as they disappear around the side of the house.*)

SCENE 3

(*GEN. MAGRUDER and ELI can be seen coming through the front gate, each of them supporting PRIVATE PARKER who has been badly wounded. He is bleeding from his left shoulder, up near his heart, and is barely conscious.*)

GEN. MAGRUDER: (*Sends ELI for help while he makes PARKER comfortable in the yard.*) Quick, go fetch somebody who knows somethin 'bout bullet wounds and be quick about it, boy! Go on, git!

ELI: (*Calls to CAROLINA, the Groce family maid, who is standing on porch*) Ca'lina, Ca'lina! Come quick, Massa Av'ry 'bout to die! Brang some rags and hot water. Y'all hurry up! (*He runs back to his dying master, and holds him in his arms.*) Massa Av'ry? Massa Av'ry, it's me Eli. Say sumpin, suh! We got he'p on d'way! Hang on, suh! . . . Massa Avery?

CAROLINA: (*On the porch tending to MRS. GROCE, CAROLINA heeds the call.*) Lawd a'mercy, what nex'?! (*To JOSH*) Run, boy, tell Georgia to brang some hot water and pleny clean rags!

(*She runs down off the porch and into the yard to tend to the wounded soldier, who is gasping for air while trying to say something to ELI, his trusted body servant.*)

GEN. MAGRUDER: Do what'cha can for 'im, gal, I gotta git back to d'field. (*Runs back out of gate to battlefield*)

PARKER: Eli, E-E-E-li, looks like . . . I-I ain't gone make it . . . ol' buddy . . . Tell my, my daddy . . . I did 'im proud out dere—an' thanks, Eli fo' . . . fo' . . . (*Dying*) E-E . . . (*Dies, with his eyes fixed on ELI*)

(Meanwhile, CAROLINA has wiped his blood with her apron; GEORGIA is in shock, standing there holding a pan of hot water and some rags; ELI is holding the dead soldier in his arms, not sad, but confused.)

CAROLINA: *(After a few seconds to soak in the reality)* Don't jus stand there gawkin, let's git this boy up f'om here and git 'im ready fo' burial.

GEORGIA: Ever'thang's happenin so fas' wit dis war an all, whew! More folks is dying dan's bein b'on. Look lak we's buryin somebody chile ever'day. Jes look at dis chile, ain't no mo' den eighteen year old, if dat much. *(Calling to field hands)* Mose, Josh, y'all come he'p us git dis so'dier up f'om out de yard, 'fo Missus hab one o' her fits! I declare, dat one woman what can't stan' no blood!

CAROLINA: Ain't it de truf? Ever since she was a little thang she can't stan' to see nobody hurt.

MOSE: Us might as well be on de battlefield ourse'fs, as to be draggin dese bodies lef' an' right.

JOSH: Tell it, brothuh Mose. Sound lak I feel a song comin on —

(Singing as MOSE and JOSH take soldier's body around the back of house. CAROLINA and GEORGIA walk behind them, singing also.)

I'm on de battlefield for my Lord,
I'm on de battlefield for my Lord.
An' I promised him dat I
Would serve him til I die,
I'm on de battlefield for my Lord. *(Repeat three times)*

SCENE 4

(CAROLINA and AUNT LIDDY, the cook, standing outside, on the side of the house discussing ELI.)

AUNT LIDDY: I tell ya de truf, dat so'dier wudden eben col' yit fo' dat boy servant o' his struck outten here!

CAROLINA: Da one dey call Eli?

AUNT LIDDY: Uh-hum, he be de one, awright.

CAROLINA: You don't mean! Where ya reckon he wuz goin?

AUNT LIDDY: He come to de back door o' de kitchen and axed me fo' as much pork and bread as I kin spare. Po' chile ate lak he wuz runnin outten time.

CAROLINA: Huh? Where he say he wuz goin?

AUNT LIDDY: Tol' me he wuz goin jine d'Union!

CAROLINA: *Say what!?*

AUNT LIDDY: I ain gots t'lie! Jes as sho as I'm standin up here fannin dis apron, he say he ain't nevah goin back where he come f'om. Say he massa wuz so mean, mek 'im sleep in d'barn in de winnertime.

CAROLINA: Uh-uh-uh. Lawd, Jesus.

AUNT LIDDY: Talked 'bout how he didn 'ave no people no where since he mammy died. Dat de only way he gone be free, is to go to war and fight.

CAROLINA: I hope he know dat dey ain't takin no colored boys.

AUNT LIDDY: I hears dey's talkin 'bout it, though. Cause our boys wants to fight fo' dey own freedom!

CAROLINA: Well, iffen dey lets 'em fight, dey's gone hafta carry guns and you knows yose'f, dat de white man don' want no niggers t'have no guns — not now, not nevah! Dem white folks up in de Norf what meks de decisions ain't lak Massa Groce. Ain't another white man lak 'im nowheres.

AUNT LIDDY: I gots to go see 'bout dat ox we got cookin. All dis cookin on accounta us having to feed dese so'diers. So much comin and goin, you don't know who's who.

CAROLINA: It's a wonder dat Eli ain't lef fore now — de way our folks is runnin off to Mexico and ebber where else. You heard 'bout dem boys down round de Wharton place what got caught livin out in de woods, huh?

AUNT LIDDY: Sho' 'nuf? Well, down in dem Brazos River bottoms ain't no tellin what cha might fin'. So many niggers is plum fed up wit de way dey's havin to wuk double extra wit dey bosses gone off to war. Plus ha'f dese missus don't know what de hell dey's doin 'ceptin orderin folks roun'.

CAROLINA: 'Bout lak my boy Jake, hired out to work Gee's place. He say he know how to raise a crop f'om de seed to de table but ol' Missus Gee can't let 'im git no res' fo' she telling 'im to go git dis and go haul dat. By de time he git to de fiel', he be lookin for a shade tree.

AUNT LIDDY: Lawd, chile, lemme go see 'bout dis ox.

CAROLINA: Yeah, and I better go see 'bout Miz Courtney. Know how she is whenever anybody die. (*Walking off*) Shame 'bout dat po' so'dier what died in de yard, huh?

SCENE 5

(*MRS. COURTNEY GROCE is in her upstairs bedroom sitting at a desk writing in her journal when a letter arrives from her son, GEORGE, who has left to fight with the Confederate Army. COURTNEY reads aloud as she writes.*)

COURTNEY: It's been 214 days since George left to go on the battlefront with Colonel Carter's Lancers, barely escaping that deadly Battle of Shiloh on April 6. And with less than six weeks before Christmas, we have yet to hear from him. Lord knows how it grieves me not to have received just one letter. (*She begins to weep silently, but stops herself, trying to have strength.*) I so wish he had left with Major General Wharton, his uncle. No less he might have fared better, wherever he is. I so remember the day he left. (*Turns pages back to read in her journal*) Ah, here it is. I must have read it a dozen times already—

Before he left, it seemed there was no end to everything that was good. It was the first of April and that morning, Aunt Liddy laid out an incomparable meal—nice fried ham, stewed chicken, excellent biscuits, lightbread, butter, buckwheat cakes that were most delicious, molasses and, oh yes, four or five different kinds of preserves. We all gathered 'round the table . . . and Leonard prayed for George's safe return. Thereafter, we retired to the music room. (*She rises and goes downstairs to the music room, preferring to comfort herself with some soft music.*)

On the day George left home I played the piano . . . and as if my piano playing wasn't good enough, Georgia sent for one of the Negroes to come in and enliven the occasion by patting and dancing something they call the juba, which brought all the Negroes who weren't doing field work around to the side window, dancing, singing, and clapping like crazy! We all ended with a jubilant "Dixie" and a hymn to ol' Bonnie Blue. And then . . . (*Musing to herself and speaking slowly*) and then . . . off went George, in his new uniform and musket, daring to trade his feather bed to sleep on the hard ground, with his knapsack as a pillow . . . (*Crying softly*) riding the horse his father had given him for his sixteenth birthday . . . If only I could bring myself to quit worrying so. This bloody war is so cruel. I pray daily as I await his safe arrival home, and yet . . . I cannot imagine, the breakdown that would occur in our perfect Southern society if slavery were wiped out altogether.

CAROLINA: (*She is excited, bearing good news, and can be heard coming up the walkway, up the steps, and into the house.*) Miz Courtney? You in here? Oh, Miz Courtney!

COURTNEY: What on earth? (*Getting up to find out why CAROLINA is so excited*) Carolina!

CAROLINA: Look what done come, Miz Courtney? One o' de captains jes brung it, a letter f'om George!

COURTNEY: Say what? Are you sure? How you know it's from George?

CAROLINA: 'Cause it says so right here, ma'am— (*Stops abruptly because she is not supposed to know how to read*)

COURTNEY: (*First looks at CAROLINA in disbelief, then immediately taking letter to see for herself*) Well, I declare, you're right it is! Quick bring me my spectacles! Oh, my prayers have been answered, my child is alive! Look at the date on it. And bring the letter opener, Carolina. Hurry up!

CAROLINA: I'se hurrin, ma'am. Where is yo' specs, ma'am? Oh, here dey is, right here. (*She hurries to give her both items, then stands there as if to share in the news of the letter.*)

COURTNEY: (*Firmly*) You're dismissed, Carolina. The Colonel and I will be needing to speak to you immediately after supper. Is that clear?

CAROLINA: Yes'm. (*Leaves sadly, fearing a strong reprimand for exposing her ability to read*)

COURTNEY: (*Composing herself for whatever news the letter will reveal, reading aloud*) "My dear Mother, I can only hope that this letter arrives to find you and father enjoying the best of health. Since injuring my hand this is only the second letter I have been able to write. I lost one finger from my right hand to misfiring a musket and the others are still very stiff. I paid a comrade to write one other letter for me. He of course charges ten cents, five cents if I furnish stationery and stamps. I am told that guerrillas and bushwhackers and even apparently inoffensive citizens are always ready to waylay the only carrier of Uncle Sam's mail sack. Therefore, I hope that this letter will arrive safely and that you will be put at ease to know that I am still alive. Give my love to all, your son, John."

(left) **The Civil War—a time of great loss. George Ranch Historical Park, Texian Market Days Festival, 1995;** (below) **The Old South—a "way of life destroyed." Sam Houston Festival, 2000**

CANE CUTTER COUNTRY
The Saga of the Lake Jackson Plantation

Written for "Viewing the Past through Different Lenses: The African American Legacy in the Lower Brazos Valley," 2000, and sponsored by Texas Parks and Wildlife

CHARACTERS
NARRATOR: middle-aged black male
SOLOMON: male field hand, age 22
RICKTER: male field hand, age 29
CALEB: boy, age 10–12
MANDY: female field hand, age 20
ABNER JACKSON: owner of the plantation, age 46
WHARTON: neighboring planter, in his midthirties
MARGARET JACKSON: wife of Abner, age 49
HATTIE: Jackson family cook, age 35
JOHN: oldest of the Jackson sons
ROSE: an attractive house servant
GEORGE: a younger Jackson son
MAJOR: an assistant overseer, age 43
PETER: the blacksmith, age 35
MALINDA: Peter's intended wife, a slave
WHITE LADY: a store customer, in her midforties
DOCTOR SMITH: a mature gentleman, age 55

SETTING
TIME: *1856–1865*
PLACE: *Cane field and sugar mill at the Jackson Plantation along the Brazos River in Brazoria County, Texas*

SYNOPSIS
For 150 years, the stories of the African Americans in the Brazos River Basin have gone largely ignored, been disregarded, kept silent. *Cane Cutter Country* seeks to give voices to these ancestors by showing their contributions to

the development of the plantation society of Brazoria County, where many Texas slaves lived. According to Randolph Campbell, "The oldest area of major slaveholding was that part of Austin's Colony extending from the Gulf coast inland along the Brazos and Colorado Rivers. This included Brazoria and Matagorda counties on the coast and the inland counties of Fort Bend, Colorado, Austin, and Washington. Taken together, these six counties had approximately one-third of Texas' slaves in 1840."[18]

Abner Jackson was no doubt a shrewd businessman. By age fifty he was the second most prosperous planter in Brazoria County. But that wealth came from the backbreaking labor of those who harvested the sugar cane on his three plantations. We honor the enslaved in *Cane Cutter Country* with glimpses into their private lives, by showing their ambition to be free, and the extent to which their labor brought affluence to the thriving plantation economy in Brazoria County and in Texas.

Many pieces to the puzzle are still missing, but we have taken facts and built them into a theatre piece that portrays the life of a slaveholding family along the Brazos. The aim of this play is to pay homage to the Jackson family—both its white and its black descendants—and to interpret the attitudes and social politics of the planter class. It is also a story of the anxiety of the impending Civil War, the fear of slaves uprising, the fierce determination to hold onto the Southern way of life, and the Underground Railroad to Mexico.

SCENE 1

(At curtain rise, music fades down as lights come up—NARRATOR enters.)

NARRATOR: Howdy. I'd like to welcome y'all to the Jackson Plantation here on the Brazos River—one of the largest sugar cane operations on the Brazos. This here is sugar cane country. The time is October 1856. It's five years before the Civil War will begin. We're out here between the fields, where they grow the cane, and the sugar mill, where they cook the juice from the cane to extract the sugar. Ya see, this here plantation was built mainly for one thing—to make sugar. Most of the world's sugar comes from sugar cane. Oh sure, there's some farmers out west that grow sugar beets and they make a little sugar from them, but it ain't even enough to sweeten all the mint juleps on Kentucky Derby Day. No, sir—this is where the real sugar comes from.

(*Holds up a piece of sugar cane*) This cane once grew all up and down the Brazos. Sugar was big business back in these days. Ya see, long before Texas started supplying beef cattle to the Confederacy and later to the rest of the United States and the world—and even longer before they discovered oil up near Beaumont and started the first big oil boom—one of Texas's primary exports was sugar. Of course this was way before saccharine and NutraSweet, too.

(*He pours sugar from his hand.*) Now, the sugar back in these days wasn't a nice pure white like this, like the kind you put in your lattes or iced tea. That won't be available for many years, when they will discover a process called vacuum distillation. All sugar in these days is a rich brown color.

(*Pours light brown sugar from his hand*) Now it's not to be confused with the brown sugar you use today in cooking or baking. The brown sugar produced back then is now called raw sugar, and today it's sold in fancy markets where it costs about two or three times what the white stuff costs. Well, that's progress. I mentioned that the sugar was brown. Well, that's fitting, I guess, 'cause so were the people who worked so hard to produce it. They cultivated and harvested the sugar cane, they crushed the stalks in the sugar mills to extract the sweet juice which they boiled in huge cauldrons, and then they loaded the sugar in large wooden barrels called hogsheads. It was long, hot, exhausting, and dangerous work. It was the work of the enslaved.

(*SOLOMON and RICKTER enter singing a song under the NARRATOR's lines.*)

Our story today is about some of the people who grew the cane and made the sugar—and also made some very sweet profits for the plantation owners. You're gonna meet some of the enslaved folks that do all this hard work. Later you'll meet Abner Jackson, the owner of the plantation, as he shows his neighbor, Mr. Wharton, around the place.

(*NARRATOR exits.*)

SOLOMON AND RICKTER: (*Singing together*)

Cane need cuttin, (uh-uh)
It done growed tall. (uh-uh)
Massa is cussin, (uh-uh)
And that ain't all. (uh-uh)
My sickle ain't sharp, (uh-uh)
Enough to make cane fall. (uh-uh)
Gone sharpen dis knife, (uh-uh)
Den leave here, y'all. (uh-uh)

SOLOMON: Rickter, some o' dose stalks we cuttin's too big to go through the juicer more than one at a time. Dey liable t'tear up da mill.
RICKTER: Yessuh, boss. I do it one at a time, now on. Ya know Brothuh Sol'mon, you gotcha a real head on dem shoulders.
SOLOMON: Why thank ya, Brothuh Rickter.

(*CALEB enters.*)

Come 'ere, Caleb, I wants you to give Brothuh Rickter a han' wid da juicer. See here, some dese stalks is too big to go thoo, 'cept one at a time. (*To both*) Now y'all knows what t'do. Go on over and git started. (*Sees MANDY enter, gets a drink of water, and sits*) I needs me a lil res'.
RICKTER: You takes your rest, boss. Me an' Caleb, we go an' do da job right.

(*RICKTER and CALEB exit.*)

CALEB: We goin do it kinda slow lak, that right Brothuh Rickter?
RICKTER: Yeah, nothin to it. Jes ease 'em on thoo—uh-hum, that's right. You learn quick don'cha boy?
CALEB: (*Proudly*) Dat's why de Massa has me working in the blacksmif shop soma de time.

(*SOLOMON crosses to MANDY.*)

SOLOMON: Mandy girl, how you been doin?
MANDY: (*Wiping her brow*) I been fine—how's you doin?

SOLOMON: Fine, jes fine. You getting yo'self a drink o' that water—takin a break from de cookin kettles?

MANDY: Yeah. It's thirsty work. Dat heat burn all the way to your innards.

SOLOMON: That it do, girl, that it do. (*Pause*) Say girl, I ever tol' you how good y'all looks to des here eyes o' mine?

(She smiles—he looks around, then kisses MANDY on the cheek.)

MANDY: (*Mock reprimand*) You better be careful Major don't see you. (*Coy*) I sho is glad to see you. I heard y'all's fine singin.

SOLOMON: Why, thank you, Mandy girl. We gots to sang to keep a goin in dis heat. Hell can't be no hotter'n dis!

MANDY: (*Wipes her forehead and fans herself with a rag*) Preacher say it be seven times hotter in Hell, but I don't think he ever done no sugar cookin befo'. Whilst I'm standin here, onliest thang make me able to hol' out is thanking 'bout dem cold nights when me and Mama was back in 'ginia. It use to snow and freeze sumpin awful back dere. (*Pause*) That was befo' me and Mama got sol'.

SOLOMON: Yo' mama and you got sol' away? Woo, gal, I's sorry 'bout that. How come y'all to git sol'?

MANDY: Mama was takin kere of the ol' Missus's baby, when it jes up an' died. Missus said that Mama had *kilt* her baby—and made de Massa sell bofe us.

SOLOMON: Did yo' mama kill de baby?

MANDY: Course not! Dat baby always sickly—from de time when it wuz bo'n. But that ain't why we was sol'. It was on account o' folks was sayin dat de Massa was my pappy, dat's why. Missus couldn't stand my mama or me. On our way down here we got separated. In New Orleans, some man bought Mama—an'—I ain't never seen her no mo'.

(They pause a few beats. SOLOMON sees ABNER and WHARTON enter. ABNER is showing WHARTON the plantation.)

ABNER: Just come over this away and I'll show you the—

(He continues talking but unheard. SOLOMON crosses toward RICKTER and CALEB. He speaks somewhat loudly to avoid suspicion.)

SOLOMON: Rickter, y'all come over here. I gots to go over some 'cedures wit y'all.

(RICKTER and CALEB enter and cross to SOLOMON.)

It's important that y'all put de big canes through one at a time. Dey so big if you puts mo' den one you liable to bust sumthin in de juicer. Now if y'all thanks ya got it, we'll git back to bizness.

RICKTER: Got it, boss!

CALEB: We got it, boss!

SOLOMON: Well, lets get back to work—we got a passel o' cane left to cook today.

(SOLOMON, RICKTER, and CALEB exit singing until they're out of sight.)

I'm a cane cutter, cane cutter
comin down de row.
Where I been,
there ain't cane no mo'.

WHARTON: *(Impressed)* Major, I gotta hand it t'ya. This here is one of the finest and highest developed properties in all o' Brazoria County.

ABNER: *(Proud)* Well, you ain't seen nothin, yet. Wait til I git dat new steam engine in here and you gonna really see some production. On dis plantation alone we brought in ovah a hundred hogsheads last year. Wait til you see what we do when we get that new steam engine fired up.

WHARTON: I come pretty near close to seventy myse'f—though I raised a lot mo' cotton than cane last year. You still leasing Retrieve?

ABNER: Yes, I am. Fact is, just this mawnin I wrote to Gov'nuh Pease 'bout buyin Retrieve—I'd jes as soon buy it seeing as how I been cultivatin cane over there all these years.

WHARTON: Sounds lak a good deal to me, Major. How many field hands you got workin now?

ABNER: Right at two hunnurd all together here and Retrieve—and the number still climbin. *(To MANDY, sarcastically)* Mandy, if you through takin in the fresh air, you think you might do a little work for me?

MANDY: (*Exits quickly*) Yessuh, Massa, suh. I was just getting a mouthful of water. I's goin right now.

ABNER: (*Watching her exit*) Lazy gal! Ya gotta watch 'em ever minute, or they'll sit down all day.

WHARTON: If'n she's all that much trouble, why 'on't you sell her to me? (*Indicating MANDY and grinning*)

ABNER: (*Looks at MANDY, then smiles knowingly*) Wharton, you just an ol' devil.

WHARTON: I reckon so. But it gits mighty lonely since my wife took sick with the fever. She ain't rightly recovered and prob'ly never will. (*Pause*) While we're on de subject of slaves, Aaron Coffee tol' me 'bout sumpin been happening up in Colorado County, prob'ly other places too. Seems a bunch of niggers been escapin from there and runnin on down cross th'border t'Mexico. 'Cordin to him, they don't know how many done escaped. You heard 'bout dat?

ABNER: (*Interested*) Escaped to Mexico, ya say?

WHARTON: Yes-sir-ee. Aaron said that the Colorado County Sheriff and a bunch of boys is plannin a expedition to go down there and round up dem runaways. We can't be too careful — them niggers are plotting against us evah minute.

ABNER: There's no doubt about that! Why you thank I had a jail built right here on my place? It's de stronges' building I got — I'd lock up any unruly nigger that needs it.

WHARTON: You might need that jail — you keep treatin your niggers lak you do.

ABNER: Yeah? How's that?

WHARTON: Working them in the field is one thang, they do that okay, long as you whip the lazy ones — keeps the others in line too. But you trainin them to do sumpin that requires a white man's skill, you askin for trouble. I hear dat you got you a nigger blacksmith, and a nigger brick mason, and a nigger engineer! I'd counsel against that, Jackson. That's lak throwin some rotten apples in your barrel o' good ones. I tell ya, Jackson, you askin fo' trouble.

ABNER: I do own a few slaves wit some skills. Dat's what I bought 'em for. They came here wit dat. An' it's worked out just fine. I got two coopers that make the finest barrels dis side of de Mississippi. I don't care what you or anybody else says. It's worked pretty fine fo' me.

WHARTON: Well, I hope ya right, I surely do. But some of them smart ones with the skills 'cide to take off to Mexico, you'll be singin a different tune.

ABNER: Hell, I got my niggers working day and night and Sundays—and they will be up til I git all my sugar in the barrels. That means evahbody on dis place is accounted for round de clock! Come take a look at my jail. I'd jes lak to see one of 'em git out of that.

(They exit.)

SOLOMON, RICKTER, CALEB, AND MANDY *(Offstage)*:

Cane need cuttin, (uh-uh)
It done growed tall (uh-uh)
Massa is cussin, (uh-uh)
And that ain't all (uh-uh)

(They enter and cross to center stage.)

My sickle ain't sharp, (uh-uh)
'Nough to make cane fall (uh-uh)
Gone sharpen dis knife, (uh-uh)
Den leave here, y'all (uh-uh)

RICKTER: *(Preoccupied with something he has heard)* Jes how far is it to Mexico, do ya think? How'd you get there?

SOLOMON: Well, I don't rightly know. But I tell ya how to find it. Mexico to south a bit. When you gets up in da mornin and see the sun a risin, that's da east. Ya turns you yo'sef aroun' until yo' lef' arm is pointin at da sun—

(RICKTER points with his right arm—SOLOMON points to his left arm—RICKTER, trying to mock him, turns around and points with his left arm.)

—this means yo' body is pointin south. You jes take runnin in that direction and you keeps runnin until you cross a big river and smell dose chili pepper . . . then, by God, you is a free man!

(They all laugh and cheer.)

RICKTER: Wait a minute, Brothuh Sol'mon. Wouldn't it be better if you was to run away at night, while the Massa and th' oberseer a'sleepin?

SOLOMON: (*A little patronizingly*) Well, I'd say you's got the right idear.

RICKTER: Well, tell me this—which hand you point toward de sun at night?

SOLOMON: Let's talk about dis later and I'll 'splain it all to you again.

(*RICKTER crosses to CALEB. SOLOMON speaks to MANDY.*)

Sometime I thinks dat boy forget where he put his brain at, las' time he use it.

(*They laugh.*)

MANDY: I think when de Lord hand out brains, Rickter thought de Lord say, "rains," so Rickter run under de porch.

(*They laugh again.*)

SOLOMON: Well, Mandy girl, I knows where you wuz, when de Lord hand out good looks—you wuz in de front of dat line!

MANDY: (*Shoos him away in mock anger*) You go on, git outta here wif dat fancy talkin!

(*The MEN get together and sing, and MANDY joins them.*)

MEN: Take dis sickle, (whoo) swang it to de left (whoo)

MANDY: Take dis ladle, (whoo) swang it to de right (whoo)

MEN: Swang it to de left, swang it to de right,

ALL: We workin dis cane day and night.

MANDY: When you look to de lef (whoo)

MEN: When you look to de right (whoo)

ALL: If you don' see me (whoo), I lef last night.

(*All laugh loudly as lights fade down and music fades up.*)

SCENE 2

(Lights fade up as the music fades down. We are in the Jackson family parlor. MARGARET is seated and ABNER is standing. They speak silently as the NARRATOR enters.)

NARRATOR: The time is still 1856. We are in the parlor of the Jackson plantation home. You've met Abner and now you'll meet his wife, Margaret. Margaret and Abner had five children—four sons, John, George, Andrew, and Abner Jr., and one daughter, Arsenath. By this time, Margaret is in very poor health. She has seen the doctor and she knows her days are numbered. Let's join Margaret and Abner. She has just sent word for him to come to the house.

ABNER: I was really busy, dear. What is so important that I needed to drop everything and come to the house in the middle of the day?

MARGARET: Don't be cross with me, Abner. *(Tries to catch her breath)* You used to be so nice to me. Have I gotten so old and unattractive that you don't want to spend time with me?

ABNER: Of course you haven't. Perish the thought. It's just that I was very busy. Couldn't it have waited until supper?

MARGARET: What I want to talk to you about is not supper table conversation. And by the time we retire, you're often so tired I wouldn't want to trouble your rest.

ABNER: Okay, my dear. You have my undivided attention.

(She struggles to catch her breath.)

Margaret, I do believe that your cough is getting worse. Perhaps you should see Doctor Smith.

MARGARET: I saw him last time I was in town two weeks ago. He gave me something to take.

ABNER: Has it helped?

MARGARET: He—he said it might take a while to begin helping.

ABNER: Maybe you should lie down. *(Starts to rise)* I'll tell Hattie to—

MARGARET: *(Stopping him)* Abner, I'm okay. I'll have a nap later. I want to talk to you, my dear. *(He sits.)* What if something should happen to me, Abner?

ABNER: What? Did the doctor find something? Did he tell you something I oughta know?

MARGARET: (*Pauses*) No, Abner. But what would you do if something did happen to me? What would become of all the property and the niggers? How can I be sure that you will divide everything fairly?

ABNER: Margaret, it hurts me to hear you say that. That is an insult to me. Why wouldn't I divide the property fairly?

MARGARET: You know as well as I do that you have never liked John. You refuse to have anything to do with him—regardless of how hard he tries to please you!

ABNER: Please me? That boy doesn't try to please anyone but himself. He is as impudent as they come. He acts like he hates me. I don't know why he can't be like George.

MARGARET: Abner, John has never been able to do anything right where you're concerned. I think that's because the two of you are so much alike. And George can do no wrong. You even treat Andrew and little Abner Jr. better than you do John. You know you do.

ABNER: Margaret, let's not argue. You know that I will treat all the children fairly. Why don't you lie down and try to get some rest—you know what the doctor said. While you're resting, I'll go over to the mill and check on things. (*Exits*)

MARGARET: (*Watches ABNER exit*) Two years ago we were so happy, watching this house being built, caring for our children, and enjoying our love. Nowadays all he thinks about is how much sugar we can get from an acre of cane. If I could be sure that Abner would be fair to the boys, I'd rest a lot easier.

HATTIE: (*Enters quickly*) Ma'am! Ma'am, you better come out to de kitchen, quick! (*Runs back into the kitchen to monitor a fight*)

MARGARET: What on earth is wrong now?

HATTIE: It's John and George, they at it agin! You got to come separate 'em, ma'am, fo' dey hurt one another. Oh, no, John knocked George down! Bus' his lip! Whoo, now George kick Massa John in his private! Oh, no, he mad now! He hit little Georgie in his eye. It gone be black by mornin! (*Runs back to the door of the parlor*) Ma'am, you better do something and I mean quick—I think they gittin mad now! (*She exits.*)

MARGARET: Lord, I do believe I've given birth to Cain and Abel.

(She is almost praying for help as NARRATOR enters.)

I don't understand why they're always fighting. I'm afraid someday one is gonna kill the other. I can't handle this. Abner's gonna have to do something.

(MARGARET tries to rise, but she is too weak and sits again—she stares downstage tearfully, going into a soft freeze.)

NARRATOR: When it came to getting on with one another, John and George weren't so much like Cain and Abel—they were more like Cain and Cain. History doesn't tell us why they hated each other, and why that hatred grew throughout the years. Maybe John was jealous of the attention their father showed George. Maybe John feared the loss of his birthright. We may never know. Our story takes up again in 1858.

(HATTIE enters with a blanket and covers MARGARET.)

Margaret's health has grown steadily worse in the last two years. The doctor has been summoned. The dark angel of death is hovering near.

MARGARET: *(Weakly)* Oh, Hattie, I was burning up a few minutes ago, and now I've taken a chill.

HATTIE: It's the fever. I thinks ya over spent yo'self, sittin here in the parlor. You needs your res'. The doctor oughta be coming soon. Massa Jackson should be back any minute now. Here, lemme prop you up a lil bit—drink some o dis water down—you needs plenty water. Jes hol' onto me—an' take it slow and easy.

MARGARET: Hattie, where are my boys?

HATTIE: George went with the Massa and Andrew over to Retrieve. I thanks Abner Jr. went wit 'em.

MARGARET: I don't know why I let Arsenath go visit her cousin. I need her. *(Coughing)* Where's John?

HATTIE: Ma'am, you need to save your strength. You's gittin all tired out. Lemme wipe yo' head wit dis cool rag. You lay back now.

ABNER: *(Enters)* How is she, Hattie?

HATTIE: Not much better, I's 'fraid ta say. Thank goodness y'all is back. Look lak you been gone forever.

ABNER: (*Crosses to MARGARET*) Margaret, my dear. I'm back. How are you feeling? The doctor should be here shortly. Have you been able to rest? (*He looks at HATTIE. She shakes her head.*) You must rest, my dear.

MARGARET: I'll have all eternity to rest. We need to talk.

ABNER: Now, now, you need to get some rest. Why don't you let me help you get to your bed?

MARGARET: I don't want to go to bed! I don't want to die in bed— (*Pausing to catch her breath*) I just want to—to sit here.

ABNER: Maybe I should go and let you rest. We can talk later.

MARGARET: Abner, I'm trying to tell you, there isn't going to be any later. We must talk now.

ABNER: Dearest, I really wish you would—

MARGARET: I want to talk about the will. Abner, did you make the changes in the will like I asked you?

ABNER: Yes, dear, I did—just like you asked.

MARGARET: You promise me, you'll honor my dyin wish—

ABNER: (*Trying to change the subject*) What's all this talk about dyin. Why, I bet in a few days you'll be up and—

MARGARET: Abner, I'm dying. Don't let me go to my grave uneasy about the will and worried about my children. (*Holding his arm, then with the last of her strength*) Promise me, Abner, promise me that you'll see fairly to the children.

ABNER: (*He's lying.*) I promise, Margaret.

(*MARGARET visibly relaxes—this exertion has weakened her.*)

DOCTOR: (*Enters and crosses to MARGARET, takes her hand*) Now, how's the patient?

(*MARGARET is too weak to reply. He looks at HATTIE—she shakes her head. He takes a stethoscope from his bag.*)

I'll take over from here. You've done a good job, Hattie.

HATTIE: Thank you, suh. I done my bes'. Can I git ya anythang?

DOCTOR: Yes, bring some more water.

(*HATTIE exits.*)

MARGARET: (*Weakly*) Can you gimme something for the pain, please? It hurts in my chest.

DOCTOR: I know, Margaret. Try to relax—let me have a look at you. (*He listens through a stethoscope for a while.*)

ABNER: (*Kneels and takes MARGARET's hand*) Margaret, my love—you're gonna be just fine, dear. (*Prays*) Please God, save her. I beg you to have mercy. Please, Lord.

DOCTOR: Don't strain, Mrs. Jackson. Try to relax.

MARGARET: I don't want the children to see me like this. After I'm gone, you tell them how much their mother loved them.

HATTIE: (*Enters with pan of water and a towel*) I brung the water, Doctor Smif.

DOCTOR: Yes, just place it on the table there. (*Holding MARGARET's hand feeling her pulse*)

(*After a beat, he lays her hand back on the bed. He motions for all to exit. HATTIE helps ABNER out of the room. After they are gone DOCTOR closes MARGARET's eyes and looks sorrowfully at her.*)

HATTIE: (*As she exits*)

Oh, Lord Jesus,
Hear my troubled cry.
Let me see some freedom
'Fore I die.
Hmm-umm

(*The lights fade down as music fades up.*)

SCENE 3

(*At curtain rise, lights fade up and music fades down. Outside the stables, JOHN is talking to ROSE silently. NARRATOR enters.*)

NARRATOR: The year is 1860, about two years after Margaret's death. We're outside the house, near the stables. John Jackson is preparing for a trip. He's talking to one of the house slaves, Rose. You'll see that maybe Rose is a little more than just one of the slaves. You'll also see that the relations between John and his father and his brother George have not changed, except maybe for the worse.

JOHN: You packed my white shirts, didn't you?

ROSE: Yes I did, 'long wit some food I packed up fo' your trip—your favorite, cornbread and pork chops, and some of them yams I cooked fo' ya.

JOHN: Thanks, Rose. I'll be back around the end of the week. (*Grins*) You be nice to me, maybe I'll brang ya somethin pretty.

ROSE: I's always nice to ya. That's why I gots this problem I needs to talk to ya about.

JOHN: Rose, I ain't got no time for no problems. I should have left two hours ago. If it can't wait til I get back, go see my daddy.

ROSE: Well, it's some kind of a daddy problem, alright. But it ain't your daddy I needs to talk to 'bout it.

JOHN: Rose, I don't have time for your games right now. It'll have to wait.

ROSE: It'll wait a few more days, I 'spect. I guess if I don't tells ya, ya find out 'ventually anyways. (*Pause*) Do Massa know you goin?

JOHN: No he don't. And there ain't no need for you to tell him, ya hear? I don't need him on my trail. (*To GEORGE as he enters*) Well, it's about time. Saddle my horse, little brother, and don't take all day!

GEORGE: Does Papa know you leavin?

JOHN: No he don't. Jus' forget about Papa and saddle my horse.

(*He takes packages from ROSE and motions for her to leave. ROSE exits as ABNER enters. JOHN turns and starts to leave.*)

ABNER: (*He sees JOHN leaving and tries to stops him.*) John, don't be leaving just yet. (*To GEORGE cordially*) Mornin, son. I'd like you to take a ride with me over to Retrieve. We need to check on the cane cutters. Go saddle up. (*Watches GEORGE exit, then yells to JOHN*) An' just where the hell do you think you're goin?

JOHN: (*Bitter*) Well, I might have gone over to Retrieve with you and George, but I wasn't invited.

ABNER: The way you're behavin right now is why you weren't invited.

JOHN: No problem, Father, dear. I've got some business of my own to tend to.

ABNER: John, why don't we quit all this bickering. Your dear mother would be sad to see you behave this way and—

JOHN: Don't you dare mention my mother to me!

ABNER: Now calm down, son. I just want us to come to some agreement —

JOHN: You and I have never agreed on anything, and I don't 'spect we ever will. Now, if that's all you have to say, I'll be going 'bout my business. You and George have a nice ride. (*Exits, angry, as GEORGE enters*)

ABNER: (*Calling after JOHN*) John! You come back here! (*To GEORGE*) I truly believe that your mother went to an early grave because of that boy. Let's go. (*Exits slowly*)

GEORGE: What's wrong with John?

ABNER: Nothing a good hidin wouldn't cure!

GEORGE: Why is he always mad at me? I didn't do nothin.

ABNER: Of course you didn't. That boy's got the devil in him. Let's not ruin our day, studying on him. We got us a plantation to run.

GEORGE: Papa? What's gonna happen if — if something happened to you? If you — passed on like Ma?

ABNER: Well, I'm not goin anywhere for a while yet. And when I do, I have a will and an expensive lawyer in town to take care of things. He will see to it that after I'm dead and gone you won't have a thing to worry about.

(*They exit as lights fade down and the music fades up.*)

SCENE 4

(*At curtain rise, lights fade up as music fades down. ABNER is speaking with MAJOR, his black assistant overseer, near the sugar mill. They are unheard.*)

NARRATOR: It is now the summer of 1861. It is a time of excitement: for the Jackson household, for Texas, for the South, for the whole country. The war that would come to be known as the Civil War and the War Between the States, has started. It would prove to be a time of great irony and sadness. Ironic because the war that many people on both sides thought would be won in a few months, lasted four long, horrifying years, and sad because it pitted brother against brother and cousin against cousin and killed more Americans than any other war in our history. It would redefine our nation. But in the summer of 1861, there was a great pride on both sides, and an eagerness to get it over with! Few people on either side could have predicted that this very war would be so good at doing what wars do best—destroying so much of what it takes so long to build, and killing lots of people. But the optimism of both sides was rampant on the Jackson Plantation that summer. While the impending war was creating change, other things remained unchanged. The great rift between Abner and John had only grown wider. We see Abner talking with his assistant overseer, Major. (*Exits*)

ABNER: Well, Major, the last of my four sons is headin off to Houston to join the Eighth Cavalry. I 'spect you'll be my head man now.

MAJOR: Meanin no disrespeck, suh, but what 'bout John? Evah since you been kinda ailing, he been actin lak he in charge.

ABNER: (*Subdued anger*) In charge o' what?!

MAJOR: All de operations, suh, de cane mill, de hands. And if you'll be pardonin my sayin so, de way he bosses George aroun' and his brothuhs, all de time, well it's causin trouble, suh.

ABNER: Well don't trouble yourself over it. I'll put an end to all o' that!

MAJOR: Far as runnin thangs go, t'ain't nothin I can't handle, suh. I been de one driving dis plantation all dese years. I don't reckon a war's gone change none o' dat.

ABNER: I hope you're right 'bout that, Major. But the war's liable to change most evahthang. Margaret's dyin was hard enough on us, and now we got a war to fight—an' to win! (*Pauses, rises and slowly looks about*) But as long as we can get all the cane cut and cooked into sugar, we should make the winter. (*To Major*) How do you think those cane cutters are comin 'long?

MAJOR: Well, suh, dem cutters, dey been cuttin f'om cain to cain't! We's about one-third cut, I'd be guessin, suh—both here an' over at Retrieve.

ABNER: (*Disappointed*) Only one-third? I thought that we'd be a lot futha along by now.

MAJOR: Massa, dem boys cain't wuk no faster. An' 'member, suh, we had all dat rain las week. (*Anxious*) And if the Massa excuse me for sayin, dat new overseer you jes hired ain't noways fittin t'be a driver.

ABNER: What 'cha aimin at, Major?

MAJOR: Well, suh, he's drivin d'folks alright—but dey ain't gone give 'im no respeck. He be usin that big bull whip of his evahtime somebody bats dey eye. They ain't no call for that, suh. Folks here work hard, they don't need no lashin all the time. Th'other day, he lashed a couple of de wimmen folk jes fuh comin up behind 'im while he on his horse! He acts lak he scared o' somethin.

ABNER: I already told 'im once 'bout doin that! I guess I'm gonna have to make my point a little stronger. (*Pause*) I been good to y'all, ain't I, Major?

MAJOR: Yas-suh. You been mighty good to us. Yas-suh, mighty good.

ABNER: Well y'all better remember one thing. You niggers don't work fuh him, you work fuh me!

MAJOR: Yes, suh.

ABNER: Gol-darn-it! I've 'bout had it up to here wit no-count overseers! They're as bad as them damn circuit preachers I been paying to preach some sense into you folks!

PETER: (*Enters*) Sorry, suh. The overseer sent me to fetch Major—if'n you through wit him, suh.

ABNER: Oh he did, did he? Well, I'll decide when I'm ready to send Major to him! Damn it to hell! If it ain't one thang it's another. I got a son who'd just soon shoot me as look at me. De niggers are workin slow as molasses. I'm tryin to run a plantation with 'n ovah-seer who ain't got the sense the Good Lord gave a goose! And now, the war's comin on. I tell you, it's more than a Christian man can suffer, sometimes. (*Pause*) Major, what he got you doin?

MAJOR: Well, suh, he got me doin a whole passel o' things. Right now, I be needin to go over and oil up de steam engines. An' suh, he ax me to tell you dat one o' dem steam engines needs a new turning belt. (*Exits*)

ABNER: Aw, hell! What else? Wit de war startin, it's liable to be a coon's age 'fore we can git a new belt. I feel lak givin up! It was bad enough Margaret died—and now all my boys is leavin me for the war. Damn Yankees! I can't stan' no more of— (*ABNER clutches his chest.*)

PETER: (*Crosses to ABNER*) Massa, you sick, suh? Here, lemme he'p ya. Come ovah here and res' yo'sef on dis bench. Major, come back, quick! It's de Massa! (*Helping ABNER to the bench, and calling MAJOR back to help him*)

ABNER: (*In pain*) It's my chest again.

PETER: Yes, suh. Kin I git you somethin, suh?

MAJOR: (*Running back onto the scene and assisting PETER to get ABNER up onto a bench*) What's wrong? Lawd, o' mercy, you alright, suh?

ABNER: No, boys—I ain't alright. It's my chest . . . Jes git me up f'om here. (*Pause, catching his breath, not wanting to admit he's in so much pain*) What you doin here, Peter? Why ain't you workin? That cane ain't gonna cut itself! Go on, Major, git back to work!

PETER: You sent fo' me, suh.

ABNER: Sent for ya? (*Pauses, trying to hide the pain but still breathing heavily*) Oh yes—I did. Peter, I need to talk to you 'bout somethin—somethin 'portant. Afraid there ain't no way around it . . . the Eighth Cavalry's needin a blacksmith—a good blacksmith to take with 'em.

PETER: Yessuh.

ABNER: Well, they been looking all over the county and they ain't found no one—so that's why I'm talkin to you.

PETER: You was thinkin of sendin me, suh?

ABNER: Look, Peter, I tried to git around it. Jake was gonna let Big William go, but he jes can't spare him—war or no war. They wanted Wally Sams t'go. Anyway, neither one of 'em—

PETER: Massa, you promised me and Malinda we could jump de broom. I cain't be leavin now . . . please, suh! Can't it wait til—

ABNER: Don't be tellin me what you cain't do. I'll decide whether or not you leave. You better not cross me, boy! You thank she needs ya? Hell, I'm the one that needs ya! (*Pauses, calmer*) It cain't be helped. Now, you go git ya tools and go on up to de kitchen n'wait. Tell Andrew to give ya dat horse I tol'im 'bout! (*Clutching his chest in pain*)

PETER: How soon will I be needin to leave? (*Looking ABNER in his eyes*)

ABNER: You leavin along with Andrew and John.

(*Peter exits upset.*)

Hey, I'll miss you, boy! You one of the finest blacksmiths in the county. (*Louder*) I want you to go n'make de South proud, boy, ya hear?!

(*ABNER clutches at his heart in pain. WHARTON enters in uniform.*)

WHARTON: (*Salutes smartly*) Capain J. A. Wharton, reporting, suh. Of Company B, Terry's Texas Rangers.

ABNER: (*Looks up at WHARTON*) Now ain't you a sight for sore eyes? I always figured you for an officer—sorta have that look about 'cha.

WHARTON: Howdy-do, Major Jackson? (*As they shake hands, WHARTON senses ABNER's weakness.*)

ABNER: Don't ask me how I feel. You don't wanna know.

WHARTON: You do look rather pale, suh. Can I get you—

ABNER: What is it, Wharton? You come for th— (*Sighs*)

WHARTON: It's my understandin that you got four young rangers who's rarin to go fight some Yankees!

ABNER: That is a fact, Captain. They're waitin for you. 'Cept for Abner Jr., my youngest—I'm sending him to Bastrop Military Institute. This war prob'ly won't last long enough for him to see action. And George, he's already joined Captain James Fry's company.

WHARTON: Cap'n Fry's, is it? They're gonna be the First Regiment of Texas Mounted Riflemen. That oughta make you right proud, Major. I'm teaming up with Colonel Terry.

ABNER: I see. Well, all you men have got my best wishes and prayers ridin with you. We all hope you roust them Yankees and git back home befo' the firs' fros'. I've outfitted all my boys wit the fines' muskets, horses, and uniforms to be found in Brazoria County.

WHARTON: We knew we could count on you, Major. The support of gentlemen like yourself is the backbone of this war. (*Pause*) Well, suh, I 'spect we need to get on the road. (*With meaning*) We got a long way to go.

(*ABNER grabs his chest in pain.*)

Are you alright, Abner? You don't look well.

ABNER: I'm okay . . . just a little touch of somethin, I 'spect.

WHARTON: You sure there isn't somethin or someone I can get for you?

ABNER: I'm fine—maybe I'm missing my boys already. With Margaret gone, and now the boys, it's gonna be a lonely place here for an old man. (*Pauses—then a show of strength*) We've already said our goodbyes. They're over at the stable gittin saddled up for th' trip. (*Calling his sons*) Andrew? John? Captain Wharton is ready to leave. (*To Wharton*) What's your opinion, Wharton? Are we gonna be able to provide enough guns and ammo to win this war?

WHARTON: Frankly, Major, I don't know. It's the question on everybody's mind. We're workin mighty hard to supply all we'll need. No one can tell how far this thang might go. Some say we'll be home in a few months. Others say it could be the longest war we've ever seen. One thang's for sure, we're gonna give it our best shot. And we know the Lord's on our side.

ABNER: Amen to that. It's our way of life we're fightin for, Wharton. (*Pause*) I expect we'll be notified if more support is needed. I don't care what it takes; I'll put up evahthang I got to see that the South wins! Y'all whup them damn Yankees for all of us!

WHARTON: That's the spirit! Sure you don't wanna go? We could always use a good man like yourself.

ABNER: I'm a might ol' for fightin. Anyway, somebody has got to stay home and make enough money to finance this war.

WHARTON: Right you are, suh. Well the Eighth Cavalry is meeting Colonel Terry and Lieutenant Colonel Lubbock in Houston. We leave for Tennessee day after tomorrow. (*Pause*) Goodbye, Major. You say a prayer for us.

ABNER: (*Shakes WHARTON's hand*) You and all our boys shall be in my prayers, nightly. Look after my boys, Captain.

WHARTON: (*Salutes ABNER, then shouts as he exits*) You boys saddle up, we got ourselves a little war to win! (*Gives a rebel yell, while the cries of "Bye, Pa!" are heard in the background*)

(*Drum cadence sound effects*)

NARRATOR: The little war that everyone hoped would be over before the polish wore off the eager young soldiers' boots lasted more than four tragic years. It killed and maimed more men than any war fought in this country's history. The nation lost 618,000 men during the Civil War. Of that number, 258,000 were from the South and 17,000 were from Texas. And all the tragedy took place on the battlefield. Within a month after his three sons left to go fight for the Confederacy in the Civil War, Abner Jackson died. Two of his sons, Andrew and Abner Jr. were both killed in the war. Abner Jr. fresh from military academy, was killed in 1862, and buried in Arkansas. Andrew died in 1865.

(*A sad melody, i.e., "One Vacant Chair," plays in the background.*)

By the end of the war only John and George remained alive. John returned home to manage the estate in 1862 after the death of his father. George returned home weakened by tuberculosis after spending a year in a Yankee prison camp.

(Lights fade down as the sad melody fades into a solo drum funeral march. The drum solo also fades.)

SCENE 5

(At curtain rise, lights fade up as PETER enters looking about the edge of the cane field to see who might be there. NARRATOR enters.)

NARRATOR: If you recall, besides Captain Wharton and the Jackson boys, there was someone else who was leaving for the war — Peter, the blacksmith. He had at least two reasons for not wanting to leave the plantation to fight. I think that you can understand why he didn't want to help the South fight a war, which, among other reasons, was being fought to preserve slavery. A more personal reason was Malinda.

(MALINDA enters.)

She was his true love and had promised to step over the broom with him. That's about as close to a marriage ceremony as slaves could expect to have.

(PETER gives a love call to attract MALINDA's attention — she looks about.)

We're here on the edge of the cane field. Why don't we watch what happened to Peter after he left Abner.

PETER: Malinda, ovah here. Quick! C'mon, gal!

MALINDA: *(Looks over her shoulder while crossing to PETER)* Peter, what you doin here? Is sumpin gone wrong?

PETER: Yeah, sumpin's wrong. Sumpin's bad wrong. *(Looking around)* Where de overseer?

MALINDA: He gone over to de Retrieve — ain't nobody here now but Major.

PETER: *(Sincerely)* Thank God Almighty.

MALINDA: Ain't nobody where dey oughta be. Why you not at de blacksmif shed?

PETER: Look-a-here, sugar, you know you's all I got in dis worl' — you and my mammy. But baby, I gots to git outta here, and I means right now!

(She is in shock.)

Now, jus hold on an' listen. Massa done tol' me dat I got to go wit Wharton and his boys to Houston to jine de 'fed'rate army. He say dey's needin a blacksmif fuh de war.

MALINDA: Oh, Peter no! You cain't leave me, honey! Oh, baby, no! *(Crying)*

PETER: I gots to go, baby — *(Pause)* But I ain't goin wit dem.

(Pause — she looks at him in awe.)

Dey's fixin to leave right now. I ain't leavin til t'night. I already got a horse Massa gimme t'ride to Houston. Befo' daybreak in de mawnin, I gots t'be takin dat trail down to Mexico.

MALINDA: What you gone do in Mexico?

PETER: Honey, you heard us talkin 'bout dat t'other night. We can be free down in Mexico. Lots o' slaves gone down there. De Meskins don't b'lieve in no slav'ry.

(She starts to cry again.)

I gots no choice, baby girl. You don't want to see me go to da war, do ya? An' end up dead?

(She shakes her head, using her apron to hide her face.)

Well, das what's gone happen to me if'n I don't take off fo' Mexico — tonight . . .

MALINDA: *(Hears someone — stage whisper)* Hush! Here come Major.

(They hold each other close, silently.)

MAJOR: *(Offstage)* Haven't I tol' you 'bout cuttin them stalks off f'om de bottom lak dat? You leaving too much cane behin'. Nigger, you don' understand a thang I say, do you? Now haul yo' black behin' down dis row and you cuts it right or I'll be cuttin you. Y'hear me?! *(To someone else)* Hey you, boy! Git dat cart out de way! Yeah, I'm messin wit yo' no-good, lazy, triflin se'f! Move it, I say! *(Voice fades as he moves further away)*

PETER: 'Member dat gun we hid under the flo' boards o' de cabin? I'm takin it wit me. I'm gone hide out in the cane brake till t'night. Some othuh boys is leavin, too. But I ain't goin wif 'em, sees as how I gots dis horse and they be runnin on foot. Tell dese boys to meet me dere after nightfall—dat is Solomon and Rickter. Hear me? Jes dose two. And whatever you do, don' let Major know what you doin. He's as much de enemy as de Massa hissef! De wrong pusson fin' out, I'm dead, Malinda—we all be dead, ya hear me, baby girl?

MALINDA: I hears ya.

(He starts to leave—she stops him and takes food from her apron pocket and wraps it into the apron making a bundle.)

Wait! Here, take dese biscuits and dis lil piece o' pork rind. God go wit you, my love.

(They embrace—she tries to stop crying and appear brave.)

Is I'm gone never see ya agin?

PETER: Lindy, love, it may not be til we gits on de othuh side, but we will meet again. Take good care o' yose'f, cause when dis war is ovah, I'm comin back here fo' you. Dat's my promis. G'bye, Lindy.

(They kiss, she waves, he looks around then exits. MALINDA then collapses in tears as lights fade down and music fades up.)

SCENE 6

(At curtain rise, music fades out as night sounds are heard. After a few beats, lights fade up. PETER is dozing in the cane break beside the trunk of a tree. He has a pistol in his hand. SOLOMON and RICKTER enter with bags and startle him and he cocks his gun.)

PETER: *(Stage whisper)* Who dere?

SOLOMON: *(Stage whisper)* Hold yo' fire, it's Solomon!

RICKTER: (*Shouts*) And Rickter!

SOLOMON: (*Slaps at RICKTER, then loudly*) Quiet! You wake up the dead and de overseer!

PETER: (*Stage whisper*) Will y'all hold it down? (*Still holding the gun on them*) Anybody wit 'cha?

SOLOMON: Naw! Hold up, it's jus' us. Put dat gun up. We got no call to lie.

RICKTER: (*Loudly*) Yeah, put dat gun down.

PETER: Rickter, will you be quiet? (*To SOLOMON*) Dey still lookin fo' me ain't dey?

SOLOMON: Hell, naw. Why should dey be? White folks is all gone off to war, 'cept Massa. De big house folks is where dey b'long—at de big house.

RICKTER: (*Loudly*) Yeah—(*Remembers to be quiet—but not very much softer*)— why should dey be?

PETER: Wait a minute, you mean to tell me the Massa and none of 'em is lookin fo' me?

SOLOMON: Nobody thinkin 'bout you. Dey was so all fired up 'bout de folks going off to war, dey ain't said nothin 'bout you. All dem folks in de quarters is wonderin how thangs gone come out, if'n dey gone be free sometime soon. Freedom sho' be a sweet thought, don't it?

PETER: Did y'all brang de provisions?

SOLOMON: Yep. I got ever'thang you said right here in dese two sacks. We're ready to go. It ain't no moon tonight. We oughter be able to git pretty far away 'fore mawnin if we don't waste no time.

PETER: I'm sorry to be leavin y'all but I'm takin dat horse Massa give me to ride into Houston an jine de Confed'rates. Lemme take a look at dem provisions. (*Sorts through sacks to get what he needs*)

RICKTER: (*Sharpening a cane knife*) What you think it like down in Mexico? I heared dey gots dat peppa food—says it burns you goin in and again when it comes back out.

(*They look at him for a moment wanting to laugh but wishing he wouldn't joke.*)

I guess we better bring our own food, huh? What y'all think?

PETER: I'm thinkin we maybe trade you for one dem Meskin boo-roses when we get down dere.

RICKTER: (*Looks at PETER for a beat or two—then to SOLOMON*) What you be thinkin, Brothuh Sol'mon?

SOLOMON: I'm thinkin we'd be lucky to fine a Meskin whose blin' in one eye and cain't see out t'othuh and maybe dumb 'nuf to give us a whole boorose for ya.

RICKTER: (*Looks at both of them—starts to laugh nervously*) Y'all funning me ain't 'cha?

(*They don't laugh.*)

I know y'all funnin'—y'all joshin ol' Rickter—ain't 'cha?

PETER: (*Getting impatient*) Rickter, git your bag! Mexico ain't gittin no closer, us standin here jawin.

RICKTER: I'm getting tired already. We wukked all day long. When we gonna stop to res'?

(*PETER and SOLOMON shake their heads.*)

PETER AND SOLOMON: (*Unison*) It's going to be a long trip.

RICKTER: What y'all brung to eat? I's hongry already. Y'all think we be there by morning? I hope dey don't have no snakes. I don't like studying on no snakes! No sir, why I remember—

(*They exit cautiously with their bags.*)

(*Lights fade down and the following chant can be heard as if in the distance.*)

NIGGERS AM A'RISIN

Run get your shotgun, run get your rifle,
Run tell the white folks the niggers am a'risin.
Run get your shotgun, run get your rifle,
Run tell the white folks the niggers am a'risin.

SCENE 7

(At curtain rise, music fades down as lights fade up. JOHN (now 28) is arguing silently with ROSE (24) inside John's Sandy Point store on the Chebang Plantation. After a few beats, the NARRATOR enters.)

NARRATOR: Well, the war has been over for some time now, but the effects of it are still being felt by the whole country. The whole economy of the South has been disrupted. And although Texas did not suffer the destruction that the rest of the Confederacy did, the hardships brought on by the war will continue for years. Of course there was a great blessing gained by the war, the abolishment of slavery. But even that would prove to be a mixed blessing for years to come. There were few jobs available for returning soldiers and even fewer jobs for the newly freed slaves who could now work for wages. The plantation owners either couldn't or wouldn't hire them to do the work that they'd been forced to do for decades for no pay. Although John inherited his stepfather's plantations, he still had to open a general store on one of the plantations to make ends meet. And that's where we are now, in the Sandy Point Store on the Chebang Plantation.

When a middle-aged white lady enters the store, John and Rose immediately stop their argument. Turns out, Rose, one of Abner Jackson's former slaves, is the mother of John's illegitimate son. John has fathered another branch of the Jackson family tree.

JOHN: *(To ROSE in his shopkeeper's voice, as if she's a customer.)* S'pose you wait over there, til I get finished with this lady. *(To WHITE LADY)* Miz Rogers, how good to see you. How are you doing?

WHITE LADY: Good afternoon, John. I'm fair to middlin, I 'spect. *(Fanning herself)* If I survive this weather. I'll swannie, it's more than a Christian soul should have to tolerate. *(She notices ROSE and lifts her eyebrow disdainfully, then turns back to JOHN.)*

JOHN: And how is Seth and the rest of your family? I trust that the Lord's blessings still shower down on the Rogers family.

WHITE LADY: Seth is down on his back again. Some mornings he can barely get out of his bed. He ain't been the same since the War.

JOHN: He's a martyr, a Christian martyr, ma'am.

WHITE LADY: The younguns are mean as ever. Little Louis has the croup and keeps cryin, "Mama, make it well. Make it well, Mama." It's all I can do to keep from crying. (*She wipes a tear from her eye.*)

JOHN: (*Trying to sound sincere*) Poor little angel.

(*ROSE grunts. JOHN expresses anger with her for doing so, and WHITE LADY looks at her with indignation.*)

WHITE LADY: (*Back to JOHN*) My Letitia is off to Miss Borden's Young Lady's Christian Academy in the fall, God willing. I'm afraid that she inherited her beauty from my side of the family.

ROSE: (*Under her breath, but loud enough to be heard*) Too bad you didn't inherit some fo' yo'sef.

WHITE LADY: What did you say, girl?

JOHN: (*Frowning at ROSE, then turning to WHITE LADY, trying to change the subject quickly*) Tell me, Miz Rogers, what brings you to Sandy Point this fine day? Got some new gingham in from one of the rebuilt mills up in Birmin'ham—blue as Letitia's own two eyes.

WHITE LADY: Perhaps another time, John. Right now I need some groceries. Let me have five pounds of sugar, some lard, and one half-pound of coffee. Now, I know coffee is scarce, so I'd appreciate whatever you can sell me.

JOHN: I'm sorry Miz Rogers, but we don't have any coffee. Since the end of the war, there are some things we still can't get. But it's gettin better—a lot better than during the war. Now, I can sell you about three pounds of sugar?

WHITE LADY: Fine, I'll take it.

JOHN: An' I can sell you plenty lard—all you want.

WHITE LADY: Two pounds should do. What about tea?

JOHN: No tea, either, ma'am. That was two pounds of lard, right?

WHITE LADY: That'll be fine.

JOHN: Will there be anything else?

WHITE LADY: No thank you, that'll be all.

JOHN: Okay. (*Finishing the package*) That'll be twenty-five cents for the sugar and twenty cents for the lard—your total is forty-five cents, ma'am.

WHITE LADY: Twenty cents for two pounds of lard? Why, John Jackson, I would just as soon buy a hog and render my own lard before I pay your price!

JOHN: (*He shrugs, trying to finish up her order and get back to ROSE.*) Oh, here, take it!

(She gives him the money and starts to leave the store but turns to ROSE.)

Say, gal. I been looking for another cook since my last one run off after the war. If you'd like the job, I have a nice cottage back of my house where you could stay. Are you interested?

ROSE: I ain't inner'sted.

WHITE LADY: Well! I don't know what's got into you niggers. Y'all are awful high and mighty since that emancipation bizness got y'all all stirred up! *(Exits angrily)*

ROSE: *(Approaching the counter)* Look, I ain't got all day. You gone gimme the flour and stuff or not?

JOHN: You can't come in here demandin nothing from me, Rose!

ROSE: I seem to remember that you was plenty demandin when you showed up at my cabin ever night. How kin you talk t'me 'bout bein demandin, John Jackson, when I'm jes tryin to feed your child!

JOHN: *(Steps toward her, but she steps back)* Why I oughta—

(GEORGE enters, limping badly—JOHN sees him and freezes.)

My God!

GEORGE: Hello, brother. *(Pauses)* I 'spect I'm about the last person you expected to see.

JOHN: What are you doin here?

GEORGE: Cain't a man home from the war visit his lovin brother?

(JOHN doesn't answer. GEORGE then turns to ROSE.)

Hello, Rose.

ROSE: George? 'Zat you?

GEORGE: In the flesh—what there is of it. How you and little Frank makin out? *(Looks at JOHN again)*

ROSE: We been better. *(To JOHN)* I thought you tol' me yo' brother was dead.

JOHN: He looks like he *is* halfway dead. He ain't no brother of mine. We just had the same mama and daddy, that's all.

GEORGE: Told you I'd be back, didn't I, big brother? I 'spect you'd rather me be dead, wouldn't ya?

JOHN: What do you want here?

GEORGE: I only want what's mine. I know Papa left a will. He told me 'bout it 'fore I left for the war. But nobody seems to know about it. Andrew couldn't find it when he came back here. I guess you wouldn't know anything about it, would ya, brother?

JOHN: Stop callin me brother. And I don't know nothin about no will. If that's what you came for, you can just limp on outta here.

GEORGE: You stealing from your own brother. I'm glad Mama ain't here to see this.

JOHN: Don't you talk about Mama to me!

GEORGE: Alright, let's talk about our daddy. You hated him, didn't you?

JOHN: That's the first thing you said makes any sense.

GEORGE: Ever stop to wonder why?

JOHN: Yeah, because he hated me!

GEORGE: Be honest, I 'spect maybe he did. But that's not why you hated him. You hated him because you're just like him.

JOHN: That's not true, damn you!

GEORGE: Just like him. He stole from you, so you're stealing from me. You are as mean as he was. I want what's mine, I want what I deserve!

JOHN: (*Comes around the counter and whips GEORGE with a quirt*) Well, I'll give you what you deserve. Take that, you filthy lyin cripple.

ROSE: Stop it! Please, John, stop it! Ain't he been hurt enough?

JOHN: You shut up! This is none of your business. (*Whipping GEORGE and chasing him out of the store*) I'll kill you if you ever come here again!

GEORGE: (*Coldly*) I'll git even with you for this. Someday you're gonna be sorry. (*Exits*)

JOHN: Go on, git outta here and don't come back! (*Returns to behind counter, exhausted*)

ROSE: (*Looking at JOHN with surprise and disdain*) You do that to your own brother?

JOHN: (*Trying to gain composure*) He ain't my brother. All we had was the same mother. I hate his daddy and I hate him. (*Cold anger*) If he comes back, I'll kill him.

ROSE: That's just the way you beat po' Silas to death, ain't it? (*Skips a beat*) Ain't it?! Dey tol' me you had kilt 'im, I jes didn't wanna believe it! (*Starts crying uncontrollably*) I hate I ever set eyes on you, John. You is the Devil — I swear it! (*Runs out of store*) Da Devil!

JOHN: Rose? Rose, you come back here! (*Runs to the door, shouting*) Rose! (*He*

watches her for a second.) Alright, you run away! Go ahead, who needs you!
(*Exits as NARRATOR enters*)

NARRATOR: Well, George Jackson did come back—but not to the store. He got himself a lawyer and, in 1867, he went to court. He applied to the court for his portion of his father's estate. The court ruled in his favor and awarded him the 6,700 acre Lake Jackson Plantation, the cattle herd, and one hundred and fifty head of horses and mules. He had been right when he told John that he'd be sorry. 'Cause he took a lot more than just his land and livestock. The story isn't over yet.

(*GEORGE enters and sits in a rocking chair.*)

It's been a year or so since the court awarded George the Lake Jackson plantation. We find George taking the air on his front porch. It's December 8, 1868—a dark day for the Jackson family. George is about to have a surprise visitor.

(*JOHN enters.*)

This was the first time the brothers had met since John whipped George and chased him out of his store.

GEORGE: Well, you're about the last person I ever expected to see, brother. Have you lost your bearings, or has Hell done gone and froze over?

JOHN: I 'spect you'd likely know more about Hell than me. No, sir, I'm here on business.

GEORGE: (*Enjoying himself*) Business, you say? Sounds important, brother. What do you plan on stealing from me this time? I guess I better start nailing down everything, and hiding the silverware. (*Enjoying his brother's rising anger*) I'm glad my teeth are still wedged in tight, or I'd likely be eating soup the rest of my life.

JOHN: I should have known better than to expect civility from you.

GEORGE: Civility, is it? (*Rises and snorts contemptuously*) I 'spose you know all about civility. Refusing to help feed your own child—stealin from your own family—whippin your kin like I was a dog, or a nigger!

JOHN: Settle down, George. I've learned that it's better to forget the past.

GEORGE: I'm sure you'd like ever'body to forget your past. I'm just glad our mama didn't live to see how you turned out.

JOHN: (*Still trying to be conciliatory*) Now, hold on. You have a right to be— (*Can't think of a word*)

GEORGE: That's rich, brother. You telling me what rights I have. Seems to me the last time you tried that, the judge took issue with it. Seems like you'd remember that, being you're on *my* property.

JOHN: Well, I tried to be kindly. I can see where that got me. (*Authoritarian*) I've come to take you to Brazoria. There are some papers I want you to sign.

GEORGE: You've come to *take* me, have you? You take me?

JOHN: Get your horse saddled, we're running out of daylight.

GEORGE: (*Controlled anger*) My dear brother, kindly remember who you are talking to. I'm not some nigger that you can talk to as you please.

JOHN: Listen to me, my crippled little half-brother—if you don't like the way I'm talkin t'ya, sir, I will whip you. I done it once, I can do it again.

GEORGE: (*Cold anger*) You whip me, brother? I think not.

(*He draws a revolver and shoots JOHN six times in the chest—He falls dead instantly.*)

I think not, brother.

(*GEORGE stares at his dead brother for a few beats, then he sits in the chair, with the gun in his lap and begins to rock. Lights fade slowly on GEORGE. NARRATOR enters.*)

NARRATOR: George never knew any happiness after that tragic day. He died of tuberculosis in 1871. The only surviving member of the Jackson family was Arsenath, the older child of Margaret and her first husband. Arsenath Strobel Jackson Groce, who married the son of Leonard Groce of Liendo plantation, inherited what was left of the Jackson estate after taxes. Frank Jackson, John's son by Rose, was of course not included in the inheritance. Frank, never shared in the Jackson fortune, but he inherited the name and was blessed with a large family of fourteen children. The Great Hurricane of 1900 destroyed or heavily damaged almost every building on the Lake Jackson plantation—only the jail was left standing after the devastating storm passed. This was rather ironic considering that today the Texas Department of Corrections operates prison units on both the Darrington and

Retrieve plantation sites. As the Bible says, "Be not deceived . . . for what-soever a man soweth, that shall he also reap. He that soweth to his flesh shall of the flesh reap corruption." On the former Lake Jackson plantation site, Dow Chemical has built a replica of the Abner Jackson residence. The Department of Archaeology at the University of Houston–Clear Lake, under the direction of Joan Few, has conducted excavations of some of the plantation ruins. This beautiful civic center and the new Lake Jackson Historical Museum are a testament to the strength and endurance of the Lake Jackson community and its people. And "he that soweth to the spirit, shall of the spirit reap life everlasting."

(Blackout)

PART
VI

EMANCIPATION

OVERVIEW

The Civil War and the Emancipation Proclamation changed everything for Americans, and even more for African Americans. With the end of slavery came the freedom the enslaved had dreamed about and prayed for, the biggest event of their lives. It led to a reorganization of African American identities, too; with their new mobility, blacks could form larger communities and affiliate with more and different types of persons. Free people and former slaves congregated. As they moved from one place to another, looking for jobs and searching out loved ones from whom they had been separated, people formed new networks and associations, often through local churches. The churches functioned like extended families. Following the Confederate surrender in 1865, missionaries from all the Protestant denominations crowded into the South to assist in the organization of African American churches.[1]

Emancipation was a time of jubilee, but following the wild shouts, dancing, and merriment, reality set in and some hard choices had to be made. *Slav'ry Chain Done Broke at Las'* is about choosing what to do with the new freedom. Sometimes the choices resulted in more family separation, as in this play.

Emancipation was a time of choices for everybody—everything had changed. There was no more slavery, no more people working for free, but there was little or no money to hire and pay folks, either. All that remained was the looming question, "What we gone do now?"

Socioeconomic woes beset ex-slaves and ex-masters, each from a somewhat different perspective. The ex-slaves were looking for gain. The ex-masters were trying to hold on to what they had. Many Confederate fathers, sons, and other male family members returned home from the war defeated and embittered, and demonstrated an overt hatred for Negroes.[2]

The Negro man was faced with the white man's determination to emasculate him. This movement was implemented and supported by some conservatives and some liberals (however subtly) from 1865 through 1965. As a result, some former slave-owners and landowners elected to negotiate contracts for work only with Negro women.[3]

The outcome of the Civil War was unacceptable to many southerners, including some Texans. Many felt their way of life had been destroyed along with whatever wealth they'd had or hoped to have. Texas, granted statehood as late as 1845, was thriving until the Civil War disrupted the growing prosperity of an area so vast that "the institution of slavery was not threatened due to natural boundaries." In the aftermath of the war, several major Texas figures advocated that the African slave trade begin again, saying "that 'until we reach somewhere in the vicinity of two millions of slaves, it is evident that such a thing as too many slaves in Texas is an absurdity.'"[4] Talk of slavery was strongly discouraged. Abolitionists were "forcibly expelled" and vigilance committees were formed to carry out those demands.[5]

Those attitudes were so prevalent that Joshua Houston and his fellow slaves decided against leaving Sam Houston and his family when they were emancipated in the fall of 1862, as *Porch Politics: Sam Houston Style* will show. This piece of living history delighted its first audiences. It was performed at the Sam Houston Memorial Museum on the back porch of the Woodland Home where Sam and Margaret once lived, steps away from an outdoor kitchen. We staged our characters to come from all directions: inside the house, from the kitchen, and from both sides of the porch where Sam sat, busy shaving and having his morning coffee.

There is an interesting, enduring myth that it took longer for the news of the emancipation to reach Texas than anywhere else. According to the memoir of Jeff Hamilton, Sam Houston's trusted slave, "It was not until June 19, 1865, that General Gordon Granger of the United States army issued a proclamation freeing all the Negro slaves in Texas." But Jeff writes that years earlier, in the fall of 1862, Sam read "every word of President Lincoln's proclamation of September 23 announcing that all slaves would be declared free on the first day of the following January." Jeff proudly states, "the General said he didn't have to wait until January to give his slaves their liberty."[6] So much for how long it took for news to reach Texas! (And after all, there was also the telegraph.)

President Abraham Lincoln's announcement of his preliminary Emancipation Proclamation on September 22, 1862, came just five days after the Battle of Antietam, up to then the bloodiest battle. Lincoln intended the proclamation to become effective in the rebel states on January 1, 1863, but the war raged on. In fact, on that date there was a battle in Galveston Bay called the Battle on the Bay. It happened that the Confederates, under the command of Major General John B. McGruder, commenced a land attack against three Union companies beginning at three in the morning on New Year's Day, and they "captured or killed all of them except for the regiment's adjutant and Galveston was in Confederate hands again."[7]

So President Lincoln's plan for the emancipation of slaves was put on hold. In *Porch Politics: Sam Houston Style,* the slaves of Sam Houston put their freedom on hold also, to preserve their safety in the face of radical opposition to emancipation. Lincoln knew immediate emancipation was not consistent with popular opinion. He even felt that "the Union men in Missouri who are in favor of gradual emancipation represented his views better than those who are in favor of immediate emancipation." Yet his own plan for emancipation would "have three main features — gradual — compensation — and the vote of the people."[8] A fourth feature to that plan was the probability of colonization, by means of sending freed blacks back to Africa.

On January 1, 1865, the shouting and jubilation elsewhere was not being echoed in Texas. Nevertheless, Lincoln's words spelled the beginning of the end: "All persons held as slaves within any State or designated part of a State, the people whereof shall then be in rebellion against the United States, shall be then, thenceforward, and forever free."[9] *New York Times* editor Henry Raymond had this to say: "President Lincoln's proclamation, which we publish this morning, marks an era in the history, not only of this war, but of his country and the world."[10]

The emancipation was so slow in coming to Texas that it seemed to gather some momentum upon arrival. In fact, it is still celebrated to this day, as in the play *Juneteeth at the George Ranch.* The ex-slave memoir of Isabella Boyd recalls:

> When we all gits free, dey's de long time letting us know. Dey wants to git through with de corn and de cotton befo' dey let's de hands loose. Dey was people from other plantations say, "Niggers, you's free and why are you workin'?" Us say, "No, de gov'ment tell us when we's free." We workin' one day when somebody from Massa Grissom place come by and tell us we's free, and us stop workin'. Dey tell us to go on workin' and de

boss man he come up and he say he gwine knock us off de fence if we don't go to work. Mistus come out and say to massa, "Ain't you gwine make dem niggers go to work?" He send her back in de house and he call for de carriage and say he goin' to town for to see what de gov'ment goin' do. Nex' day he come back and say, "Well, you's jus' as free as I is."[11]

According to Austin Grant, another ex-slave, when his "old boss" called them up, "he read the verdict to 'em" and "the' wasn't but one family left with 'im. The rest was just like birds, they jus' flew."[12] In *Slav'ry Chain Done Broke at Las'* there is considerable restlessness among the slaves when their rejoicing gives way to making decisions about what to do with their new freedom. Some wanted to stay and others wanted to fly.

"Forty acres and a mule" would have made a considerable difference to freedmen if it had in fact materialized, in Texas or anywhere. But since it did not, many contemporaries wonder where the notion came from. But it wasn't just a notion. Dorothy Sterling makes it plain:

> In 1865 forty acres of land for each ex-slave and his family was not a dream born in the delirium of sudden freedom. Months before the treaty of peace was signed, the government had promised this to the freedmen — only to renege a year later. The promise had come from an unlikely source. When General William T. Sherman's army marched across Georgia, tens of thousands of slaves left the plantations to follow him. Ragged, hungry, and homeless, they clogged the roads and slept under bridges at night, threatening the health and discipline of his men. The stern-visaged general was no philanthropist, but something practical had to be done with the freedmen. When Secretary of War Stanton visited Savannah in January 1865, twenty of the city's black leaders were summoned for a conference. Sixteen of the men who came to Sherman's headquarters had been slaves; only the Reverend James Lynch was a Northerner. The interview was conducted Army-style, with the black men receiving written questions and their spokesman, ex-slave Garrison Frazier, supplying written answers to questions.[13]

Questions included, "State what manner you think you can take care of yourselves," "Would you rather live among whites or by yourselves," and "Do you think there is intelligence enough among the slaves to maintain themselves?" Answers included, "We want to be placed on land to work until we are able to buy it," "We prefer to live by ourselves because of prejudice," and "There is sufficient intelligence among us to do so."[14]

Sterling writes that "four days later Sherman issued a Special Field Order that set aside the islands and coastal lands from Charleston, South Carolina, to the St. Johns River in Florida for black settlements."[15] Forty thousand freedmen soon were cultivating three hundred thousand acres of their own land.

The good news was followed by sad news. "In March 1866 a new order was issued: 'The former owners of the land in the Sea Islands on the coast of South Carolina and the owners of land on the Main embraced in General Sherman's Special Field Orders will be permitted to return and occupy their lands.'" By spring of 1866, the freedmen who refused to sign contracts with the planters were driven away by squads of black soldiers. A year or two later, the freedmen were again working for the white planters.[16]

Meanwhile, in northeast Texas something else was brewing. Bob Lee was a Texas Confederate soldier who once rode with Nathan Bedford Forrest, a wealthy slave trader and one of the founders of the Ku Klux Klan. Lee was like many embittered Confederates, and he declared that he would never surrender to Union forces and continued the Civil War until his tragic death. In Corners Country—which includes Grayson, Fannin, Hunt, and Collin counties in northeast Texas—Lee and his band of Klansmen declared war on "the Southern Unionists, Yankee soldiers, and the newly freed slaves." More than two hundred white and black men and women were killed because of the terrorism waged by Lee and his raiders.[17]

Things were not that bad in all of Texas but there were problems in other areas. William Watkins, born in 1850, told interviewers the following:

Dey's ghosts dere—we seed 'em. Dey' a w'ite people wid a sheet on to scare de slaves offen de plantation. We wears charms to keep us well. De first time we sees de Ku Klux is right after de war. Dey whips de slaves what leaves de plantation, dey don' wan' dem to be free.[18]

President Lincoln initiated the Bureau of Refugees, Freedmen, and Abandoned Lands to assist all refugees and to aid former slaves with employment, health care, and education. These federal agencies became known as Freedmen's Bureaus and were instrumental during Reconstruction. However, in some isolated areas in Texas, the Freedmen's Bureaus were rendered powerless to do their job because many of their agents were killed or run off. Northeast Texas, with its thick piney woods and uncultivated lands, was so remote that the Union soldiers could scarcely subdue renegades like Lee, who regularly "looted the homes of blacks, stealing food, clothing, arms, and anything of value. They assaulted freedmen and raped freedwomen," frightening them away from their homes and making it almost impossible for them to do any work. Lee and his gang terrorized and murdered Freedmen's Bureau agents.[19] Many crimes went unreported and many reported crimes received no attention.

Years after the war and even today, the feelings of some Confederate sympathizers prevail in an overt racism that refuses to acknowledge the progress made by African Americans. During the 2008 presidential election, that racism—and even some sexism—reared its ugly head. Nevertheless, as opinions and deep-seated beliefs are continually subsiding in favor of a more compassionate worldview, change is the brother of hope. Over time the views of Abner J. Stroebel, like the excerpt below from 1926, will fade away:

The freeing of the slaves did, in effect deprive the Southern people of about two thousand million of dollars (2,000,000,000.00) of property, computing four million slaves at five hundred dollars each, and this was prompted by altruistic motives, it may be. The economic loss from confiscating the labor of the slave, great as it was, is but an item in the total loss which the Southern people sustained during the war and Reconstruction.

By 1880, fifteen years after the close of the war, the original owners of these plantations, and their heirs, had practically ceased to own them. In those fifteen years, we had nothing that would operate against farming in the way of nature's eruptions . . . it was the war and the aftermath of war that caused their ruin.

In 1870 the Fifteenth Amendment to the constitution (enfranchising the Negro) was perhaps the utmost limit of legislative folly. At the time, it was regarded in the North as beneficent and wise. It sought to place the Anglo-Saxon people in the South under the rule of their former slaves. The result was only harmful to the negro as well as the whites, as everybody now knows. It was the Act that started the race trouble. The freed men, left to themselves, would have solved the labor question and their social status and the race problem.

From this act came the crimes committed by the negroes, and

frequent lynchings followed as a result. What a change! As a Slave, he
was the faithful protector of his Mistress and her family. The child of
that slave became the terror of unprotected women. The negro, when
introduced into this country, was a stupid animal, speaking a jabbering
lingo. He was taught and trained in civilization until he was adjudged, in
the North, if free, as being capable of assuming the duties of citizenship.
Every blunder possible for a partisan Congress to make, prompted by the
zealous fervor of the reformers, who knew nothing of the task in hand,
was made that could be made by law.

   At the close of the War Between the States, the Ex-Confederate
soldiers took their stand for Anglo-Saxon civilization and saved the
South from the fate of Haiti and the West Indies. Their service in the
years succeeding the war was as truly great as those they rendered from
1861 to 1865.

   What of the New South?

   It has been said, and not without historical authority, that the builders
of this nation have been largely the descendants of the Puritans, of
Massachusetts, the Cavalliers of Virginia, and the Hugenots, of the
Carolinas.

   May the New South carry human achievement to the farthest point
mankind has ever known. To do so, she must ever observe the principles
and ideals of the Old South, upon which our country is founded, and the
observance and preservation of which, including the worship of God and
the purity and supremacy of the Anglo-Saxon strain, are essential.

   And the time will come when the rich and fertile creek and river
bottom-lands of old Brazoria County will again be famous for the
production of cane and cotton. [20]

   *Dedicated to the survivors of the Confederate Army, who stood like a stone
wall for white supremacy and preserved and gave us our present civilization,
to whom we owe a debt of gratitude that can never be repaid.*[21]

   The celebration of emancipation, or Juneteenth as it is called, has resumed
not only in Texas but in nearby Louisiana, Oklahoma, Kansas, and a number
of other states including New York, California, South Carolina, and Delaware,
where it has become a state holiday, like in Texas. Celebration lapsed for a
while during the 1950s and 1960s as the struggle gave way to the civil rights
movement, ironically. Then the celebrations resurfaced as an opportunity to

have barbecues, blues festivals, social events, and parades. Of late, however, there has been more emphasis on the history behind the celebration. In many areas such as Commanche Crossing, near Mexia in north Central Texas, and at Barrett Station near the Gulf Coast, authentic commemorations of "free at last" have continued since emancipation.

SLAV'RY CHAIN DONE BROKE AT LAS'

Written for the George Ranch Historical Park Texian Market Days Festival, 1994

CHARACTERS
JANE: a slave descendant
AMELIA: her daughter

SETTING
TIME: *10:00 a.m., June 20, 1865; the morning after emancipation*
PLACE: *Slave quarters of the Jones Plantation, Fort Bend County, Texas*

SYNOPSIS
The morning after the reading of the Emancipation Proclamation, Jane has trouble deciding whether to stay on or leave the plantation. This vignette examines the consequences of both, and how difficult it was for slaves to decide.

(It is mid-morning and JANE is alone in her garden, a plot she has been allowed just behind her cabin for growing vegetables. She has just returned from being emancipated and told by her master that she can either stay on at the plantation and work for food and shelter, or that she is free to go with those who have chosen to leave. She is trying to make a decision about her future and prays for divine intervention. We come up on her hoeing away the weeds when she throws down her hoe.)

JANE: Thank God A'mighty, I'se free at las'! *(Dancing and singing)*

SLAV'RY CHAIN[22]

Slav'ry chain done broke at las', broke at las', broke at las',
Slav'ry chain done broke at las', goin' to praise God til I die.

'Way up in-a dat valley, prayin' on my knees;
Telling God about my troubles, an' to he'p me ef-a He please.

I did tell Him how I suffer, in de dungeon an' de chain;
An' de days I went wif head bowed down, an' my broken flesh an' pain.
    But brethren,

Slav'ry chain done broke at las', broke at las', broke at las',
Slav'ry chain done broke at las', goin' to praise God til I die.

(*Picking up hoe and chopping away*) Happy as I is, I'se mo tired than any-thang. I be's too tired anyhow to leab dis place . . . eben if I is happy. I can't go home, to Africa, only place lef' for me to go is heaben. I'se jes a stranger here. (*Humming softly, then singing*)

PILGRIM'S SONG

I'm a poor wayfarin stranger,
While journeyin through this world of woe,
Yet there's no sickness, toil and danger,
In that bright world to which I go.
Hum-um umm

JANE: Lawd, what do dis 'mancipation mean? When you done wukked as long and hard as I has, it's hard to b'lieve you is fin'ly free. Free to do what? Free to go where? Go somewhere I don't know where is? I hear dey got places where we can wuk in de towns but I ain't got no schoolin. It's been 'gainst de law for me to read and write, cipher, or do any of dat.

    Hear me Lawd, Jesus, as I stan' here. I ain't a stranger callin yo name. You knows the soun' of me when I ain't eben talkin and you hears me all d'same. (*Stands still listening*) Jes listen at 'em ovah dere in de praise grove:

(The strains of distant singing can be heard:
"Lincum rode a big black horse
Davis rode a mule
Lincum is a nobleman
Davis is a fool")

(Laughing) Dey's singin Massa Lincum's praises so hard dey ain't eben stopped to consider dat dis here freedom is mo' dan a notion. When my grandmama come here she wuz a young woman. Tol' me she wuz b'on at Norf Ca'lina. When she weren't cooking, cleaning, and taking kere o' dey chilluns, Massa Henry and Miz Nancy wukked her in dem fields yonda lak she wuz a man, eben when she wuz so big havin her babies she could hardly stoop over. All of 'em wuz sleepin in de barn, de men, de women, chilluns an' all, right in dere wit de animals til Massa Henry fin'ly figure dey needs cabins. If I wuzn't no cook, I nevah woulda had dis cabin o' my own. Jes the same, I thanks God for it ever'day.

Some of us is jes rarin' t'go way f'om here. An' some o' us ain't gwine nowhere. I nevah been off dis place. Was bo'n here and ain't been no further den my eye can see down de road to Wyly Martin's place. You'd hafta point me to de Norf—or de Souf. I member lak it was yestiddy when my pappy ran off to Mexico. Dey say dat to de Souf. I 'members it was back when Massa tol' de overseer to loosen his hide for thinkin he was a big nigger, dat he tied his hands to his foots and run a stick under der knees and ovah de arms at de elbows. Pappy was kicked over and whupped worse'n a dog. All us could do wuz cry. He had to be carried away. Mama nursed him wit de elderberry leaves and camphor til he got well. And no sooner did Massa send him back in de field, he lit out f'om here lak lightening. *(Pauses)* Las' we evah seen of 'im.

All dese white folk, de bad ones and eben de good ones knows dey ain't done us right! *(She starts to sing.)*

YOU BETTER MIN'

(*Chorus*)
Oh, you better min' (You better min')
Oh, you better min'. (You better min')
Cause you got to give an account in de judgment,
You better min'.

You better min' how you talk,
You better min' what you talkin about,
Cause you got to give an account in de judgment,
You better min'.

(*Repeat chorus*)

You better min' how you walk,
You better min' what you walkin through,
Cause you got to give an account in de judgment,
You better min'.

(*Repeat chorus*)

JANE: Colly can't wait to leab here. Swear he gone take my daughter, Amelia, and all dem chirren on account o'dat baby she jes lost f'om being made to git up too soon. He f'om Africa and ain't nebber fergit what freedom lak. Unca Owley, he ain't gwine nowhere cause he jes loves ol' Miz Nancy. Dat fool blesses de very groun she walks on and she been walkin all ovuh him for don't know how many years. Me mysef, been stepped on so much, I-I tell'ya, what wit tryin to keep up dis place durin d'war, it's done wore us all plum out. Yet and still, dey tell me d'Yankees is subjeck to come in here and set fire to d'las' of it!

How you s'pose I gwine to fergit all dat? Tuck it under where, when all dat suffrin and pain layin so heavy on my heart, huh?

Dese legs would have to walk me a mighty long way f'om here for me to be really free. Talk t'me lawd. Don't nobody hear me but you. Eben though I is glad, I jes don't know how to 'cept it, dat's all. (*She begins to sing.*)

COULDN'T KEEP IT TO MYSELF

Said I wasn't gonna tell nobody but I-I
Couldn't keep it to myself, (Oh, I)
Couldn't keep it to myself, (Oh, I)
Couldn't keep it to myself.
Said I wasn't gonna tell nobody but I-I
Couldn't keep it to myself
What de Lord has done for me.

Ev'ry time I feel the spirit
Movin in my heart I will pray-ay-ay!
Ev'ry time I feel the spirit
Movin in my heart I will pray.

JANE: (*Walks around holding her body tight, then kneels beside her praying stump*)
Lord, what do dis 'mancipatin mean? What is I free to do? I sangs yo'
praises day and night. But I cain't eben write my name. Dis what dey call
me ain't my name. Where I am, ain't my home. I hardly knew my pappy fo'
he up and ran'd 'way, my mammy long since been gone, jus plain wukked
to death. Onliest one of my chirren I got lef' is Amelia, and she plannin
to leab here. De mos' family I got lef' is dese othuh slaves roun' here. Hab
mercy on po' George, who starved to death in de stockhouse cause he tried
to run away. An' Lawd, hab mercy on po' sistuh Rachel who had her tongue
cut out cause she sassed the missus. Bless ol' Aunt Harriet who is crazy
from still hearing dat bell dey made her wear so many years behin' always
sneakin off. Take pity on all yo' chirren who's jes fumblin roun' in de dark
like cattle, waitin for you to show us de light. Show me an' dese othuhs
what t'do, which a'way t'go. But Lawd, what-so-ever happens, Please, he'p
us to walk togedder.

(*JANE gets up feeling relieved and renewed. She sings.*)

WALK TOGEDDER CHILDRON[23]

Oh, walk togedder, childron, (Don't yer get weary)
Walk togedder, childron, (Don't yer get weary)
Oh, walk togedder, childron (Don't yer get weary)
Dere's a great camp meetin' in de Promised Land.

(JANE is joined by her daughter, AMELIA, on these last two choruses.)

Dere's a better day a comin', (Don't you get weary)
Better day a-comin' (Don't you get weary)
Dere's a better day a comin', (Don't you get weary)
Dere's a great camp meetin in de promised land.

(The audience is invited to join in on this last chorus which is repeated.)

Oh feel de spirit a-movin (Don't you get weary)
Feel de spirit a-movin (Don't you get weary)
Oh feel de spirit a-movin (Don't you get weary)
Dere's a great camp meeting in de promised land.

A family reunited. George Ranch Historical Park, Texian Market Days Festival, 1996

Naomi on a bale of cotton. George Ranch Historical Park, Texian Market Days Festival, 1995

PORCH POLITICS
Sam Houston Style

Written for the Sam Houston Folk Festival at the Sam Houston Memorial Museum, 1999

CHARACTERS

SAM HOUSTON: Hero of San Jacinto, president of the Texas Republic, Texas senator and governor, age 69

JEFF HAMILTON: house servant, carriage driver and personal assistant to General Houston, age 22

ELIZA: cook for the Houston family, age c. 50

HANNAH: maid and cook for the Houston family, age 35

JOSHUA HOUSTON: servant to Sam Houston, carriage driver for General Houston and blacksmith and wheelwright, age 40

COLONEL ROGERS: neighboring farmer

MARGARET LEA HOUSTON: wife of Sam Houston, age 42

TOM BLUE: coachman, age 43

WALTER HUME: co-conspirator in escape to Mexico, age 30

MARY: nursemaid for the Houston children, age 16

SETTING

TIME: *October 1862*

PLACE: *Back porch of the Woodland Home (on grounds of Sam Houston Museum), Huntsville, Walker County, Texas*

SYNOPSIS

It's business as usual at the Houston household with Sam Houston, his wife Margaret, their eight children, and ten slaves. However, the politics of the Civil War brought some unexpected changes. Because Houston had opposed Texas's secession and joining the Confederacy, his term as Texas governor was cut short. One of his most trusted slaves, Tom Blue, escapes to Mexico, and in the wake of the Emancipation Proclamation, the General frees his slaves.

(It is morning at the Houston home and there is the usual coming and going in and out of the kitchen, on and off the back porch while GENERAL HOUSTON is busy shaving. It is on the steps of the back porch that JEFF delivers his first speech.)

JEFF: *(Whittling on a piece of soft pine)* I'm Jeff Hamilton and my master, General Sam Houston, saved me from the auction block when I was jes a lil thirteen-year-old slave boy. I said *saved* me, not *bought* me. Oh, yeah, he *bought* me for $450, but it was his human kindness that saved me.

See, along with Uncle Joshua, I am one of the General's most trusted slaves. I sleep on a pallet beside the door to his room. I even saved him from being shot one night when he was in the governor's office in Austin.

There are two things that are sure to draw a crowd here in Huntsville: a circus and my master, Sam Houston. *(Pointing)* That's the General, there, shaving himself, as he is fond of doing here on the back porch. Miz Margaret, his wife, likes to keep the mess out of the house and out here, on the porch. That way, the General can talk to his friends and visitors while he's shaving and having his mawnin coffee. *(Continues whittling)*

ELIZA: *(Coming from the kitchen, chastising ANDY)* Little Andy, leave that dog alone and quit running! You gone hurt yose'f. Mawnin, Massa Houston, suh, I'se awful sorry but you got to send Uncle Joshua into town for mo' coffee and sugar. We's plum outten it, suh.

HOUSTON: More coffee and sugar?! What's happening to all this coffee and sugar: We bought coffee last week and it's up to $3.75 a pound!

ELIZA: Well, suh, you'll have to ask Hannah about that. She makes de coffee. I he'p de Missus wit de chirren and cook. *(To ANDY, who almost spilled soup)* Watch out there! I'm tryin to tek dis soup so's I kin feed Temple Lea. Dat po' chile is sufferin from de consumption for sho'. An-drew, quit chasing dat po' dog! *(Going into the house)* S'cuse me, suh.

HOUSTON: Jeff, go in the house and bring me some writing paper, a pen and some ink, will ya? I need to write a letter to the Confederate secretary of war.

HANNAH: *(Calling from the kitchen door with her hands on her hips)* Liza, what 'bout de coffee?

JOSHUA: *(Comes up on the porch, carrying a tool from the blacksmith shop)* Yep, General, that wheel was the problem, awright. Tom said it was wobblin from the last trip. I took it off de front of de family coach and put on another one, so now it's all ready for the trip to Independence.

HOUSTON: Joshua, without your skill as a blacksmith, we would have been let down many times on the road. Thanks to you, most all of our trips throughout Texas have been made without the usual hazards.

JOSHUA: Massa, I need to meet the stagecoach in town today and replace a wheel I repaired. Will you and the Missus be needing anything, suh?

HOUSTON: Yes, mo' coffee! And sugar. And oh yes, wait til I finish this letter for you to mail. Maybe it can get out on today's stagecoach. I don't know what this town would do without one such as yourself. Hand me my cane.

JOSHUA: Here you are, suh. When you see Tom Blue, tell 'im I'm waitin for 'im. I'll be in the blacksmith shop, suh, when you need me. (*Leaves for shop*)

COL. ROGERS: Howdy, Gov'nor.

HOUSTON: Morning, Colonel Rogers. You're out awful early.

COL. ROGERS: I thought I'd pass by on my way back to the farm. Stayed in town last night fo' news f'om the Confed'rate Army. Ever since the start of this here war, thangs ain't been looking too good for us. You heard anything?

HOUSTON: Ask me no questions, I'll tell you no lies, Colonel. At the least we hoped to hear some news about Sam, Jr. by now. He was wounded and left for dead last we heard. Lucky for him some doctor came 'long—so, far as we know, he did receive some medical attention 'fore it was too late. Maggie's worrying herself t'death 'bout the boy.

COL. ROGERS: I am sorry 'bout yo' son, General . . . It's mighty unsettling—first succession, then war. I felt it coming for a long time. Down here, we need our slaves and that's all there is to it.

HOUSTON: Is that a fact?

COL. ROGERS: Well, Sam, let's face it—do you b'lieve that yo' wife and daughters oughta be scrubbin their clothes at a wash tub and cookin meals in pots over a hot fire? Before I suffer my wife and daughter to cook and scrub, I'll wade in blood up to my neck!

HOUSTON: Cooking and scrubbing is honorable work and I don't know of any white woman that's ever died from it. Do you?

COL. ROGERS: Ya'see, Sam, that's why you ain't governor today. We people of Texas and evah other Southern state has a right to own slaves. It's a way of life for us that the Union has no bizness tryin to change!

HOUSTON: Where there is union, there is strength, Rogers, and when you break the Union, you wreck the whole fabric of the Constitution. No, I never agreed to sign Texas away as a seceding state and I never will! Good day, Colonel!

COL. ROGERS: To you, too, suh! (*Throws hat on his head and walks away, in anger*)

JEFF: Massa, here's the paper. We only have dis elderberry ink that Eliza made for you, and I sharpened you this quill for writin. Lemme set it all ovah here.

HOUSTON: Thanks, Jeff. Just he'p me get t'the table.

JEFF: Yessuh. (*Helping to make HOUSTON comfortable with his lame leg*)

HOUSTON: That'll be all. War, secession, I do not believe in human slavery nor in secession — or disunion either! By golly, no sooner'n I get one thang done —

MARGARET: (*Coming onto porch*) Sam, dear, I brought your clothes so you can change in the bedroom here. (*Pointing to room just off porch*) This will be much better than your having to walk back upstairs.

HOUSTON: Yes, yes — (*Regrouping*) Maggie, my dear, you are so considerate of an old man. (*Gently laughing*)

MARGARET: (*Scolding*) You're not getting overheated out here, are you? I heard you talking to that Colonel Rogers.

HOUSTON: Rogers is a yellow dog, itching from too many fleas. How's my lil soldier boy, Temple Lea? (*Beginning to write letter*)

MARGARET: Better, but still coughing a lot. Eliza was up with him all last night.

ELIZA: (*Coming out of house with soup bowl*) Miz Maggie, I thank his fever done broke and he fell asleep jes now in my arms, so's I put 'im to bed. I'm going 'head wit dinner now. (*Stopping on her way back to the kitchen*) Will there be any guests tonight, ma'am?

MARGARET: Not tonight, Eliza. Why hasn't Hannah served the General his coffee?

ELIZA: (*Apathetic at first*) That, ma'am, is sumpin you should ask her. You didn't git it fom me, but her and Mary has been makin off wit a lil o'dat coffee evahday, til it ain't none lef'.

MARGARET: What, no coffee?! Well, get Tom Blue to go into town and pick up some — (*Holding up the GENERAL's clothes and giving them a final inspection*) — along with a few other things I need. Where is Tom, anyway?

ELIZA: Any other time he'da been up here for breakfast long 'fore now, but I ain't seed him all mawnin. Him nor dat dog what's always followin him 'round. Shall I have Joshua go look for 'im, ma'am?

MARGARET: Please. There's been some change in our plans for the trip. And tell Hannah to iron this shirt for the General. (*Giving ELIZA a white shirt*)

ELIZA: Yes'm. (*Starts to leave, turns around to notice HANNAH, and shakes her head*)

HANNAH: (*Bringing GENERAL's coffee*) I'se sorry we outta coffee, suh. I thought we had some put back and when I found out we didn't, I roasted some sweet pertater hulls and made dis fo'ya, Marster. I used molasses for sugar. I sho hope you fin it to yo likin. (*Attempts to leave without being questioned*)

HOUSTON: Hannah, don't let this happen again. I thank I know what's been happening to all this coffee and sugar. You and Mary know, too. (*Takes a sip*) Whew! That'll wake up anybody! (*Returns to his letter writing*)

ELIZA: (*Going out into the yard and calling toward the blacksmith shop*) Joshua! Oh, Uncle Joshua! Lawd a'mercy, what is goin on here, dis mawnin. Umph-umph-umph!

MARGARET: Andrew, go inside and have Mary change your clothes. That's right. (*Watching him go up the stairs and into the house*) And leave the dog outside! (*To HOUSTON*) Anyway, dear, as much as I would like to visit with Mother and the girls, since both you and Temple Lea aren't feeling well, our trip to Independence will just *have to be* postponed. Besides, I really don't want to leave you.

HOUSTON: Now, now, Maggie, I'm an old soldier at taking care of myself. My only worry is that the war makes things a little unsafe for travel. But if I didn't trust Tom Blue to *take* you and the children, I would say so. Fact is, with Union troops advancing into Galveston Bay, I think you all will be a lot safer in Independence.

MARGARET: Shall I help you inside so you can get dressed?

HOUSTON: That you shall, my dear. (*HOUSTON stumbles to his feet and calls JEFF to help him.*) Help me up here, Jeff. If I could'ove bought me another leg after San Jacinto, I wouldn't be in such bad shape. (*To JEFF*) That'll do. Go see if you can find Tom Blue. Tell 'im I need to see him right away. Oh yes, give this letter to Joshua to mail and put my journal back inside.

(*HOUSTON and MARGARET go inside, leaving JEFF on the porch.*)

JEFF: (*Begins to narrate the escape of TOM BLUE*) Now, I want to tell ya 'bout Tom Blue an' why we couldn't find 'im. The way I found out about it was from reading one of the letters my Marster received from a friend o' his.

(*Picking up journal, begins to read a letter and make casual comments*) The letter reads, Sam, from all indications, that slave of yours, Tom Blue ran off to Mexico where he could be free. Since Mexico *still is* a free country.

(*Looking away from the letter*) Blue was one of the most remarkable colored men I ever knew. He was my master's coachman and I must admit, a tall, impeccably well-dressed mulatto. That's him, right there, coming out onto the porch. He always did wear a pair of white gloves and a top hat.

Everybody liked him. Go on, (*To the audience*) shake his hand. Now, if he coulda had the same sort o' chances that most white boys have, he would prob'ly have been a great promoter and made a fortune. He's right friendly, wouldn't you agree?

Yep, Tom Blue was a tall, fine-looking mulatto, nearly white. My master bought him on a trip to Washington nearly 20 years 'fore he bought me. Blue was born in the West Indies and had a good education and fine manners like a high-class gentleman. He used to entertain all the famous people who came to see my master when he was the Texas president and later United States senator. After the General and Miss Margaret Lea of Alabama got married in 1840, Master bought a big yellow family coach and four fine horses. Knowing Tom Blue, he had probably been planning to escape, long before he really did. See him checking all the papers he carries in his pocket, as he walks back up on the porch? As Blue had been trained to ride and drive, the General made him his coachman. He's the one who always drives Miz Margaret and the children—and was s'posed to be driving'em to Independence to visit her folks.

According to the letter, this is how Blue pulled off his escape. No sooner than President Abraham Lincoln issued his 'liminary Emancipation Proclamation last month, the news reached Huntsville. Blue figured that Proclamation made him a free man, although under the laws of Texas and the Confederate nation, he was still a slave.

Like most all of Houston's slaves, Blue could read and write. There he is, reading that Proclamation.

Tom Blue knew all too all too well that Mexico didn't allow slavery under its laws. And just like slaves in the North used the "Underground

Railroad" to reach Canada, he figured that if he could escape to Mexico, he would be free — and that's just what he did.

(TOM BLUE and WALTER HUME reenact getaway.)

Now that's Walter Hume coming from around the side of the house. First, Tom Blue started talking to Hume off and on, finally convincing him to run away. Blue gave Hume an old jacket and hat to wear. Hume put on those garments. Both men were enthusiastic about this clever scheme.

Blue knew he was gone have a mess of trouble getting across the Rio Grande River. See Blue pointing to the River? This is the Texas side and that yonder is the Mexico side of the River. Blue had decided to pass himself off for a white man and have Walter pose as his slave. Like I told ya, Blue's skin is so nearly white that he looks like a Spaniard, while Walter is a full-blooded African.

The letter says that Blue and Hume approached a white official who asked for identification papers that Blue pulled from inside his coat pocket. Then the two men crossed to the other side of the river. The white man crossed the river also, behind them. That's when the deal went down. Blue and the white man talked and talked.

Blue knew that it would take some ready money to live in Mexico like a "white gentleman." So on the day he crossed the bridge into Mexico, he sold his "slave" Hume, at the bargain price of eight hundred dollars cash — about one-third his market value. Uh-hum, it says so right here in this letter.

Looking at Walter with a devilish grin, Blue negotiated to sell Walter Hume to the white man who paid Blue, then tied Walter's hands and lead him off, probably back to Texas to sell him for more money.

(WALTER and his new owner disappear back around the side of house, while BLUE wipes his hands, pulls off gloves and goes inside house.)

I know for a fact that the General and the Missus laughed over the escape. And you know why? Cause Tom Blue and his "slave" went to all their trouble to escape just about ten days too soon. One morning soon after their disappearance, the General sent word to all of his slaves to come to the front of the house after breakfast.

My master was freshly shaved and had on his Sunday suit. Mrs. Houston, with several of the children, stood beside him on the porch. (*JEFF now begins calling all slaves by name.*) "Uncle Joshua, Eliza, Hannah, Mary and all y'alls children, come to the front porch. The General needs to talk to us right away!"

(*All of the enslaved crowd around the porch as called, wondering why. This ends the narration/pantomime.*)

(*After the crowd has been relocated, and the slaves have assembled themselves to face the front porch, GENERAL SAM HOUSTON, MARGARET, and the children come onto the front porch. MARGARET is holding a handkerchief because she has been crying.*)

HOUSTON: (*Taking a newspaper out of his pocket and wiping off his spectacles with his handkerchief*) I want each one of you to listen very carefully to what I read to you. What I have here is a preliminary proclamation of emancipation from Abraham Lincoln, president of the United States. It reads:

EMANCIPATION PROCLAMATION

That on the first day of January 1863, all persons held as slaves within any State or designated part of a State, the people whereof shall then be in rebellion against the United States, shall be thenceforward and forever free: and the Executive Government of the United States, including the military and naval authority thereof, will recognise and maintain the freedom of such persons, and shall do no act or acts to repress such persons, or any of them, in any efforts they may make for their actual freedom . . .

And by virtue of the power and for the purpose aforesaid, I do order and declare that all persons held as slaves within the said designated States, and parts of States, are, and henceforward shall be, free; and that the Executive Government of the United States, including the military and naval authorities thereof, will recognise and maintain the freedom of said persons.

And I hereby enjoin upon the people so declared free to abstain from all violence, unless it is necessary in self defence; and I recommend to them that, in all cases when allowed, they labor faithfully for reasonable wages. And I further declare and make known that such persons, of suitable condition, will be received into the armed service of the United States, to garrison forts, positions, stations and other places, and to man vessels of all sorts in said service.

And upon this act, sincerely believed to be an act of justice, warranted by the Constitution upon military necessity, I invoke the considerate judgment of mankind, and the gracious fear of Almighty God.

In testimony whereof, I have hereunto set my name and caused the seal of the United States to be affixed.

Abraham Lincoln
Jan. 1, 1863, Washington

HOUSTON: (*Pauses briefly after reading*) I don't have to wait until January to give you your liberty. The laws of Texas, the United States, and the higher law of God Almighty give me the right to free you whenever I want to, and I am glad to do that *right now*, in the name of God Almighty. (*Pointing to each of them*) You, you, each of you, are now free. You know I am your friend, and I know you are my friends. (*Wipes his eyes*) I'll always be ready to help you when I can. If you want to stay here and work for me, I will pay you good wages as long as I can.

(*There is deep silence for a minute. MISSUS HOUSTON is crying and there is not a dry eye among the slaves. ELIZA begins to moan and sway from side to side.*)

JOSHUA: General, you been mighty good to us down thoo the years and as for me, I plan to go right on working for you just like I have always done.
JEFF: I got no intentions on leaving.
HANNAH: (*Weeping softly*) Me neither, Marster Houston.
MARY: I'se staying too, Marster. I gots nowhere to go . . . no fambly, nothin at all. Y'all *is* my fambly, the *onliest* one I'se evah had, so, *here* I stays.
ELIZA: What if the Union soldiers comes to tek us 'way f'om the Houston

family? Oh, Marster! Oh my God, Missus Maggie, I don't want no 'mancipation. I'se happy wid you all an' de chillun. I ain't gwine ter be 'mancipated. God, help us all! Have mercy!

JOSHUA: (*Going to comfort ELIZA*) Come on, 'Liza, now be strong.

HOUSTON: One thing I can assure you, that no soldiers, neither Union nor Confederate, are going to come on this place and make *anybody* do *anything*. I'm offering any and everybody who wants to stay on here a job. And like I said, I will pay you good wages as long as I can. May God Almighty protect us all. (*He turns and walks back into the house, followed by MARGARET and his children, all of them weeping softly.*)

(*The slaves all slowly leave, not a dry eye among them. The men comfort the women and they retreat to the kitchen, left, behind the house. JEFF stays and goes up onto the porch to deliver the Epilogue.*)

EPILOGUE

JEFF: Besides our loyalty to the Houston family, Joshua and the rest of us was smart enough to know that the war was still goin on—it was October 1862—and there was deep hostilities among whites towards us slaves. We knew deep inside ourselves that the safest place for us was wit the Houstons, where we could look out for one 'nother like we'd always done. That's why we stayed here—'cause under the state constitution adopted by the Confederate government, it was against the law in Texas for the General to free us and Texans didn't want a bunch of free colored folk runnin 'round, free to do as they pleased. Although the General had done everything in his power to make us free, if he was freeing us, where was our free papers? The General died less than a year later on July 26, 1863. And why were we still listed as property in his last will and testament?

(*JEFF turns and goes inside the house, shutting the door.*)

(top) **James Faulkner as Jeff Hamilton. Sam Houston Festival, 1999;** (above left) **Larry Durbin and Kit Fordyce portray Sam Houston confronting Col. Rogers. Sam Houston Festival, 1999;** (above right) **Devonae Servance as Eliza, the Houstons' cook. Sam Houston Festival, 1999**

PART

VII

RECONSTRUCTION

OVERVIEW

Reconstruction was undeniably one of the most difficult periods in American history. The essence of the word means to reconstruct, to rebuild, to put back together. What had been was gone. At least 618,000 Americans died in the Civil War, and some experts say the toll reached 700,000. Furthermore, a whole way of life had been sacrificed. It was going to take time to bring southern states back into the Union. States' constitutions had to be re-written and ratified. The Union itself required some reorganization. And what about the former slaves? How far was Congress allowed to go, under the Civil War amendments, when regulating what it saw as violations of equal protection, due process, and other basic liberties? And why did it take three amendments to the United States Constitution to make black folks free?

CONSTITUTIONAL GRANTS OF POWERS TO CONGRESS UNDER THE CIVIL WAR AMENDMENTS

Amendment XIII
Passed by Congress January 31, 1865. Ratified December 6, 1865.

Section 1.
Neither slavery nor involuntary servitude, except as a punishment for crime whereof the party shall have been duly convicted, shall exist within the United States, or any place subject to their jurisdiction.

Section 2.
Congress shall have power to enforce this article by appropriate legislation.

Amendment XIV
Passed by Congress June 13, 1866. Ratified July 9, 1868.

Section 1.

All persons born or naturalized in the United States, and subject to the juris-diction thereof, are citizens of the United States and of the State wherein they reside. No State shall make or enforce any law which shall abridge the privi-leges or immunities of citizens of the United States; nor shall any State de-prive any person of life, liberty, or property, without due process of law; nor deny to any person within its jurisdiction the equal protection of the laws.

(Sections 2–4 omitted.)

Section 5.

The Congress shall have the power to enforce, by appropriate legislation, the provisions of this article.

Amendment XV

Passed by Congress February 26, 1869. Ratified February 3, 1870.

Section 1.

The right of citizens of the United States to vote shall not be denied or abridged by the United States or by any State on account of race, color, or previous condition of servitude.

Section 2.

The Congress shall have the power to enforce this article by appropriate legislation.

Appropriate legislation eventually resulted in the following:

1. As the Civil War ended in 1865, Congress created the Bureau of Refugees, Freedmen, and Abandoned Lands, popularly known as the Freedmen's Bureau, to help former slaves make the transition to freedom. Throughout the South, the Freedmen's Bureau established schools and hospitals, helped negotiate labor contracts, leased or sold confiscated lands to the freedmen, and generally tried to protect them from former masters.

2. The summer of 1865 found Lincoln assassinated and Andrew John-son, his successor, became president. Johnson, described as a "'poor' white from Tennessee," had no particular affection for southern aristo-

crats, nor equality for blacks."[1] He went so far as to issue two of his own proclamations. One granted "amnesty and pardon, with restoration of all rights of property, except as to slaves" to the Confederate rebels, including officials. The second proclamation took away the forty acres and the mule compensation that freed slaves had received.[2]

These actions and the unrest in northern states over the abolition of the three-fifths compromise (eventually laid to rest by the Thirteenth Amendment) prompted action by the Congress. The struggle was now about the voting rights of blacks.

When it became apparent that the post-war Confederacy was regaining ground from Johnson's relaxed policies on amnesty and forgiveness, Congress took control of Reconstruction. (It should be noted that Andrew Johnson was impeached in 1868.) In order to protect the civil liberties and voting rights of African Americans, the Fourteenth and Fifteenth Amendments were a necessity. In addition, the Civil Rights Acts of 1866 and 1875 were enacted: one to ensure all persons the rights to make and enforce contracts, to sue, and to testify in court, and the other to guarantee all citizens equal rights in hotels, theaters, restaurants, trains, transportation facilities, and other public accommodations. Federal troops were stationed in the southern states to enforce this legislation and the reconstruction process. They gave limited protection to the Freedmen's Bureaus and protected the voting rights of the freedmen who voted for Republicans, both black and white, who belonged to the party that freed them. Following the election of 1876, the federal troops left the South, and policies put in place to assure Republican reconstruction began to fail.

During Reconstruction, Texas lawmakers and the Texas Rangers responded to the federal government's policies by enacting their own restrictive laws and by structuring a convict leasing system that eventually became one of the most repressive anywhere. It was intended to maintain the "bottomland cotton and cane plantations of East Texas" (many of which became and are still prisons) and sustain the old slavery "traditions of hard labor, corporal discipline, racial subjugation."[3]

During the decades that followed Reconstruction, African Americans lost the right to vote and throughout the South freedmen were essentially re-enslaved through sharecropping, convict leasing, and

Black Codes that barred them from exercising their freedom. Black Codes, laws passed on the state and local levels with the help of the Ku Klux Klan and other white supremacist groups, helped racial segregation once again became the law.

The Supreme Court later ruled the civil rights acts and the Thirteenth, Fourteenth, and Fifteenth Amendments unconstitutional with the *Plessy v. Ferguson* decision in 1896. This case, which made segregation legal, was overturned in 1954 by *Brown v. Board of Education.* The current Voting Rights Act was signed in 1965 by President Lyndon Johnson, exactly one hundred years after the end of the Civil War—and in sharp contrast to the policies of President Andrew Johnson.

While historians may be familiar with these facts, I repeat them here for the benefit of students. Why are they so relevant? Because freedmen, as ex-slaves were called, were struggling to become independent following the Civil War—they were reconstructing themselves. This included a strong desire to acquire land because land was power. Land ownership meant you could work for yourself and get out from under the lash, the control of a system determined to keep you in your place of second-class citizenship. Second to the desire for land ownership was a strong desire to acquire education, heretofore illegal in most instances. Therefore blacks pooled their efforts to build churches and schools, more often than not a multipurpose building that could serve as a school, church, and place of community.

Authorities concerned with enticing or coercing black labor into white cotton fields often disapproved of freedmen who set out to obtain their own land to farm. Aware of white public opinion, the Eleventh Legislature, in 1866, passed a homestead law granting up to 160 acres of free public land to white persons only, blocking this route to black landownership. According to Texas Reconstruction historian James Smallwood, "As much as any other factor, this land act explained why more blacks did not become independent yeomen, but instead remained tied to white landlords. As late as 1871, not one in a hundred Negroes owned land." In Travis County, "night riders" attacked black landowners, hoping to force them out of the community.[4]

After a lengthy study of reports of Freedmen's Bureau subagents, army garrison commanders, and the American Missionary Society, the story that Texas officials and newspaper editors had so little to say about emerged from historian Barry Crouch who generalized,

Violence surrounded all aspects of a former slave's life, from work to school, from politics to social relations. In the labor arena violence continually surfaced from signing of the contract to the division of the crop. Whether attending religious meetings harassed or broken up by disgruntled whites, or school where white assailants attacked the children, blacks found mundane activities dangerous. Transgression of established white mores led to physical conflict, and political participation by blacks intensified white racial attitudes engendering more violence.[5]

The Bureau of Refugees, Freedmen, and Abandoned Lands began to function in Texas during December of 1865 and passed out of existence early in 1870. No confiscated or abandoned lands were redistributed to blacks, so they remained "farmers without land," a phrase of C. Vann Woodward, echoed by Leon Litwack.[6]

In spite of these consequences, many freedmen's colonies sprang up, including some independent black landowners. Not all whites were mean, and there were many blacks who did not succumb to the system of oppression.

According to Herman Wright, Jr., author and producer of *thelongblackline* film and website,

> From 1920 to 1935 African American families lived in thousands of communities (freedom colonies) which they created after Emancipation in 1865. These individuals, many with little or no education, built over 5,000 schools throughout the southern United States. Millions of children went from its classrooms into the world to become teachers, doctors, lawyers, scientists, business people, and military leaders.
>
> It was a crusade that rivaled any crusade in human history led by ordinary people in their rural and small town communities who accomplished the extraordinary. By the twenty-first century it was little remembered the enormous faith these families had in themselves and their children in the face of racism, poverty, ignorance, and government indifference to their plight decades after the end of slavery.[7]

In Clyde McQueen's book, *Black Churches in Texas,* he chronicles 375 historic congregations, many dating back to early Reconstruction. These freedom churches are synonymous with the freedom colonies. It is in one such church that *Juneteenth at the Ranch* takes place. Although the play is set in

Table 7.1. **Population in Fort Bend County
Following the Civil War**

Year	Whites	Blacks
1860	2,007	4,136
1870	1,604	5,510
1880	1,712	7,503
1890	1,605	8,981
1900	5,724	10,814

Source: Pauline Yelderman, *The Jay Birds of Fort Bend County: A White Man Union* (Waco: Texian Press, 1979), 41–42.

1930, it could well have been 1890 or 1870, and could have occurred in any number of counties, though owing to population density, there were more of these settlements in East Texas than in South Texas. The songs and the services are unmistakably a transference of African cultural traditions. In these services there is a freedom of expression: an unleashing of spiritual energy that transcends space and time, condition and circumstance.

Social Politics in Victorian Texas was written following research and workshops for a group of historians funded by the National Endowment for the Humanities. We had several tasks, and mine was to create an interpretive piece that would showcase the J. H. P. Davis home for its visitors. The timing made it possible to showcase this play at the 1998 Juneteenth celebration at the George Ranch Historical Park. It was very intimate and the audience liked that. It was like a reality show that flashed back to the past.

The research team assisted me with all sorts of political and social facts about the Victorian period, which, by the way, is also a period during which Jim Crow politics were thoroughly entrenched. The piece was also embellished by several oral history interviews I was able to conduct with the descendants of people whose families had been enslaved at the ranch. Fort Bend was and still is an interesting county whose racial demographics are a key factor in its politics.

The Democratic Party in Texas always had been a "lily white" party. Before the adoption of the Fifteenth Amendment, the Negro could not vote and after its adoption, he found his political birth in the Republican Party. However, there was no general state law providing for an all-white Democratic Party until 1923 when the Ku Klux Klan-dominated legislature passed a law providing for a white primary for the Democratic Party. The law stated:

> In no event shall a negro be eligible to participate in a Democratic party primary held in the State of Texas and should a negro vote in a Democratic primary election such ballot shall be void and election officials shall not count the same.[8]

As the above population statistics reveal, Fort Bend County boasted a large population of Negroes at the close of the Civil War—Negroes outnumbered whites. The election of 1869 launched the long and successful political careers of three Negroes, namely Walter Moses Burton, L. H. McCabe, and John Cobbin.

A number of Negroes held offices with some degree of regularity from 1869 to 1888 including London Branch, Charles Head, Tom Taylor, J. B. Roberts, Henry Phelps, J. Stansberry, H. E. Ganaway, G. Garner, C. H. Brown, Tom King, William Eaton, H. G. Green, H. W. Ballard, and William Henry. For the most part, the Negroes in this group were illiterate—former cotton and sugar cane field hands—and were not capable of handling the duties of the offices to which they had been elected. Their offices were run by white scalawag Democrats or white Republicans, often called carpetbaggers. Generally, old timers refer to the Republican-Negro regime that took control of county government in 1869 as the "carpetbagger-negro gang," but no one has been able to identify any of the white office-holders as carpetbaggers.[9]

According to Pauline Yelderman, the Jaybird-Woodpecker Battle of 1889 was the culmination of the Democrats' resentment against black progress and enfranchisement. Following this shootout on the streets of Richmond around the county courthouse, which was nothing short of something straight out of a Jesse James movie, the political climate for blacks changed entirely. During the shootout, little Robie Smith, who had been sent on an errand by Mrs. M. Newell to the J. M. Moore home, was killed in the crossfire crossing Jackson Street, where she lay dead until sometime after the fight was over.[10] In a matter of twenty minutes, several hundred volleys were fired by about thirty-five cursing and shouting men, and then it was all over. Morton Street in front of the courthouse—the scene of the battle—was an awful sight. The dead, dying, and wounded lay there in their spilled blood.

Looking back at the intensity of the shooting, one is amazed that there were so few casualties and that so many bullets missed their targets. The men of Richmond were noted for their prowess with guns. It was said that:

There were more men in Richmond who would stand up before shotguns and pistols than in any other town of its size in the United States. And if anybody doesn't believe it, just let the doubting Thomas go over and claim himself "Bad Medicine from Bitter Creek" and make a gun play and if somebody don't call him, it won't be at this time and generation.[11]

A short while after the smoke of battle had cleared, news of the frightful event reached the outside world. Governor Ross received two frantic wires: Judge Weston wired "Troops Needed"; Sergeant Aten wired "Street Fight Just Occurred Between The Two Factions. Many Killed Send Militia."

The governor acted at once. He telegraphed the following message:

Austin, Texas, August 16, 1889

To Captain E. A. Reichardt, Commanding Houston Light Guard:
Take Your Company Armed And Equipped To Richmond At Once. I Will Get There On First Train. Report To County Judge.

L. S. Ross, Governor

Finally, a Negro man, no doubt trembling with fear, carried the body of little Robie Smith away. Who buried little Robie Smith is not known. One presumes that it was the J. M. Moore family, as she was a maid in their home.[12]

Juneteenth at the George Ranch, set in 1930, is the only play in this book that occurs years after emancipation and, as such, makes a statement for how much and how little things changed following slavery. It takes place at a church, a building that could well have served as a school during the week. It could have been located in an independent freedom colony.

Freedom colonies, or freedmen's towns, were places where black people got busy building places for themselves following the Civil War.[13] Lincolnville, one such colony that is named for the Great Emancipator, existed in Coryell County. When the newly freed slaves in neighboring Hamilton County were told they were no longer wanted, they walked to Coryell County and joined other freedmen in establishing the Lincolnville community. Blacks desired to live alone in many instances, in places free from racial discrimination and beyond the control of whites who moved quickly to take back all the rights blacks had earned. In these independent settlements, blacks worked to earn enough money to buy land and to build churches that also served as schools. Several hundred of these Texas Freedmen's settlements began between 1870 and 1890.[14]

In *Juneteenth at the George Ranch,* emphasis is on education and political awareness. This is one of two plays in this book that has not yet had a premiere (the other is *Plantation Liendo*), but it contains a number of characters in an audience of churchgoers, making for great viewer participation.

SOCIAL POLITICS IN VICTORIAN TEXAS
A Living History Interpretation of African Americans
and Their Responsibilities

Written for Juneteenth 1998 performance at the George Ranch Historical Park

CHARACTERS

FRANCIS BURTON: cook, age 32

WASH ROPER: gardener, age 35

LOUISA JONES TYLER: maid, daughter of Robert, age 30

MARY MOORE POLLY JONES RYON: age 65

JOHN HARRIS PICKENS DAVIS: Judge J. H. P., age 39

ROBERT "UNCLE BOB" JONES: Once a slave and now a freedman, he was given to Mary M. "Polly" Jones Ryon as part of her inheritance from her parents, Henry and Nancy Jones, owners of the Jones Stock Farm.

TOUR GUIDE

SETTING

TIME: *1890*

PLACE: *The home of rancher and farmer J. H. P. Davis, Fort Bend County*
  Scene I: Yard, in the gardens closest to the kitchen and in back of the big house
  Scene II: In the hallway between the parlor and J. H. P. Davis's study
  Scene III: In the kitchen
  Scene IV: In the upstairs bedroom

SYNOPSIS

From 1869 to 1889 African Americans in Fort Bend enjoyed some prosperity and leadership at the local and state level. Following the Jaybird-Woodpecker War of 1889, the Democrats took over and blacks no longer held public offices. This was the climate of social politics in 1890. In spite of the Ku Klux Klan Act of 1871, the KKK was very effective in cutting down Negro participation in elections. (It should be noted that the period known as Reconstruction, during which the Freedmen's Bureau was in operation, only lasted until 1877.)

In this vignette, Polly Ryon, owner of Ryon Farm and Pasture Company, seeks to settle once and for all a long-standing deed dispute with her former slave and carriage driver, Uncle Bob Jones.

(Under the direction of the TOUR GUIDE, when visitors enter the back yard, they observe WASH, the gardener, busy working outside of the kitchen, bent over with hoe in hand.)

FRANCIS: *(From inside kitchen)* Oh, Wash! Bring me some onions from the garden. *(She comes outside.)* Did ya hear me, Wash? *(Fans herself with her apron)*

WASH: Yes'm. *(He goes to the garden just below the kitchen to gather them.)*

(While FRANCIS waits just outside the kitchen door, LOUISA comes out onto the porch in back of the house to tell WASH and FRANCIS some good news.)

LOUISA: Papa, Uncle Bob is coming to visit Miz Polly today. She ain't feeling too well and wants to talk some bizness with 'im. She actin like she too tired to go on living.

WASH: It's high time some things be talked about 'tween him and her — mainly 'bout that property and the house on it.

LOUISA: You don't forget nothing do you?

WASH: Neither does Uncle Bob.

FRANCIS: I hear that yo' papa *(Pointing to LOUISA)* and brother, Y.U., are really prospering. They got some kind o' partnership where they buys property. Uncle Bob always was smart.

WASH: That boy o' his done bought up more property than you can shake a stick at.

FRANCIS: Him and that cute lil yeller wife o' his.

LOUISA: Papa and Y.U. own pretty near one thousand acres o' land at the least.

WASH: And that wife o' his, well now, she sho' is fine, but she ain't got nothing on you, Louisa.

LOUISA: *(Blushing)* You really need to quit all that.

FRANCIS: *(To LOUISA)* You like it and you know it. Wash, when Lawyer goes into town for Mr. Davis, I have a few things on my list for him to pick up at the grocer for Sunday dinner. Miz Polly is having her church ladies over again. *(Shakes her head, uh-uh-uh)*

LOUISA: Tell me 'bout it. I can't seem to get evahthang dusted . . . then starch and iron them doilies, and if that ain't all, put fresh linen on all the beds.

FRANCIS: I ain't two minutes ago, hollered out here to Wash to brang me some mo' onions.

LOUISA: Lord knows I'll never get out of here for that meeting Saturday evening at th' church. Don't dese white folks know we has a life of our own?

WASH: Whatever we got to do 'round here, we sho' got to be at that church meetin. We s'pose to be discussin what to do bout some of dis Klan violence. Tobis and Mahaly n'ems barn was burned down th'other night!

LOUISA: Say what?!

FRANCIS: Uh-huh, like that Jordan man over in Brazoria who was lynched last month and left a widow wit six chil'ren to care fo'. We got to keep our eyes on what's happenin round here.

WASH: Things wasn't so bad when we had some black folks in state and local government, but that Jaybird-Peckerwood War done changed all that. Look like the war ain't over.

FRANCIS: Ain't no tellin what dese white folk is up to. They want you to do the work but they don't want you to be in charge of nuthin. Anyway, let me get on. Honey, I wish you could see dis menu she got me cookin up for Sunday.

WASH: (*Who continued his working while they talked*) Here's your onions, Francis. I gots to go to the carriage house and tell Lawyer that Mr. Davis needs to go into town to pick up de papers for dat big herd o' cattle he shippin up north first thang in de morning.

LOUISA: Miss Polly got t'have ever'thang just-so in here, (*Pointing back inside house*) so I better get back to wuk m'self.

(*FRANCIS returns to kitchen, LOUISA goes inside house, WASH goes to carriage house. TOUR GUIDE takes visitors around to the front of the house for entry. By that time, LOUISA has gone into parlor where she is busy dusting and attending to POLLY. MISS POLLY is doing some needlework. Alongside her sits a big basket of lace, etc. POLLY calls to J. H. P. DAVIS, her son-in-law, who is across the hall in his study. Visitors stand in hall so they can view action in both rooms.*)

POLLY: (*To J. H. P.*) I hope you checked through those ledgers for the years 1865–70 and found the deed to that property William and I gave Uncle Bob when we freed him and Fenton.

J. H. P.: I'm checkin on it. (*Continues studying his papers, not wanting to be bothered.*)

POLLY: You're checking on what?

J. H. P.: What is it?!

POLLY: Well, did ya locate it? (*He does not answer immediately.*) Did ya, Judge?

J. H. P.: (*Preoccupied*) Did I what?

POLLY: Did you locate the deed to Uncle Bob's property?

J. H. P.: I hope you realize that locating that deed is not the most important thing I have t'do.

POLLY: Not important?!

J. H. P.: Lookie here, Miz Polly, I got a shipment a'cattle that has got to leave Ryon Farm and Pasture Comp'ny by six o'clock in the morning in order to reach Kansas City by noon, day after tomorrow. I'm right now trying to—

POLLY: Don't you have time to do anything I ask?

J. H. P.: As I was saying, I'm jes tryin to supervise half-a-dozen cowboys to git 'em cows loaded in the boxcars, plus send Lawyer in t'town to pick up some papers I need t'sign. Now, if you'll have a lil mo' patience, Miz Polly, I'll get to ya deed in due time. (*Rises to go to kitchen but is stopped by POLLY*)

POLLY: (*Standing to confront him*) I need a word with you, Judge, can you step in here? (*To LOUISA*) Louisa, please bring me a glass of lemonade and do something 'bout this fly that keeps pesterin me!

(*Meanwhile, J. H. P. begins to pace impatiently.*)

LOUISA: S'cuse me, Miz Polly, but you hasn't drank the last lemonade. (*Pointing to a tray and glass half-full*)

POLLY: Louisa, just go to th'kitchen and bring me some fresh! (*Fans at fly*)

(*LOUISA exits and POLLY turns her full attention to J. H. P.*)

Now, Judge, if you'll take a coupla minutes out of yo' too busy schedule and listen! When I turnt this place over t'you t'manage, mind ya, we agreed that some thangs has importance over other bizness and right now Uncle Bob is one a'those.

J. H. P.: I don't hafta be reminded—

POLLY: Bob an' his wife, Fenton, took good care o' me til I let 'em go after my prairie house burnt down—which is how and why I come to be livin here wit you and Belle, anyway—instead of my own place!

J. H. P.: I am very well aware of all that!

POLLY: And be aware, Judge, that Ryon Farm and Pasture Comp'ny has already put many a silver dollar into yo' account, so since when do you get too busy to handle some of my most important business, I would like to know?

J. H. P.: (*Backing down*) I beg yo' pardon, ma'am. I never intended to overlook the deed—

POLLY: Overlook, mind ya—

J. H. P.: (*Trying to be a little calmer*) I simply hoped it could wait til I got this big shipment of cattle on th'train. Just why are you so anxious 'bout dis? I know Uncle Bob and Aunt Fenton wuz your two mos' important colored folks but they can at least wait one more day!

POLLY: Bob is on his way over here to pick up that deed today! Me and William, God rest his soul, give 'em that house and property when they wuz first freed. Course, William didn't want 'em to abandon me, so he made me promise not to turn over th'deed till after I had died, leaving instructions in my will.

J. H. P.: If you'll remember, I promised to he'p you make a will.

POLLY: I see how you carry out my will, Judge Davis!

(*J. H. P. attempts to interrupt her but is unsuccessful.*)

Well, I am *not* dead and while I can still take care of some of my affairs, I wants them to have what's rightfully theirs, Bob and Fenton. (*Stares at him firmly*) And I'd 'preciate you t'locate that deed, suh!

(*J. H. P. storms out of the parlor and goes back into his study.*)

I wonder what's keeping Uncle Bob? He's never late.

LOUISA: (*Returning with lemonade then picking up feather duster*) He ain't even late now, ma'am. You said he'd be here shortly after noon. Cook ain't even served you and the cowhands, so it mustn't be noon yet.

POLLY: Louisa? The lemonade, please! And I'll thank ya to thread these needles fo' me. I'm plannin t'work on my embroid'ry this evenin. Jes put the dusta down! (*LOUISA puts down the duster, takes the basket back to the sofa, and sits to thread needles.*)

UNCLE BOB: (*Enters the study and takes off hat to greet J. H. P.*) Howdy, Mr. Davis.

(He is interrupted in paying his respects by LOUISA, who is thrilled to see her father.)

LOUISA: Hello, Papa! *(Running to hug him)*
UNCLE BOB: Baby girl!
LOUISA: How's Mama and ever'body?
UNCLE BOB: Well, you know your Mama suffers with that arthritis and can't eat no mo' pork. Other than that, she sends love and some vegetables I brought you from de garden. I lef' 'em in de kitchen wit Francis.
LOUISA: Thank you, Papa. I'd love to talk to ya, but lemme finish what I'm doin for Miz Polly. *(In a half-whisper, more for the benefit of the audience)* You know how she is, I swear, dat woman!
UNCLE BOB: Now, now, be of good cheer.
J. H. P.: *(Realizing that UNCLE BOB is in the house, makes it his business to speak to him briefly, then make a quick exit)* Well now, if it ain't *the* Uncle Bob. What you been up to, Uncle?
UNCLE BOB: Jes trying to stay 'bove water, suh. And yourself?
J. H. P.: I ain't one t'complain. What with over ten thousand head a'cattle and hopes for a good cotton crop, ain't much I can say, now, is it. I 'spect you here to see Miz Polly?
UNCLE BOB: Yessuh, I am.
J. H. P.: Well, I ain't gone keep you from her. *(Turning away)* Miz Polly, I'm goin git Lawyer t'drive me to th'bank. I need t'sign some papers concernin dat shipment in th'mornin. *(Hollers back to LOUISA)* Louisa, tell Francis I won't be eatin 'til suppuh. *(Turns and leaves through front door)*
LOUISA: Yessuh, Mr. Davis. You want yo' hat, suh? *(As he was in such a hurry to get away from POLLY, he almost forgot it.)*
J. H. P.: *(Clearing his throat)* Course I do. *(Leaves rather angry for having to be reminded)*
POLLY: Come on in, Uncle Bob. Pour you a cool glass o' lemonade and res' yose'f. Louisa, you may go help Francis.

(LOUISA reluctantly exits to kitchen.)

UNCLE BOB: *(Helping himself to the drink)* Miz Polly, you looks 'bout as good as the first time I met 'cha.

POLLY: Now, now, Bob Jones, yo eyesight mus' be failin ya. I done worked so hard dese las' few years, it's 'bout t'catch up t'me.

UNCLE BOB: Well, you coulda fooled me. (*Taking something out of a sack*) Lookie here what I brought 'cha, some of Fenton's fresh basil an' I dropped off some of our new potatoes in the kitchen wit Francis.

POLLY: Oh, do let me have a smell. (*Reaching for basil*) You know how I always did love the smell of basil. Tell Aunt Fenton I'm obliged to her and you. I s'pose you know why I sent for ya?

UNCLE BOB: No ma'am, I don't.

POLLY: Well, as I'm getting up in age, I feel a need to put some things in order as it concerns property and such, 'specially dat piece Mr. William an' I gave t'you and Fenton, years ago, t'build y'alls house on—right afta we gave y'all yo' freedom.

UNCLE BOB: Yes'm. Y.U. and I jes finished puttin a fresh coat o' paint on th'house.

POLLY: Well, 'fore he died, Mr. William reminded me 'bout dat deed. I expected to let you have it today, 'ceptin' the Judge cain't seem to take th'time t'find it.

UNCLE BOB: Is that right?

POLLY: I tell you, no sooner'n Belle lef' here fo' Kentucky t'go visit her folks, did he start t'git saucy wid me. As much as I did fo' th'bofe of 'em, him and Belle—raisin Mamie and Bud long afta their mother, Lizzie, died—and I don't know what all else . . .

(*She starts to get sentimental and cry. UNCLE BOB rises to comfort her but does not go in her direction at all. He was forbidden from touching POLLY.*)

UNCLE BOB: I know ma'am. Susan Elizabeth . . . that was you and Mr. William's onliest child . . . and she died so young, just twenty-nine, wasn't it? (*He knew her intimately and perhaps loved LIZZIE from a baby.*)

POLLY: (*Finishes her crying and is sorry for letting herself go like that*) Course I know he means well, J. H. P., I mean . . . but he's just not gotten roun' to lookin through all dem papers to fin' it!

UNCLE BOB: Now, don't go gittin yourself all worked up over it, Miz Polly. Course it do need to be settled an' I ain't gittin a day younger, m'self. If it wasn't for m'son, Y.U., who's got such a good head on 'im, I'd be los' as a rabbit in a briar patch. He just 'bout takes care of ev'rythang for me dese days. He owns close to five hundred acres o' property now.

POLLY: All here in Fort Bend?

UNCLE BOB: Right here in Fort Bend. We got quite a few prosperous colored folk in dis county.

POLLY: Who are you tellin? I tried to convince dat big-headed son-in-law of mine, when he went and joined up wit that renegade Jaybirds Democrat Association, that they should have lef' well enough alone. He did, however, use his influence to protect some o' y'all.

UNCLE BOB: Some folk think the Jaybird-Woodpecker War ain't settled yet, Miz Polly . . . Course we colored folk are bound and determined to stay and vote Republican cause dat's the party what freed us.

POLLY: And as you well know, for the las' twenty years, right here in Fort Bend, we had some forty-odd colored men serve at all levels of county government — includin sheriff and justice o' th' peace.

UNCLE BOB: Yep, we served in public office right up til last August . . . and that's when the Jaybird Young Men Democrats and the Republican Woodpeckers had that big shootout in front o' the Richmond County Courthouse.

POLLY: It wuz awful! Don't remind me.

UNCLE BOB: And dose two fellas got kilt . . . (*Deep in thought*)

POLLY: How well do I remember! But don't you forget one minute now, how the Judge stepped in and tried to help y'all by speaking up —

UNCLE BOB: (*Not exactly interrupting her, but still in concentration*) Not long after th'war, 'round 1869 jes afta my baby girl wuz bo'n, we took our place right 'long side th'whites in dis county, and round the state in gen'ral.

POLLY: I know, I know.

UNCLE BOB: Oh yeah, we helped y'all run thangs, an', I might say, we did a holy good job. But let's face it, Miz Polly, yo' got some whites who ain't never gone be satisfied t'have a colored man in a position o'power. They plum don't wanna work wit us — dey works against us ev'ertime . . . Mos' we can do is own our own land.

POLLY: An' I aim t'see to it that you git dat deed. The Judge is a good, hard-working man, it's jus that him an' me, we don't see eye t'eye on some thangs. But no soona than he locates it, I'll have Lawyer ride over and let'cha know, so we can put it to res', once-and-for-all!

UNCLE BOB: I 'preciate it, ma'am. Take good care o' yo'self. (*Rises with his hat in his hand*)

POLLY: Tell Aunt Fenton thanks for th'basil and t'come see me sometime.

(UNCLE BOB comes out of the parlor and exits into the kitchen where the TOUR GUIDE leads visitors. Upon their arrival in kitchen, UNCLE BOB is busy talking with FRANCIS and LOUISA.)

UNCLE BOB: Now dat's what I lak t'see, my wimmenfolks in the kitchen stirrin and churnin.

(FRANCIS is stirring cornbread and LOUISA is churning.)

FRANCIS: Just making some cornbread. Miz Polly wouldn't think o' eatin widdout it.

LOUISA: Yesterday, she sent me back in here for two more pieces, wid d'butter, which we ran out of, so Francis had to ask Wash to milk de cow again. Hey y'all, I thought Miz Belle had taken all her keys to th'linen closet so I couldn't change th' sheets on the beds—but guess who has a key?

FRANCIS: A key? Nobody but her has a key to anything.

LOUISA: Dat's what you think. Old Lawyer took me dis mornin, when I was complainin 'bout it and opened the closet right up!

UNCLE BOB: That Lawyer is a character. *(Laughing)* I could've told you he had a key. Where is he now?

FRANCIS: Lef' right after you came. He's gone t'drive the Judge t'th'bank.

POLLY: *(Calling from the parlor)* Louisa?! *(WASH may have to call, due to proximity of parlor to kitchen.)*

LOUISA: What is it now? *(Answering POLLY)* I'm coming! I'll see ya, Papa. *(They embrace briefly.)* Tell Mama and n'em I'll see 'em Saturday evenin at dat church meeting. Hope nothin don't happen 'fore den.

WASH: *(Entering kitchen)* Bob Jones! Looking good, old man!

UNCLE BOB: You ain't doin too bad yo'self. *(They shake hands.)* Look forward to seein you and all th'folks at dat meetin we havin down at th'church Saturday evenin.

WASH: Yessuh. We knows 'bout it and done made plans to be dere.

UNCLE BOB: We needs this meeting t'talk about some of dis Klan violence round here, as well as bout getting a new schoolteacher for dese chil'ren.

WASH: They shore do need some schoolin. I got five of 'em myself. We got t'be able t'do more'n dig and plow.

FRANCIS: An' cook!

UNCLE BOB: That young Professor Mitchell was run off when dose Kluckers set th'place on fire. An' dat buildin where we has church and school is all we got for a meetin place. Lucky he was there to put out th'fire 'fore it got any worse.

FRANCIS: Our kids needs schooling just lak th'white. So many of dese kids, workin right 'longsides dey folks in d'fields. Dey don't bit mo' go to school lessen it rains so bad all th'work has to stop. My Virginia is de one what taught me what little reading and writing I know. I'd thank God to help me an' John send her off t'school someplace so she could become a teacher . . . leastwise so she wouldn't have to work fo' dese white folk all her life, lak us.

UNCLE BOB: Well, Y.U.'s wife got a cousin who may come in here from Houston three or four days a week, but we got to repair dat part o' th'church what's burned 'fore she gits here. Y'all do what you can to be there Saturday evenin. I'd better mosey on over towards home. Fix me up a jar o'dat cool lemonade to take wid me.

FRANCIS: I got it right here. You know we always takes care o'you, Uncle Bob.

UNCLE BOB: Yes'm, y'all do, indeed. Thank you, kindly.

(She sees him out the back door and returns to her baking, rolling out some dough.)

(Following this episode, the TOUR GUIDE should take the visitors upstairs to view the bedrooms. LOUISA, busy making up the beds and talking to herself as though she is alone.)

LOUISA: I longs to one day have me a bed dis fine. Dose old corn-shuck mattresses we use don't hold a candle to dese new cotton ones. But I say my mama's quilts is as fine as any . . . which reminds me I need to starch and iron all those doilies o'Miz Belle's 'fore Miz Polly has her church ladies over here. I can jes hear 'em goin on wit their 'mirations, "Look at dese fine stiches . . . must o'been made by someone with small hands." Them wit their lace gloves and all . . . most of 'em ain't never touched a broom handle. They husbands won't let 'em. I wish my husband was still alive, but no . . . he had to go and get shot in front of the Richmond County Courthouse in dat Jaybird-Woodpecker War. I was sitting up late waitin on 'im

that night. When the sheriff come bringing me the news . . . I had put ma-
ma's lace quilt on the bed that day and was waitin to turn the covers down
'fore Vasey come home . . . but he never come. Rest his soul in peace, Lord.
Yeah, I wish I could quit wukkin here. I wish I had a pair of lace gloves.
But I gots no choice in the matter now. He'p me, Lord Jesus, to put up wit
Miz Polly jes a lil longa.

*(She continues her musings and mumblings under her breath. TOUR GUIDE
proceeds with tour through upstairs rooms then returns back downstairs,
exiting through back door, where WASH is outside working the gardens.
At this point, WASH can show the Carriage House and Blacksmith Shoppe to
the group.)*

Naomi Carrier doing research at J. H. P. Davis home. George Ranch Historical Park, 1998

JUNETEENTH AT THE GEORGE RANCH

Written for the George Ranch Historical Park, 1998

CHARACTERS

REV. J. W. DAVENPORT: preacher, age 60
SISTER ADDERLY: schoolteacher, age 25
BUSTER JACKSON: cowboy, age 25
JOSEPHINE THOMAS: maid, married to Johnny Thomas, age 34
ARTILIA TAYLOR: cook, age is estimated at early 30s, married

SETTING

TIME: *June 19, 1930, midday*
PLACE: *Fort Bend County, Texas. George Ranch Church; Cook's House; and Yard*

SYNOPSIS

This celebration of independence begins with an old-time prayer meeting in a one-room schoolhouse that doubles as a church on Sundays. The songs, the prayer and sermon, games, and food depict the meaning of emancipation and what it meant for African Americans to gain their freedom at the end of the Civil War. The barbecue is reminiscent of family reunions and church picnics over the years with smells of hickory smoked meats, fried chicken, catfish, and collard greens with ham hocks, sweet potato and pecan pies, molasses cakes, watermelon, homemade ice cream, all those foods that sustain the soul—soul food. No celebration of this kind would be complete without some foot stomping spirituals, gospel and blues—soul music. The celebration of Juneteenth is a celebration of the survival of souls.

(It is Juneteenth and members of this small black community always begin their celebration of independence with a prayer service in a building they have built to serve as both a church and a school — like a community center. The minister leads in the call and response tradition.)

REV. DAVENPORT: Lord, you brought us from a mighty long way and we is gathered here today to give your name the glory. *(Leads the congregation in song)*

I LOVE THE LORD

(Verse 1)
I love the Lord. He heard my cry and pitied ev'ry groan.
Long as I live, while troubles rise, I'll hasten to His throne.

(Verse 2)
I love the Lord. He heard my cry and pitied ev'ry groan.
O let my heart no more despair while I have breath to moan.

(REV. DAVENPORT prays, one knee bent, one hand gesturing.)

This evenin, our dear heavenly Father, once more and again

We come bowed down befo' You, in a place where we ain't never had no flowers.

Almighty God, You no stranger to perform yo' miracles in dis place. I beg you to shed some light on dese dark days we's living in. Father, I stretch my hands to Thee, no other help I know. If Thou withdraw thy help from me, whither shall I go.

The mountains are high and the burdens are heavy. The rivers are mighty wide and the night gets mighty dark. We know that you are everywhere at the same time. Free those who are still under the watchful eye of the overseer. And when the victory is won, We want to hear your voice say, "Servant, well done." Yeah. Oh yeah! Hallelujah!

Wipe the tears from our eyes. Hear our prayer, accept our petitions, and finally, let Thy will be done. Amen, and thank God.

(Preaches) Today is our day, a day of rejoicing in the name of freedom. Amen. No longer do we wear d'shackles on our feet and hands. Lord, You has loosed d'chains from round our necks, and in d'name of your son, Jesus, we pray for you t'take dese chains off'en our minds. We's thankful for yo' grace and yo' mercy—that we no longer works dese same fields under the lash and whip. While we no longer has to run 'way to the north t'be free, we got work t'do right here tryin to ed-u-cate dese chirren and tek kere o' our families. Give us d'strength to go all d'way. No ha'f-steppin.

Our beloved sistuhs and brothuhs, we has come this far by faith, leaning on the Lord. We do meditate day and night on his precious word. Today is a great day! A day of shoutin, an' dancin an' jubilation! Lest we forget why we's free, wasn't but a few sho't years ago t'was 'gainst de law fo' us to read—eben de Holy Bible. Now we is free to go and come, we don't wanna tek yo' blessin fo' nothin. We thank you dat we is fin'ly free to keep our families together, free to teach our chilluns. Thank God Almighty for sending us this teacher, for you is gone send us many teachers so we can finally take our place in this ol' worl'. We know we is equal in yo' sight, Lord, and we know, too, that you can take us the rest of the way. Yo' grace has brought us this far and grace shall lead us on.

(Singing and leading the congregation)

I WANT TO BE READY

(Refrain)
I want to be ready
I want to be ready
I want to be ready,
To walk in Jerusalem just like John.

(Verse)
John said Jerusalem was four square
Walk in Jerusalem just like John.
I hope good Lord, I'll meet you there,
Walk in Jerusalem just like John.

(Repeat refrain.)

REV. DAVENPORT: (*Continues speaking*) Brothuhs and sistuhs, befo' we git on wit today's festivities, I want to tek dis time to introduce to some and make known to others Miz Coreen Adderly, the cousin to Brothuh Y.U.'s wife. She comes to us from nearby Kendleton, over in Fort Bend County, where dey got the onliest colored high school anywhere near 'bouts. May she come in her own way and tell y'all how she plans to he'p us wit our school dis year. Sistuh, you may tek de flo'.

(*She comes wiping her brow with a lace handkerchief.*)

SISTER ADDERLY: Giving honor to God, the Reverend Davenport, Deacon Jones, members, and Christian friends: It was on this day in 1865, some sixty-five years ago, that our fathers and mothers were freed from their bonds as slaves to the land and the lands owners. Our mission to educate our people is still just beginning. I want to let each and every one of you know how pleased I am to be chosen to be the new teacher here in Fort Bend. With God's help and your prayers I promise to faithfully fulfill this assignment as best I can. Thank you. (*She turns to go back to her seat but is stopped by the following question.*)

MAN I: (*From audience*) Ma'am, just where do you thank we can git some more books for our youngstuhs?

SISTER ADDERLY: The county school board is suppose to pass down whatever books the white schools have used—

WOMAN: Our chilluns needs to be protected from having rocks thrown at 'em when they passes the white school. What we gone do 'bout dat?

(*MISS ADDERLY begins to look helpless.*)

MAN II: (*From audience*) And we jes fixed up dat part o' de buildin dat was set fire to a coupla weeks ago. One of us men's gone hafta stand watch to mek sho' dat sumpin lak dat don't happen again whilst you and dese chillun is in here.

(*SISTER ADDERLY is noticeably frustrated, and wiping her forehead with a handkerchief. REV. DAVENPORT comes to her rescue.*)

REV. DAVENPORT: Thank you, Sister Adderly.

(She resumes her seat.)

That's why I have axed a man f'om each o' you families to stay here a lil longer to discuss dese very issues. We won't be too long, but we has to tek advantage of what time we has here today to put some thangs in place — to make education possible. 'Course we'll take time for the freedom parade; den de womenfolk can be dismissed to go wuk on d'meal; the chillun can get up a game o' baseball and 'mediately following, us mens will have a bizness meetin, here and now. Shall we bow our heads in dismissal.

    (Prays) And now, Heavenly Father, as we prepare to leave yo' throne of mercy, go wit us each and ev'ry one, f'om de oldest to de youngest, and guide our steps lest we stumble, pick us up if we fall. Bless be the tie that binds us, til we meet again. Dis we ax in yo' son Jesus' name, Amen? Amen!

(They break up.)

TOUR GUIDE: *(Instructions to all)* Please join us outside for the freedom parade!

(All sing a medley of songs while orderly lining up and taking part in the parade. A couple of song leaders are needed and two folks play tambourines and one plays a bass drum. This parade is reminiscent of a New Orleans style second line. The only thing missing is a trumpet and trombone.)

THIS LIL LIGHT OF MINE

This lil light of mine,
I'm gonna let it shine
This lil light of mine,
I'm gonna let it shine.
This lil light of mine,
I'm gonna let it shine.
Let it shine, let it shine, let it shine.

Ev'rywhere I go,
I'm gonna let it shine.
Ev'rywhere I go,
I'm gonna let it shine.
Ev'rywhere I go,
I'm gonna let it shine.
Let it shine, let it shine, let it shine.

Jesus gave it to me,
I'm gonna let it shine.
Jesus gave it to me,
I'm gonna let it shine.
Jesus gave it to me,
I'm gonna let it shine.
Let it shine, let it shine, let it shine.

OH, FREEDOM

Oh, freedom! Oh, freedom!
Oh, freedom over me!
An' befo' I'd be a slave,
I'll be buried in my grave,
An' go home to my Lord an' be free.

No mo' moanin', No mo' moanin',
No mo' moanin' over me!
An' befo' I'd be a slave
I'll be buried in my grave,
And go home to my Lord an' be free.

(Breaking into a real shout and ring dance)

SLAV'RY CHAIN DONE BROKE AT LAS'

Slav'ry chain done broke at las',
Broke at las', broke at las',
Slav'ry chain done broke at las',
Goin' to praise God til I die.

(*Led by a high soprano*)
Way up in-a dat valley
Prayin' on my knees;
Tellin' God about my troubles,
An' to he'p me if-a he please.

Slav'ry chain done broke at las',
Broke at las', broke at las'.
Slav'ry chain done broke at las'
Goin' to praise god til I die.

GIT ON BOARD, LITTLE CHILDREN

De gospel train's a-comin,
I hear it jus' at han'
I hear de car wheels rumblin
And rollin' thro' de lan'.

(*Refrain*)
Git on board, little children,
Git on board, little children,
Git on board, little children,
Dere's room for many a mo'.

I hear de train a-comin,
She's comin roun' de curve,
She's loosened all her steam an' brakes,
An' strainin eb'ry nerve.

(*Repeat refrain.*)

De fare is cheap an' all can go,
De rich an' poor are dere,
No second class aboard dis train,
No diff'rence in de fare.

(*Repeat refrain.*)

(*One of the older children calls out "Let's play ball!" The children gather to play; the women leave to prepare and serve the meal; the men return to the church for a meeting concerning the welfare of their families.*)

(left) **The Union flag. George Ranch Historical Park, Texian Market Days Festival, 1995;** (below) **"They fin'ly tol' us we was free." George Ranch Historical Park, Texian Market Days Festival, 1999**

CONCLUSION

The museums and historic sites that commissioned these plays realized that there was a need to put a face to slavery, a need to include the experiences and contributions of African Americans to Texas's history. Talking Back Living History Theatre was born out of this need, continues out of this need, and hopes others will use this manual as a reference for developing living history plays for their communities.

The history of African Americans in Texas has leaked out in spurts and occasional drips and was still moving along at a slow pace until recently. The enslaved in Texas were the last to be freed, hence Juneteenth celebration. Perhaps their stories are some of the last to be told. But in the twenty-first century these stories are flowing out somewhat faster. Around 2005 there was a noticeable renaissance among known and unknown artists, both home-grown and transplanted to this great state, because of the abundance of opportunities here. People from everywhere began to show a keen interest in the history of African American Texans, black cowboys, rodeos, trail riders, Buffalo Soldiers, Brazos Valley plantation sagas, historically black colleges, and the Underground Railroad from Texas to Mexico. Educators, historians, journalists, authors, athletes, and scientists have become involved in the interpretation of black Texas stories. The plays in *Go Down, Old Hannah* represent just a few of the stories surrounding some of Texas's historical events. It is my hope that these stories will inspire readers to search for and preserve more stories to fully realize the rich heritage of African American Texans. Our children need to hear these stories from the mouths of the people who lived them. In the words of the African proverb, "Until the lion writes his story, the tale of the hunt will forever glorify the hunter."

I am reminded of how little folks know about African Americans and their place in American history. While they are seen on television singing and dancing, laughing and telling jokes about themselves, what folks see, in many ways, is what black people have become. Folks know what they see, but is that what African Americans feel? What has commercial appeal is not always real. Many television viewers, black, white, and of other races, honestly believe that the African Americans they view in television sitcoms, commercials, and movies are the same as the African Americans they meet in the streets, live in neighborhoods with, and work with. Hence, African Americans are responded to as if they are the same as the people seen on television. While black language and slang phrases are often adopted, and black music becomes more and more commercial, the general public doesn't really know much about how African Americans came to be how they are, or how they are perceived to be. Some don't like to think about slavery or the Jim Crow years or the "whites only" days, which were not so long ago—just fifty years have passed. It's too shameful or embarrassing. The pain is easier to forget than deal with because reconciliation requires communication, negotiation, and surrender. But where did all that pain and anger go? In many cases it just sank into the subconscious of America and has become what some call covert racism. We cannot be disconnected from our past. To make up for slavery's horrific realities, people often say, "Well, your own African ancestors sold you to the slavers," or "My great-granddaddy gave all his slaves some land when the war was over." Granted, there were some great-granddaddies that *did* bequeath land to their black folks and many others who were the vanguard for human rights and black education. But the overwhelming majority of landowners bemoaned the passing of a "way of life" that, for the privileged, no longer existed, and for poor whites, made life harder because they now had to compete with the freedmen.

African Americans have had to be invisible, are pressured to forget about the past, and nobody wants to know how they feel for fear they might express anger or hostility because of what happened to them during the empire of slavery. This too is changing and must change because it inhibits progress. In spite of the odds against education in the area of African American history and culture, there are over four thousand museums and cultural institutions in America dedicated to research, documentation, preservation, interpretation, and distribution of black history and culture, and my own organization, the Texas Center for African American Living History, is one of them.

There is so much to encourage us to believe in change. Throughout the world, old ways are giving in to a new order, a new technology, a new belief in mankind. We believe we can clean up the world, renew energy, stamp out racism, feed the world's hungry, take care of children, elevate women, get rid of dictators, and find cures for human ailments. There is that echo in Maya Angelou's poem, "And still I rise." No matter what happens, we rise to conquer anything that stands in the way of evolution. We believe in our innate ability to fix things, whatever is wrong or not working. The indomitable spirit of African American Texans has allowed them to endure, to achieve, and to surpass insurmountable obstacles. Our experience is the experience of the past and the potential of the future.

My son Robeson, upon seeing me dressed in nineteenth century clothes of the enslaved, asked, "Mom, I just don't see what you get out of doing all this." And I had to think about it, because others may wonder why I have put so much time and attention into interpretations of slavery. I know now. This work is important because slavery was and is our greatest triumph — our most outstanding victory! This victory belongs not only to blacks, but to America. This triumph belongs to hundreds of abolitionists and free people of color; to farmers, teachers, ministers, writers, journalists, politicians, and to ordinary folks working behind the scenes who believed in justice and freedom.

What African American Texans have achieved, as was so eloquently stated by Herman Wright, Jr., "was a crusade that rivaled any crusade in human history led by ordinary people." It is a victory for Texans that should be continually embraced, confronted, and fulfilled.

APPENDIX
Lesson Plans and Additional Resources

PART I: CELEBRATIONS

We can learn a lot about people and their history by studying the songs they sang. We can learn how they worked, what they did for entertainment, and about their daily lives, because songs tell stories. Understanding a people's songs helps us understand their feelings, their attitudes, and their beliefs. The Africans in a strange, new land created yells and hollers, cries and calls. Later on there were work songs, praise songs, and love songs; there were folktales, game songs, and rhymes. In the spirit of African musical and storytelling traditions, the enslaved used music to accompany everything. Yells, hollers, cries, and calls helped express feeling in the absence of language; it was unrestrained, free expression for an enslaved individual. Work songs lessened the monotony of the work; spirituals sang of heaven, and the sweet by and by where slavery would be no more; love songs often mourned the sadness of a lover sold away, runaway, beaten, or living on a plantation too far away to visit. Game songs and dance rhymes enriched rare and cherished opportunities for entertainment.

Jumpin' Juba: Uncle Bubba and Mammy Bell Jump de Broom

VOCABULARY

barn—a farm building used to shelter animals and to store farm equipment

big house—home of the slave master's family

broom jumpin—an African wedding ceremony where a couple literally jumps over a broom and symbolically jumps from the old life over into the new life

ceremony—celebration, festival, harvest

fiddle—violin; a stringed instrument

freedom — the ability to do as one chooses

frolic — to run or dance around playfully

headpiece — a wreath of flowers, berries, and leaves a woman wears
on her head during a slave wedding

juba — a dance where slaves clapped and patted their bodies to make
music

kidnap — to capture or take away

mammy — enslaved African American woman; a word used instead of
"mama"

massa — owner of a plantation and slaves

missus — wife of plantation owner

molasses — a thick dark syrup produced when sugar is refined

plantation — large farm worked by slaves

pray — to speak to or request something of a spiritual being

quarters — home of the enslaved

quilt — a bed cover made of two layers of cloth with a soft substance
in between. Quilts could be made in a pattern that might be used
as a signal or directions for travel on the Underground Railroad.[1]

sparkin — being affectionate or loving

tradition — knowledge passed down from one generation to another;
a way of doing things that becomes a habit

Underground Railroad — a network of secret pathways that slaves
followed to freedom, often traveling as far away as Canada, Mexico,
or the Caribbean

QUESTIONS

In what year did Stephen F. Austin's Old Three Hundred begin to populate
Texas?

Where did they settle and why?

What was Austin's arrangement with the Mexican government?

Was slavery allowed in the new Mexican colony of Texas?

Where did Bubba and Bell come from? Who did they belong to?

How many miles did Brothuh Solomon and Sistuh Sarah walk to get to the
wedding?

What wedding gifts did Brothuh Solomon and Sistuh Sarah give Bubba and
Bell?

What did the enslaved eat? From where did they get their clothes?
What kinds of work did slaves do?
Did slaves have to work on Christmas?

YELLS AND HOLLERS, CALLS AND CRIES

Each of these forms of expression was a celebration of personal freedom in spite of bondage.

Since the Africans came to America through forced migration, their culture and folkways were maintained through music, dance, and storytelling. In slavery days, the *field calls* doubtless had a special importance. They were a means by which the slaves could keep in touch with one another, and perhaps get around regulations of the overseer that isolated one work party from another. In early slave days, these calls undoubtedly were in African dialects, insofar as actual words were used, and they must have been a source of irritation to white overseers who could not understand them.[2]

The Negro cries and calls of the open spaces are known by different names in different places. Sometimes they are called "corn field hollers," "cotton field hollers," or just "hollers."

The *cry* does not have to have a theme, or to fit into any kind of formal structure, or to conform to normal concepts of musical propriety. It is often completely free music in which every sound, line, and phrase is used in any fashion that appeals to the crier. A cry differs from a call in both expression and intent. As an expression its tone may be high or low, smooth and mellow, or ragged and syncopated. It could be held for a long while or vanish in thin air. However it sounds to the listener, the singer's intent is to express emotions too heartfelt to keep inside, whether they be sadness or sorrow, hopes for tomorrow, sickness or pain, love lost, or shame. A cry needs no words or form and for the enslaved it was, unlike their bodies, totally free, a pure and unadulterated expression of how one feels. There is no better example than the following lyrics that date back to the *common meter* hymns sung in a cappella:

> I love the Lord,
> He heard my cry
> and pitied every groan.
> Long as I live

and troubles rise,
I'll hasten to His throne.

Types and Examples of Yells and Hollers, Calls and Cries
Work Song

Many work songs were question and answer singing, wherein a leader or caller makes a musical statement or calls out a lyric and a group responds to or answers that call. Here is an example:

SHUCK THAT CORN BEFORE YOU EAT[3]

Caller: All dem purty gals will be dar,
Chorus: Shuck dat corn before you eat.

Caller: They will fix it for us rare,
Chorus: Shuck dat corn before you eat.

Caller: I know dat supper will be big,
Chorus: Shuck dat corn before you eat.

Caller: I think I smell a fine roast pig,
Chorus: Shuck dat corn before you eat.

Caller: I hope dey'll have some whisky dar,
Chorus: Shuck dat corn before you eat.

Caller: I think I'll fill my pockets full,
Chorus: Shuck dat corn before you eat.

The enslaved used these kinds of rhythmic call-and-response work songs to step up the pace of their work and to lessen the monotony of mechanical, robotic labor. Sometimes these songs were an opportunity for the enslaved to talk about their condition and the masters and overseers who controlled the circumstances of labor without pay. This made it necessary to use "coded" lyrics for fear of punishment, in which case an overseer might be referred to as "Pharoah," a Bible character who was a cruel dictator. Animal names, like fox and possum, were also used.

The next example shows how important rhythmic music was to keeping up morale. Here a caller might sing the first line and the group would sing the second:

PICK A BALE O' COTTON[4]

Gonna jump down, turn around to pick a bale o' cotton
Gonna jump down, turn around to pick a bale a day.

Oh Lordy, pick a bale o' cotton;
Oh Lordy, pick a bale a day.

The large plantations in the South were based on West African agricultural models and the black slaves used work songs on the plantations exactly as they had used them before they were taken prisoner and sold. Just as rhythm and repetition exist in African textile patterns, art objects, music, and dance, they were also prevalent in work habits. Music and song helped move the work along. *Work songs* lessened the monotony of robotic movements and repeated strokes, and they inspired the workers. This was a cultural response that produced expedience, which was very valuable when employed on a plantation. An additional advantage was achieved when a slow worker needed encouragement. These songs kept everyone working together, helped prevent injuries, and prevented slow workers from being singled out for punishment.

These traditions carried over to the work songs of Texas prisoners and railroad workers, also called Gandy Dancers: "Gandy" from the name of the company that produced the tools, and "Dancers" from the workers' rhythmic movements. In almost the same way that the cultural traditions continued, so did the conditions of African Americans: from slavery, to sharecroppers, to second-class citizens, to the segregated disenfranchised.

"Go Down, Old Hannah" is a prison work song with music and lyrics by Huddie "Leadbelly" Ledbetter. It was recorded by Alan Lomax at the Sugar Land prison in Fort Bend County, Texas. The Brazos River, mentioned in the lyrics below, was the location of state prison farms, and the reference to the year 1910 relates to the days of the convict lease system. In addition, Old Hannah is a pseudonym for the sun.

GO DOWN, OLD HANNAH[5]

Go down Old Hannah, well, well, well!
Doncha rise no more.
If you rise in the mornin',
Bring Judgment Day.

You ought come on this Brazos
Nineteen and ten,
They was workin' women
Like they do the men.

Well, I looked at Old Hannah,
She was turnin' red,
And I looked at my partner,
He was almost dead.

So go down, Old Hannah, well, well, well!
Doncha rise no mo',
If you rise in the mornin'
Set the world on fire.

Praise Song

A lot of praise songs, or spirituals as they are more appropriately called, tell about victories. Examples include "Didn't My Lord Deliver Daniel," "Go Down, Moses," "Joshua Fought the Battle of Jericho," "Wade in the Water," and "I Ain't Goin't Study War No More," better known as "Down by the Riverside."

DOWN BY THE RIVERSIDE[6]

Goin' to lay down my sword and shield,
Down by the riverside,
Down by the riverside,
Down by the riverside.
Goin' to lay down my sword and shield,
Down by the riverside,
To study war no more.

Chorus
I ain't goin't study war no more,
Ain't goin't study war no more
Ain't goin't study war no more. (*Repeat*)

Love Songs

This early love song, "Hesh Little Baby," began as a lullaby sung by a father to his little baby, but in later years was used for hand-clapping games and as a children's jump rope chant. It conveys the attitude that no matter what happened, Papa could fix it. Many African American males were denied an opportunity to be responsible for their families during and after slavery. Some psychologists believe the paternalistic nature of the slaveholding system, separating fathers from families, transferring all responsibility to the landowners and slave masters, foreshadowed the welfare system of entitlements and absentee fathers.

HESH, LITTLE BABY[7]

Hesh, little baby, don't say a word,
Papa's gonna buy you a mockin'bird.

If that mockin'bird won't sing,
Papa's gonna buy you a diamond ring.

If that diamond ring turns brass,
Papa's gonna buy you a lookin' glass.

If that lookin' glass gits broke,
Papa's gonna buy you a horse and yoke.

If that horse and yoke fall over,
Papa's gonna buy you a dog named Rover.

And if that dog named Rover won't bark,
Papa's gonna buy you a horse and cart.

If that horse and cart don't pull,
Papa's gonna buy you a baby bull.

And if that baby bull falls down,
You'll be the cutest little baby in town.

Another love song, "Careless Love," was popularized by many blues singers, from Leadbelly to Bessie Smith.

CARELESS LOVE[8]

(*Chorus*)
Love, o love, o careless love,
Love, o love, o careless love,
Love, o love, o careless love,
Cain't ya see whut love hez done to me?

(*Verse*)
I love my mammy an' my pappy too.
I love my mammy an' my pappy too.
I love my mammy an' my pappy too.
Gonne leave 'em both an' go wid you.

(*Chorus*)

Dance Rhyme

To prevent communication across distances, slaves were forbidden from playing drums. It must have angered overseers to hear Africans speaking their native language for fear they might be communicating something else forbidden. Nevertheless, some form of physical relief and mental reprieve was essential after the harsh work and living conditions the enslaved were required to endure. Dance might have sufficed to relieve some physical anxieties, but required extra energy from tired souls and for most slaves didn't occur with any regularity. Fortunately, the rich cultural heritage of Africans enabled them to combine music, storytelling, and dance motions. Keeping rhythm without instruments required ingenuity. To improvise, they patted various parts of the body and made instruments from available resources like rib bones, hollow logs, gourds, and makeshift string instruments. Over time banjo players, percussionists, and fiddlers evolved.

When one patted the body to accompany a song, he or she was said to "pat juba." Singing, patting, and beating to the juba "in a tattoo upon the ground with the feet and simultaneously executing a graceful dance"[9] works to great effect at the end of the play *Jumpin' Juba;* our audiences have never tired of this simple wedding celebration and dance. The following poems are examples of music that might have employed patting juba.

JUMP JIM CROW[10]

Git fus upon yo heel,
An' den upon yo toe;
An' ebry time you tu'n 'round,
You jump Jim Crow.

Now fall upon yo knees,
Jump up an' bow low;
An' ebry time you tu'n 'round,
You jump Jim Crow.

Put yo' han's upon yo hips,
Bow low to yo beau;
An' eb'ry time you tu'n 'round,
You jump Jim Crow.

It needs to be re-emphasized here that while some may find these lyrics full of clown antics and too comical to be intelligent, if one takes into account the times, the need for entertainment, the transformation of traditional culture, these lyrics may be likened to modern poetry or even rapping.

Different verses are added to these rhymes as time goes forth and as they are transported from region to region. When writing *Jumpin' Juba*, the original lyrics of "Juba" could not be found and I took the liberty, as a poet, to compose some verses of my own. But, for the record, here are the verses offered by Thomas W. Talley from his book *Negro Folk Rhymes*, a jewel of a book written with a special perspective, as he was born the son of former slaves and was reared in the culture he studied.

JUBA[11]

Juba dis, an' Juba dat,
Juba skin dat Yaller Cat. Juba! Juba!

Juba jump an' Juba sing.
Juba cut dat Pigeon's Wing. Juba! Juba!

Juba, kick off Juba's shoe.
Juba, dance dat Jubal Jew. Juba! Juba!

256   APPENDIX

Juba, whirl dat foot about.
Juba, blow dat candle out. Juba! Juba!

Juba, circle, Raise de Latch.
Juba do dat Long Dog Scratch. Juba! Juba!

Activity Directions

Try putting yourself in the times and circumstances of the slavery days and compose one of these calls. You can decide whether to do a yell or holler, a cry or call. You don't have to call or sing it aloud, but it can have a special meaning just for you, yourself. Try to imagine what it was like "in dem days."

Left in Africa were families, ancestors, material possessions, and everything familiar. What was transported to the New World with the Africans was what they had inside their heads and hearts—their folkways, their cultural traditions, their stories, and their music. Ultimately, these cultural traditions and folkways—the *inevitables*—were what survived and, like cultural traditions everywhere, were and are ever changing to meet the challenges of new environments, new technology, attitudes and beliefs.

Christmas at Varner-Hogg: Patton Plantation Memories

VOCABULARY

anticipate—to look forward to

big house—home of plantation master and family; the place of authority

boil down—process for reducing the juice of sugar cane

Christmas gif'—a surprise game played by slaves. When two people met for the first time on Christmas Day, the first to call out "Christmas gif'!" was the winner of a small present to be supplied by the loser.[12]

field slave—a slave who worked in the fields

heap—a lot of, as in "a heap of trouble"

house slave—a slave who worked in the big house

make sugar—the process of boiling sugar cane juice until it thickens into a syrup

mock—to imitate

pacify—to soothe or to settle

parboil—to boil briefly before baking to help tenderize

possum—a small mammal eaten as a food supplement by the enslaved

sold—the transfer of slaves as property from one owner to another

summon—to call to a meeting; to send for

sweet potatoes—a sweet, yellow, edible root vegetable

tone—the quality of sound that indicates mood or attitude

FOOD ACTIVITIES

These cooking activities may require adult or teacher assistance.

Cornmeal Pancakes

1½ c. yellow cornmeal

1½ tsp. salt

1½ c. boiling water

¾ c. flour

1 T. baking powder

2 eggs

3 T. honey or molasses

1 c. milk

3 T. melted butter

Mix cornmeal with salt and stir in boiling water. Let stand while you assemble other ingredients. Sift flour and baking powder together. Beat eggs and mix with honey, milk, and melted butter. Mix liquid ingredients with cornmeal mixture. Stir in flour and baking powder. Pour onto hot, lightly oiled griddle.

Look for bubbles to form throughout batter and the edges to harden before flipping cakes.

Tip: Put a dishtowel on the cookie sheet. As you complete 3–4 pancakes, place them on the towel in a single layer and keep them warm in the oven. Keep doing this until you complete the whole batch. (If you run out of room on the cookie sheet, drape another towel over the first layer of pancakes and start a second layer.) Then serve. Yield: 12–16 pancakes.

Make a special sauce for the pancakes by heating together a cup of blueberries, ¼ cup sugar, 1 teaspoon cornstarch, 1 tablespoon lemon juice, and about ¼ cup water, depending on the consistency you desire. These pancakes are also excellent with maple syrup or molasses as topping.

Sweet Potato Chips

3 to 4 sweet potatoes (red skin)
vegetable oil spray
cookie sheet

Scrub sweet potatoes to remove any soil. Slice, in rounds, very thin. Spray cookie sheet with vegetable oil. Lay rounds on sheet and spray the tops. Place in preheated 350-degree oven and bake until crisp. Make several batches and store in airtight plastic. Have a Southern tea party with chamomile tea and sweet potato chips.

Chamomile Tea (1 serving)

1 c. water
1 t. dried chamomile flowers
lemon juice
honey

Bring the water to a boil in a saucepan. Sprinkle the flowers onto the water and boil for a further half-minute with the saucepan lid on. Remove from heat and stand for another minute. Remove flowers by pouring the tea through a strainer into a pretty teapot. Serve with honey and a little lemon juice.

WORD FINDS

Use the blank example word find to make a word find of your own, or you may fill in the empty squares of the example word find with letters to camouflage the vocabulary words. A blank grid is just an example of how small or how extensive you can make a word find. The vocabulary words for any of these plays can be used in a word find.

HISTORY OF THE EX-SLAVE NARRATIVES

During the 1930s, America experienced the Great Depression and out of the desperation of those troubling times the Works Progress Administration (WPA) was born. It employed writers and journalists, among others, to create

Blank Word Find

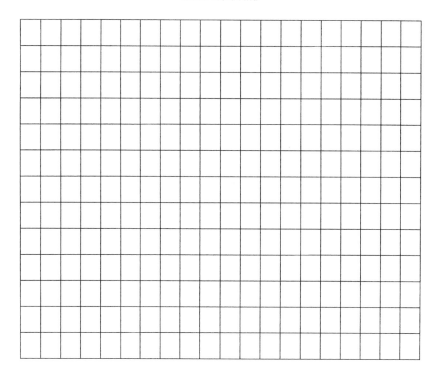

some lasting projects, including the oral history recordings of over 2,300 ex-slaves, many of whom were born in the last years of the Civil War. This project has become known as the WPA Ex-Slave Narratives. Even today there is not a more significant source of information for plantation life, family trials, spiritual inspiration, resistance, running away, work roles, and relationships than these stories from the mouths of America's four million slaves.

The Library of Congress Web site provides an opportunity to read a sample of these narratives, and to see some of the photographs taken at the time of the interviews.[13] The entire collection of narratives can be found in *The American Slave: A Composite Autobiography,* edited by George P. Rawick.[14] Many libraries have these books in their reference section and a reference librarian will be helpful in locating them.

For an example of the WPA narratives, consider the following excerpt from Sarah Ford, an ex-slave from the Patton Plantation, which later became the Varner-Hogg Plantation:

Word Find Example

											P	A	R	B	O	I	L
N	E	W	Y	E	A	R	S				A						
					N						C						
S	W	E	E	T	P	O	T	A	T	O	I		F				
					I	M	I	T	A	T	E	F		I		P	
					C						H	I	R	E	D	O	
			B	I	G	H	O	U	S	E	Y		L		S		
			A	P					O	A			D		S		
			B	A					L	P			U				
			Y	T	O	N	E		D					M	O	C	K
			E														

Us don't have much singin' on our place, 'cepting at church on Sunday. Law me, de folks what works in de fields feels more like cryin' at night. Us chillen used to sing dis:

Where you gon', buzzard,
Where you gwine to go?
I's goin' down to new ground,
For to hunt Jim Crow.

De overseer was Uncle Big Jake, what's black like de rest of us, but he so mean 'spect de devil done make him overseer down below long time ago. Dat de bad part of Massa Charles, cause he lets Uncle Jake whip de slaves so much and some like my papa what had spirit was all de time runnin' 'way. And even doe your stomach be full, and does you have plenty clothes, dat bullwhip on your bare hide make you forgit de good part and dat's de truth.[15]

CROSSWORD PUZZLE
Christmas at Varner-Hogg

Across:

1. The transfer of slaves as property from one owner to another
3. To imitate
6. A sweet, yellow edible root vegetable
9. To look forward to
11. Worked in the big house
12. Worked in the fields
13. Home of plantation master and family; the place of authority
15. A small mammal eaten as a food supplement by the enslaved

Down:

1. To call to a meeting; to send for
2. Process of boiling sugar cane juice until it thickens into a syrup and crystallizes
4. A game
5. The quality of sound that indicates mood or attitude
7. To boil briefly before baking to help tenderize
8. Process of reducing the juice of sugar cane
10. To soothe or to settle
14. A lot of

Slave clothes were meager. Many times they wore hand-me-downs from the big house, or clothes homemade from homespun materials or feed and seed sacks. The best of soul food was served at rare slave gatherings, which could include wild game like baked possums with sweet potatoes, squirrels, fried chicken, pork chitterlings, greens with ham hocks, crackling cornbread, okra gumbo, jelly cakes, and, in Texas, pecan pies made with molasses. This "Hoe Cake an' Hominy" rhyme says it all:

Hoe cake an' hominy
Pass dem collahd greens.
Spill dat gravy ovuh me—

Lak fo' tas'e dem beans.
Stomach 'low mah th'oat done cut,
Bin so long 'tween meals,
Jes' could eat dat whole ham butt,
Dat's de way I feels.
C'on pones, I lubs yuh so,
Yams, you is my frien's,
Bacon rin's, come on, le's go!
Hope dis nevuh ends.[16]

Some do not like to be reminded of the language in these rhymes because it appears unintelligent, but if you consider the times, you will find the wisdom locked inside these meager lyrics comical, though often serious.

Folk Songs and Tales

Among the most important distinctive cultural forms in the quarters were folk songs and tales. In some instances these have received less attention than the spirituals, but were equally important expressions—about work and punishment, lovers and longings, hopes and fears—that relate to the reality of oppression. In these songs and tales one could be what he was not allowed to be: proud, courageous, and defiant. Rebels and runaways were heralded as heroes and heroines, mocking cruel masters and stupid patrollers. The Reverend John Long wrote that Maryland slaves sometimes sang:

William Rino sold Henry Silvers;
Hilo! Hilo!
Sold him to de Gorgy trader;
Hilo! Hilo!
His wife she cried, and children bawled,
Hilo! Hilo!
Sold him to de Gorgy trader:
Hilo! Hilo![17]

Frederick Douglass recorded one song indicative of the slave's sense of the planter's oppression:

We raise de wheat,
Dey gib us de corn;
We bake de bread,

Dey gib us de cruss;
We sif de meal,
Dey giv us de huss;
We peel de meat,
Dey gib us de skin;
And dat's de way
Dey takes us in.[18]

PART II: FAMILY BREAKUP

Arcy Makes Room for Judith Martin: The Breakup of a Slave Family

VOCABULARY

acre—a measure of land

bed tick—the fabric case of a mattress

cabin—a small, simple one-story house

card—an instrument for combing cotton fibers; the process of combing cotton fibers

cart—a small, wheeled vehicle; can be pulled by a horse or donkey

coo—a soft, low sound

corn shucks—the green covering of the cereal grass or yellow vegetable

creek—a stream smaller than a river and larger than a brook

grind—to reduce to small particles with a machine by turning a crank

hiring out—temporary use of enslaved labor for which the owner is paid

import—to bring in from another country or place

mercy—a blessing resulting from divine favor or compassion; compassion shown to victims of misfortune

molasses—the thick brown syrup that is separated from raw sugar in the sugar-making process

much obliged—to very much appreciate a favor

petition—make an earnest request; a formal written request made to an authority

reckon—suppose; guess; think

rosemary—a plant, the leaves of which are used as a seasoning

sacrifice—to accept loss or destruction for a cause or ideal

sew—to unite or fasten with stitches by a needle or machine

spinning wheel—a small machine for making thread or yarn

spin—to draw out fiber and twist into thread

wagon sheet—large piece of fabric used on a covered wagon

weave—the process of making threads into fabric

wilderness—an uncultivated and uninhabited region; a forest

OTHER SUGGESTED ACTIVITIES

Practice weaving with a piece of cardboard and some yarn.

Name ten things made of cotton in thirty seconds.

Name and locate the parts of a shirt: sleeve, yoke, front, back, cuff, buttons, and buttonholes.

Plant an herb garden using rosemary, parsley, sage, basil, and thyme.

Study the impact of the cotton gin on the growth of slavery in the south.

COTTON SONGS

The following cotton songs excerpts, printed with the permission of Folkways Music Publishers, Inc., are by the beloved American composer Huddie "Leadbelly" Ledbetter, who was born in Louisiana and also lived in Texas.[19]

COTTON FIELDS

When I was a little baby
My mother would rock me in the cradle
In them old, old cotton fields at home. (*Repeat twice*)

Chorus
When them cotton bolls get rotten
You couldn't pick very much cotton
In them old cotton fields at home,
It was down in Lou'siana
Just a mile from Texarkana,
In them old cotton fields at home.

CROSSWORD PUZZLE
Arcy Makes Room for Judith Martin

Across:

3. Mattress
5. A plant used as a seasoning
9. To reduce to small particles
10. Small one-story house
15. A small machine for making thread
18. A small stream
19. To accept a loss for an ideal
20. Small, wheeled vehicle
21. Long-bodied limbless reptile
22. Finely ground and sifted meal of a grain

Down:

1. To unite or fasten by stitches
2. Dish of meat and vegetables served in gravy
4. Seeds of a cereal grass
6. To twist fiber into thread
7. Measure of land
8. An uncultivated forest
11. Pail; an object for carrying something
12. Thick brown syrup
13. To bring in from another country or place
14. Temporary use of labor
16. To make threads into fabric
17. To suppose; guess; think

BOLL WEEVIL

Farmer said to the boll weevil,
"Yes I wish you well,"
He said to the boll weevil,
"I hope you burn in hell."

Boll weevil said to the farmer,
"I'm gonna treat you mean,
When I get through with your cotton,
You buy no gasoline."

BRING ME LI'L WATER, SYLVIE

Bring me li'l water, Sylvie,
Bring me li'l water now.
Bring me li'l water, Sylvie,
Ev'ry li'l once in a while.

A Little Slave for Sale—Cheap!

The study of this play and the following activities satisfy requirements of Texas Essential Knowledge and Skills (TEKS): 113.23 Social Studies, Grade 7; 113.6 Social Studies, Grade 4.

PRODUCTION NOTES
Time Period

Think about how life differed for all people living in the nineteenth century, including but not limited to: electricity; transportation; indoor plumbing; social life; racism; entertainment; family structure; food; health care and disease; life span; work roles and occupations; gender roles; economics; international politics. Take yourself out of the present and put yourself into the times and the culture of the play, in front of the T.&S. Gibbs general store in Huntsville, Texas, on a hot day in 1853.

Characterization

Remember, characterization is more important than skin color when casting parts in plays. Experiment with diversity and relax gender casting. Everything about time and timing was different in the nineteenth century. Most people didn't wear watches and did not talk fast. Black people did not look white people in the eye because this was considered disrespectful. They needed permission to speak; obedience was essential, and they had better keep working. The enslaved could be imprisoned or killed for any reason at any time and could not testify against whites in court. Marriage wasn't always sanctioned and people were often sold away from their families for economic reasons.

McKell was an alcoholic and could not be trusted. His slaves were afraid of him. Jeff, the boy enslaved, never smiles, is noticeably sad and scared, has no lines, and only leaves the stage to say goodbye to his mother, Aunt Big Kitty, who is overcome with sadness and grief. Sam Houston is a hero and should be portrayed as a larger-than-life character. There is a marked contrast between Jeff Hamilton, the little boy, and Jeff Hamilton, the emancipated storyteller. As an adult, Jeff is dressed like a well-to-do gentleman, and has considerable pride, integrity, and respect for Sam Houston.

Props and Costuming

JAMES MCKELL: hat, stick or pointer, and vest or coat

JEFF HAMILTON, the boy: barefoot, no shirt, rope around neck, another rope used to hold up his pants

JEFF HAMILTON, the adult: hat, coat, nice shirt

GENERAL SAM HOUSTON: white beard, hat, coat, cane

AUNT BIG KITTY: apron, head wrapped

CROWD of onlookers: early-nineteenth-century period clothing

MR. MORELAND: hat, vest, watch

Two **WHITE BOYS** who tease Jeff: may wear caps and plaid shirts

Two **BIDDERS:** may wear hats

Two **COMMENTATORS:** hats, vests, plaid shirts

DISCUSSION QUESTIONS

Why do we study history?

What makes history relevant for today?

Why was America so torn during the nineteenth century?

Have we recovered from slavery and the Civil War?

What was Jeff feeling while he was on the auction block?

Why was Jeff being sold? Did he ever get his freedom?

What happened to his family?

What kind of man was Sam Houston? Why did he buy Jeff?

Why was slavery abolished?

Did the discrimination of slavery contribute to racism against African Americans today?

ADDITIONAL DISCUSSION TOPICS

How did the economic structures of the North and South play a part in stimulating the Civil War?

What were the dynamics of family separation?

Compare the following cultural aspects of life in the nineteenth century to those of life in the twenty-first century: work roles; clothing; food and folkways, including celebrations and accompanying music.

Explain the similarities and differences in these slave celebrations: hoedowns, corn shuckings, cotton and cane harvests, and log rolling celebrations.

Explain how a jumping the broom wedding differs from modern weddings. Do people still jump the broom? What does jumping the broom symbolize?

Explore the evolution of terms and names for African Americans.

Did the lifestyles and culture of the participants in the play cause them to have different values than we have today?

VOCABULARY

Use a dictionary to define the following words.

apron	creditor	runt
auction	dicker	sale, sell, sold
bid, bidder	enslaved	separate
bill of sale	field hand	slave
buggy	general store	slave block
cabin	hoe	slavery
commentator	narrator	two-bits
cotton sack	pallet	younguns
courthouse square	property	

ADDITIONAL RESOURCES
Books for Grades 3 and Up (Ages 9-12)
Nightjohn by Gary Paulsen
Pink and Say by Patricia Palacco
Christmas in the Big House, Christmas in the Quarters by Patricia McKissack
Sarah and the Freedom Quilt by Deborah Hopkinson
The People Could Fly by Virginia Hamilton

Books for Middle and High School (Ages 13-18)
Slave Dancer by Paula Fox
Black Hands, White Sails: The Story of African American Whalers by Patricia C. McKissack and Frederick L. McKissack
Wolf by the Ears by Ann Rinaldi
Rebels Against Slavery: American Slave Revolts by Patricia C. McKissack and Fredrick L. McKissack
The Autobiography of Jane Pittman by Ernest Gaines

Research References
I Am Annie Mae: An Extraordinary Black Texas Woman by Annie Mae Hunt and Ruthe Winegarten
I Am Annie Mae: The Musical by Naomi Carrier and Ruthe Winegarten
From Slavery to Freedom: A History of African Americans by John Hope Franklin and Alfred A. Moss, Jr.
An Empire for Slavery: The Peculiar Institution in Texas, 1821–1865 by Randolph B. Campbell
Twelve Years a Slave by Solomon Northup
Incidents in the Life of a Slave Girl by Harriet Jacobs
In Search of the Promised Land: A Slave Family in the Old South by John Hope Franklin and Loren Schweninger
Black Texans: A History of African Americans in Texas, 1528–1995 by Alwyn Barr
The Slave Community by John W. Blassingame
Slave Testimony: Two Centuries of Letters, Speeches, Interviews, and Autobiographies by John W. Blassingame, editor
Voices from Slavery: 100 Authentic Slave Narratives by Norman R. Yetman, editor
American Negro Slave Revolts by Herbert Aptheker

A Documentary History of the Negro in the United States by Herbert Aptheker
Denmark Vesey by David Robinson

Legislation

1998 — Underground Railroad Network to Freedom Act

2001 — HCR 245 enacted by 77th Texas Legislature, by Naomi Carrier and
Allen Grundy, for study of the resistance movement of enslaved from
Texas to Mexico

1820 — The Missouri Compromise

1857 — *Dred Scott v. Sandford* legal case. The Supreme Court ruled that no
person of African descent, slave or free, could be granted citizenship and
therefore was not able to sue in a federal court. This case also overturned
the Missouri Compromise of 1820.

Audio

Steal Away: Songs of the Underground Railroad by Kim and Reggie Harris
Wade in the Water: African American Spirituals, The Concert Tradition by
Various Artists
The Long Road to Freedom: An Anthology of Black Music by Various Artists

Suggested Films (Parental Permission Advised)

Nightjohn
The Autobiography of Miss Jane Pittman
Roots, The Miniseries
A Woman Called Moses
Africans in America, film for public television
P.O.V.: Traces of the Trade, film for public television

Sweet By and By: Barrington Farm Chronicle

TEXAS HISTORY TIMELINE FOR ANNEXATION AND STATEHOOD, 1845

March 1 — U.S. Congress passes the Joint Resolution for Annexing Texas to
the United States.

July 1 — The Texas Constitutional Convention votes to accept the United
States annexation proposal; it drafts an annexation ordinance and state
constitution to submit to the voters of Texas.

October 13—Texas voters overwhelmingly approve annexation, the new
state constitution, and the annexation ordinance.

December 29—The U.S. Congress approves, and President James K. Polk
signs the Joint Resolution for the Admission of the State of Texas into the
Union. Texas becomes the twenty-eighth state.

TIMELINE ACTIVITY

Make a timeline for the following important events. Discuss their relevance
for Texas annexation.

Le Code Noir as established in the Louisiana Territory
Missouri Compromise of 1820
The decision in the case of *Dred Scott v. Sandford*
The Compromise of 1850 and the Fugitive Slave Act
Anthony Burns's capture and release
The Kansas-Nebraska Act

VOCABULARY

Use a dictionary to define the following words.

annexation	harvest	overseer
burden	homegoin	property
Congress	independence	republic
cradle	manage	statehood

HYMNS OF DELIVERANCE

Hymns of deliverance, like "Sweet By and By," were prevalent during and
after slavery. As you'll see in the below example, "Go Down, Moses," the recurring refrain is, "Let my people go."

When Israel was in Egypt's land,
Let my people go;
Oppressed so hard they could not stand,
Let my people go.

Refrain
Go down, Moses, way down in Egypt's land;
Tell ole Pharaoh
Let my people go.

"Thus saith the Lord," bold Moses said,
Let my people go;
If not, I'll smite your first-born dead,
Let my people go.

(Repeat refrain.)

No more shall they in bondage toil,
Let my people go;
Let them come out with Egypt's spoil,
Let my people go.[20]

(Repeat refrain.)

So much of the imagery and ideas that the slave singers used came from the Christian Bible. "There is great strength in the assurance" that an oppressed people may internalize when they believe "they are the children of destiny."[21]

Embedded within the lyrics of other deliverance hymns are numerous references to "the river," to "warfare," to "the battlefield," and the laying down of a "sword and shield." These recurring images also help to distill the delayed gratification that was a part of "hell on earth" and the need to look forward to the "pearly gates," where they would receive "a robe." The "over yonder, after while" psychology not only helped the enslaved to cope with the trials and tribulations of slavery, it was an emotional adjustment that continued through several generations of sharecroppers, through Jim Crow segregation, even into the civil rights movement of the 1960s, due to the long-delayed justice and broken promises that not even legislation could correct. Many of these songs may be found in church hymnals, including the near extinct *Gospel Pearls*.

Other Hymns of Deliverance

SWEET BY AND BY

In the sweet (in the sweet) by and by, (by and by)
We shall meet on that beautiful shore; (by and by)
In the sweet (in the sweet) by and by, (by and by)
We shall meet on that beautiful shore.

Questions

In this song, what does "by and by" refer to?
Do you think the enslaved had different feelings about death than what
    people do today? Describe.
Could the constant reference to water in these songs have anything to do
    with the Middle Passage and the yearning to go back to Africa?

DOWN BY THE RIVERSIDE

Gonna lay down my burdens (down by)
Down by the riverside (down by)
Down by the riverside (down by)
Down by the riverside (down by)
Gonna lay down my burdens (down by)
Down by the riverside (down by)
To study war no more.
I ain't goin' t'study war no more,
ain't goin' t'study war no more,
ain't goin' t'study war no more-ore-ore.
I ain't goin' t'study war no more
Ain't goin' t'study war no more
Ain't goin' t'study war no more.

Questions

To what war does this song refer?
Does the composer see himself or herself as a soldier?
What does the riverside symbolize?
Has there been a victory?
Compare slavery to a war from the perspective of the enslaved.

GLORY, GLORY HALLELUJAH

Glory, glory hallelujah
Since I laid my burden down;
Glory, glory hallelujah
Since I laid my burden down.

Fighting on, hallelujah!
We are almost down to de shore.
Fighting on, hallelujah!
We are almost down to de shore.

Questions

What does "hallelujah" mean and why is there a constant reference to it?
To what does "burden" refer?
What does "down to de shore" mean?

"Deep River"

The reference to a river deserves some special mention. Howard Thurman wrote that "Deep River" "is the most intellectual of all the spirituals because it thinks of life in terms of a river." He goes further to point out that not only does life flow like a river but that it has a "simple beginning" and gathers more water along the way in its "process" toward the sea. He continues the analogy with an explanation of how "a river has times of drought and times of flood," using examples of rainfall, rocks, and graduated channels through which it flows. He completes his analogy with "the goal of the river is the sea" where the river answers its call.[22]

DEEP RIVER

Deep River, my home is over Jordan;
Deep River, my home is over Jordan.
O don't you want to go to that Gospel Feast
That Promised Land where all is Peace?
Deep River, I want to cross over into camp ground.

Activity and Questions

Locate the Jordan River mentioned in the Old Testament of the Bible.

Is the Jordan River mentioned in any other spirituals?

What do you think "cross over" means, and why is the final destination a "camp ground"?

"Joshua Fought the Battle of Jericho"

This song deserves special mention here because it not only shows how the enslaved equated their condition to that of soldiers in a war zone — on the battlefield fighting for freedom — it especially shows how much the enslaved identified with the persecution of the Israelites. This biblical symbolism is also shared with the lyrics of other songs, i.e., "Go Down Moses," "Rocka My Soul in de Bosom of Abraham," "Didn't My Lord Deliver Daniel," and "Jacob's Ladder." In the following lyrics, the word "fought" has been changed to "fit."

JOSHUA FOUGHT THE BATTLE OF JERICHO

Refrain
Joshua fit de battle ob Jericho
Jericho
Jericho
Joshua fit de battle ob Jericho
an' de walls cam' a tumblin' down.

Verse 1
You can talk about ye' man ob Gideon,
You can talk about ye' man ob Saul,
Dere's none like good ol' Joshua
an' de battle ob Jericho.

Refrain

Verse 2
When the chillun of Israel begin to march
Seven times roun' an' roun'
Ol' Joshua commanded de sun to stan' still
An' de sun did never go down dat mornin'

Refrain

Other Traditional

Here are some other songs that may be included in this study.
"Wade in the Water"
"Roll, Jordan, Roll"
"I'm On de Battlefield"
"Good News, de Chariot's Comin'"
"Great Day"

PART III: RUNNING AWAY

Arcy Attempts Escape

VOCABULARY

buenos días — Spanish for "good day" or "good morning"

buenos noches — Spanish for "good evening" or "good night"

buenos tardes — Spanish for "good afternoon," meaning after twelve o'clock midday

compadre — Spanish for friend or partner

cowhide — made of leather; a coarse whip of braided cowhide

gall — nerve; audacity

hasten — to move or act quickly

hesitate — to pause; hold back

independent — showing self reliance and personal freedom; not requiring or relying on something else or somebody else

mira — Spanish word meaning to look; pay attention

oblige — to do a favor for or do something as a favor

por favor — Spanish for please

render — to give to another; to cause to be

risk — exposure to possible loss or injury

señora — the Spanish equivalent of Mrs., a married woman

señorita — the Spanish equivalent of Miss, an unmarried woman

señor — the Spanish equivalent of Mr.

sí, amigo — Spanish for "yes, friend"

suspicious — inclined to suspect; mistrust; doubt

vaya con Dios — Spanish phrase meaning "go with God"

wench — a female servant

QUESTIONS

Is it important to learn to speak another language?
How prevalent is the Spanish language in Texas?
Do you know any Spanish phrases?
What was Arcy trying to get Father Muldoon to do?
Why did she think he would help her? Was she unrealistic?
What was the Mexican government's position on slavery?
Did the colonists agree or disagree with the Mexican government? Why or
  why not?
What would you have done in Arcy's situation?
How important was the Catholic religion in the prohibition of slavery?
Why was it against the law for blacks to learn to read and write?
Did anyone get a public education during slavery?

MAKE A SPANISH WORD FIND

Create a Spanish word find. You may need a Spanish-English dictionary.

Fugitives of Passion: On the Texas Underground Railroad to Mexico

VOCABULARY

abolish—to do away with
abolitionist—one who seeks to do away with something; working
  against slavery
annexation—process of attaching as an addition
approach—to move nearer to
axe—a chopping or cutting tool with sharp-edged head
beckon—to summon or signal
bolt—to move suddenly as in a fright or hurry
caucus—a meeting to decide upon policies
cautiously—carefully
clearing—a tract of land cleared of wood and brush
embrace—to hug
conductor—a leader of slaves on the Underground Railroad
hostage—a person taken by force to secure the taker's demands
mortgage—a transfer of rights to a piece of property

	Spanish Word	English Word (best translation)
1.		
2.		
3.		
4.		
5.		
6.		
7.		
8.		
9.		
10.		
11.		
12.		
13.		
14.		
15.		
16.		
17.		
18.		
19.		
20.		

peering—looking intently or curiously

praise grove—a secret place in the woods where slaves met to have church or other meetings

Underground Railroad—a secret network for conveying slaves to freedom

whuppin—same as whipping; a technique often employed for punishing slaves

wild game—animals hunted for sport or food

QUESTIONS

Why was Cudjo being sold?

Why was Hannah so late arriving at the praise grove?

What was a praise grove?

Why was Little Prince afraid?

What questions did Prince ask his mother?

Did Hannah want to be free?

Why did she hesitate to leave with Cudjo?

Do you believe Cudjo would have left without her?

What would have happened to Cudjo and Hannah if they had gotten caught without a traveler's pass?

What was it that Hannah wanted Prince to know before she left?

Why couldn't she take him with her?

On what condition did Miz Havlacek give Cudjo and Hannah some food?

Where was Miz Havlacek's husband?

How would you have liked for this story to end?

How did the bounty hunters spot Cudjo and Hannah?

ADDITIONAL RESOURCE

Harriet Tubman: Conductor on the Underground Railroad by Ann Petry

CROSSWORD PUZZLE

Fugitives of Passion

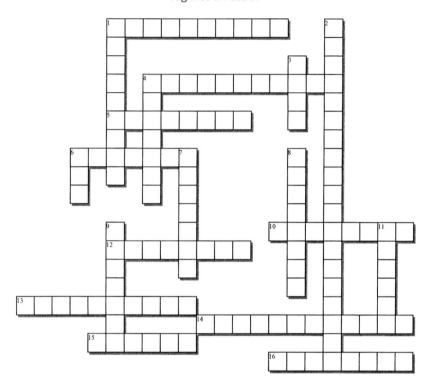

Across:

1. Carefully
4. A secret place in the woods where slaves met
5. A tract of land free of wood and brush
6. To do away with
10. To move nearer to
12. A transfer of property rights
13. Process of attaching as an addition
14. One who seeks to do away with something
15. To summon or signal
16. Animals hunted for sport or food

Down:

1. A leader of slaves on the Underground Railroad
2. A secret network for conveying slaves to freedom
3. To move suddenly as in a fright or hurry
4. Looking intently or curiously
6. A chopping or cutting tool with sharp-edged head
7. A person taken by force to secure the taker's demands
8. A technique often employed to punish or control slaves
9. To hug; an encircling with the arms
11. A meeting to decide upon policies

PART IV: BATTLES

Hell or High Water: Brit Bailey Heads Off Stephen F. Austin

VOCABULARY

buckskin—the skin of a buck

cakewalk—a dance with a high prance and backward tilt

clear—to remove wood and brush from land

clever—showing skill or resourcefulness

decorated—adorned

discreet—showing good judgment

fiddler—player of the violin

fiends—wicked or cruel persons

firewater—intoxicating liquor

frolics—parties; dances; celebrations

gunpowder—an explosive powder used in guns

harvest—the season for gathering crops

holster—leather case for a firearm

homestead—the home and land occupied by a family

ledger—a book showing money collected and due

ma'am—respectful form of address for a woman

meticulous—extremely careful with details

mount—to seat oneself for riding

musket—a heavy, large, shoulder firearm

powder horn—a pouch for storing and carrying gunpowder

quadrille—a square dance

singed—scorched on the outside to the point of removing hair

sir—respectful form of address for a man

suit—to please

FILL IN THE BLANKS

Work in teams to create sentences with blanks that could be filled with the vocabulary words. Allow the members of different teams to trade sentences and have a contest.

CROSSWORD PUZZLE
Hell or High Water

Across:

3. A book showing money collected and due
5. Adorned
7. Respectful form of address for a man
9. To seat oneself for riding
10. The home and land occupied by a family
13. A dance with a high prance and backward tilt
14. To please
15. Intoxicating liquor
16. Leather case for a firearm
17. To remove wood and brush from land
18. Player of the violin
19. The season for gathering crops
20. Scorched on the outside

Down:

1. A pouch for storing and carrying gunpowder
2. Wicked or cruel persons
4. Showing good judgment
6. An explosive powder used in guns
8. The skin of a buck
9. A heavy, large, shoulder firearm
11. A square dance
12. Extremely careful with details
13. Showing skill or resourcefulness
15. Parties; dances; celebrations

QUESTIONS

In what way do you think Brit Bailey and Bubba were friends?
In what way were they not friends? How did slavery affect relationships?
Read about the life of Stephen F. Austin. Why did he settle in Texas?
Why were settlers attracted to Texas?
What were the difficulties of being a pioneer?
Write a short story in which you and your family are journeying to Texas in
the 1820s. Describe how you travel, what items you bring with you, the
people and the animals, and what your priorities are upon arrival.

Still Am A'Risin': The Battle of Velasco and the Vigil at Bolivar

VOCABULARY

ammunition—explosives used in guns and warfare
auction block—place for public sale of slaves to the highest bidder
chain gang—a gang of slaves or convicts chained together
companion—an intimate friend
crop—something that can be harvested; the yield at harvest
descendant—proceeding from an ancestor
jug—a large, deep container with a narrow mouth
lame—having a disabled limb that restricts movement
land grant—legal right to ownership of property
mission—a place where a church carries out its work
outlaw—a lawless person
overseer—supervisor; inspector
petticoat—a skirt worn under a dress
quarters—slave lodgings
reputation—overall quality of character as judged by people
scavenger—person or animal that collects, eats, and disposes of trash
  or waste
schooner—a rigged sailing ship
throne—the chair of a high dignitary; royal power
venture—an undertaking involving chance or risks
vigil—a time of keeping awake when sleep is customary; keeping
  watch

CROSSWORD PUZZLE
Still Am A'Risin'

Across:

2. A gang of slaves or convicts chained together
4. A large, deep container with a narrow mouth
6. A skirt worn under a dress
9. A time of keeping awake when sleep is customary; keeping watch
10. Having a disabled limb that restricts movement
11. A place where a church carries out its work
15. A legal right to ownership of property
16. Slave lodgings
18. Proceeding from an ancestor
19. Supervisor; inspector

Down:

1. A lawless person
3. Place for public sale of slaves to the highest bidder
5. An intimate friend
7. The chair of high dignitary; royal power
8. Explosives used in guns and warfare
9. An undertaking involving chance or risks
12. A rigged sailing ship
13. Overall quality of character as judged by people
14. Something that can be harvested; the yield at harvest
17. A person or animal that collects, eats, and disposes of trash or waste

QUESTIONS

Was Kian happy with her position as a slave?

What was her real name and who gave it to her?

What were Bubba's views on being enslaved?

How were Bubba's and Kian's relationships to their masters similar? How were they different?

What are the differences in Brit Bailey's and Stephen F. Austin's personalities?

Is Jane Long sensitive to Kian?

What is the occasion that brings these five persons together?
Who were some of the other early Texas heroes that visited Mrs. Long's inn?
How did Mrs. Long's inn differ from today's hotels? How are they similar?
What was the reason for the Battle of Velasco?

PART V: CIVIL WAR

Plantation Liendo: Civil War Reenactment

VOCABULARY

blockade—the isolation of a place by troops or ships

body servant—a personal servant for a soldier

bushwhacker—one given to ambush or waiting to attack by surprise

commander—one who gives the orders; leader; chief

commission—a warrant granting certain powers and imposing certain duties

conscious—aware; known or felt by one's inner self

dismiss—to send away; put aside or out of mind

distract—to draw one's attention or mind to a different object

enliven—to give life, action, or spirit to

flyboy—an enslaved child whose job was to fan flies away from food or people

fumble—to grope about clumsily

gawk—to stare stupidly

grieve—to feel sorrow

guerilla—one who engages in irregular warfare

incomparable—beyond comparison

inconspicuous—not readily noticeable

inoffensive—safe

juba—a dance performed by the enslaved that involved patting different parts of the body to music

knapsack—a bag strapped on the back for carrying supplies

literacy—ability to read and write

monument—a lasting reminder of a person or event

potential—capable of becoming actual

CROSSWORD PUZZLE
Plantation Liendo

Across:

2. Leader; chief; one who gives the orders
3. An enclosure for confinement or defense
6. A lasting reminder of a person or event
9. Ability to read and write
10. Eyeglasses
14. Newly enlisted member of the armed forces
15. To give life, action, or spirit to
16. One given to ambush or waiting to attack by surprise
20. To feel sorrow
21. An enslaved child whose job was to fan flies away from food or people
24. Capable of becoming actual
25. Aware; known or felt by one's inner self
26. To grope about clumsily
27. To show respect

Down:

1. To stare stupidly
2. A warrant granting certain powers and imposing certain duties
4. A personal servant for a soldier
5. One who engages in irregular warfare
7. Beyond comparison
8. The isolation of a place by troops or ships
11. A first performance
12. A dance performed by the enslaved that involved patting different parts of the body to music or singing
13. To draw one's attention or mind to a different object
17. A play that acts out a significant historical event
18. Safe
19. To lie in wait for
22. A bag strapped on the back for carrying supplies
23. To send away; put aside or out of mind

premiere—a first performance
recruit—newly enlisted member of the armed forces
reenactment—a play that acts out a significant historical event
salute—to show respect
spectacles—eyeglasses
stockade—an enclosure for confinement or defense
waylay—to lie in wait for; to attack from ambush

RESEARCH THE FOLLOWING TEXAS CIVIL WAR EVENTS

Battle at Nueces or The Nueces Massacre, March 1862
Great Hanging at Gainesville, October 1862
Battle of Palmito Ranch, "The Last Battle of The War," May 12–13, 1865

Cane Cutter Country: The Saga of the Lake Jackson Plantation

VOCABULARY SET 1

Put the following words in *ascending* alphabetical order, then use a dictionary to define them.

inherit	distill	intervene
birthright	clutch	civility
cane	extract	fetch
devastating	eternity	hogshead
composure	lard	innards
disrupt	bicker	lashing
conciliatory	corruption	joshing
cross	illegitimate	procedures
action	visibly	ladle
daybreak	exertion	ironic
barrel	authoritarian	liable

VOCABULARY SET 2

Put the following words in *descending* alphabetical order, then use a dictionary to define them.

reprimand	rampant	mason
perish	replica	stethoscope
stalk	livestock	subdue
martyr	saccharine	sugar mill
consumption	saddle	summon
optimism	cooper	suspicion
passel	sarcastic	tuberculosis
cadence	sickle	unruly
plot	cultivate	will
pulse		

TOPICS FOR DISCUSSION AND FURTHER RESEARCH

Study the process of making sugar during the antebellum period in Texas.
Research the uprisings of Nat Turner and Denmark Vesey.
Were the whites justified in being afraid of the Negroes?
Were there any uprisings in Texas? In Louisiana?

WAR SONGS TRIVIA

The African American Civil War Museum and Memorial in Washington D.C. is a recognized authority on the involvement of African Americans in the Civil War. According to their information "209,145 United States Colored Troops (USCT) served in the Civil War," on both sides of the war, and on the front lines and behind the scenes. In the South, there was a constant vigilance against black uprisings especially after the loss of so many white men. The control they once had over African Americans began slipping away. So entrenched was the fear among whites that ex-slaves would turn against them that more than a few blacks were murdered unjustifiably. However, "in East Texas and in the river bottom plantations the Negroes remained peaceful." It is not known from whom this next song sprang, whites or "blacks humorously calculating to throw a scare into whites."[23]

CROSSWORD PUZZLE
Cane Cutter Country No. 1

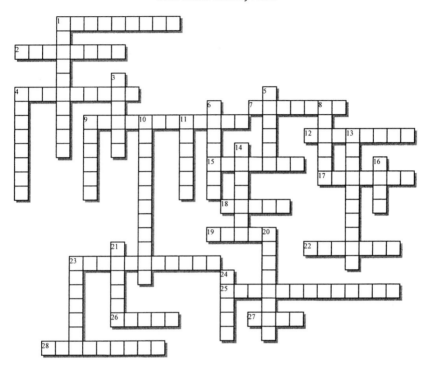

Across:

1. To encourage the growth of crops
2. Forever
4. Calmness
7. To purify a liquid
9. That which brings into agreement
12. Dawn; the first sign of light that follows night
15. The internal organs of a human being or animal
17. To draw out
18. Marked by a bad temper
19. To go after
22. Stroking with a whip; attacking verbally
23. Bringing to ruin, chaos, or helplessness
25. Favoring the principle of blind obedience to authority
26. A deep-bowled, long-handled spoon used to take up liquids
27. A tall woody grass or reed, like sugarcane
28. To come between in order to stop, settle, or modify

Down:

1. Characterized by evil; morally degenerate
3. Expressing the opposite of what one really means
4. Politeness, courtesy
5. To engage in a petty quarrel or argument
6. Teasing; joking
8. Likely; apt
9. To grasp with the hand
10. Born of unmarried parents
11. Combat; battle
13. Possession to which one is entitled by birth; inheritance
14. To receive from one's ancestors
16. A soft, white fat obtained from fatty tissue of the hog
20. A barrel
21. A round, bulging cask with flat ends of equal diameter
23. To interrupt; break apart; throw into disorder
24. A skilled worker who builds with stone, brick, or concrete

CROSSWORD PUZZLE
Cane Cutter Country No. 2

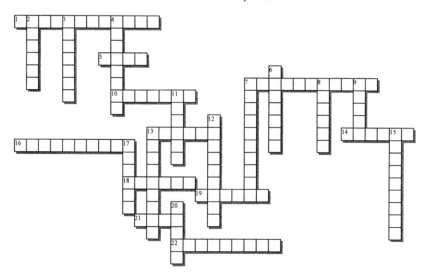

Across:

1. A disease affecting the lungs
5. A legal document declaring to whom one's possessions are to go after death
7. An instrument used to listen to sounds in the body
10. Use of cutting remarks; ironic criticism
13. Padded leather-covered seat for a rider on horseback
14. To be destroyed or ruined; to die
16. A series or steps followed in a regular order
18. A person who makes a great sacrifice for the sake of a principle
19. A large number
21. A secret scheme or plan
22. Farm animals kept for use and profit

Down:

2. Not submissive to rule or restraint
3. Unchecked in growth or spread
4. Anticipating the best possible outcome of actions or events
6. An exact reproduction
7. A white compound used as an artificial sweetener
8. A cutting tool with a curved metal blade and short handle
9. Rhythmical beating caused by contractions of the heart
11. To bring under control
12. A severe reproof; can result in punishment
13. Place where sugar is processed; factory
15. The act of suspecting something wrong without proof
17. A call to a meeting
20. A plant stem

NIGGERS AM A'RISIN'

Go tell Aunt Jane, go tell ever'body,
Go tell Aunt Jane the niggers am a'risin'.
Go tell Aunt Jane, go tell ever'one,
Go tell Aunt Jane the niggers am a'risin'.

Run get your shotgun, run get your rifle,
Run tell the white folks the niggers am a'risin'.
Run get your shotgun, run get your rifle,
Run tell the white folks the niggers am a'risin'.

Hitch up the team, load up the wagon,
Run tell the sheriff the niggers am a'risin'.
Hitch up the team, load up the wagon,
Run tell the sheriff the niggers am a'risin'.

PART VI: EMANCIPATION

Slav'ry Chain Done Broke At Las'

FREEDOM SONGS

Compare the freedom songs of slavery to the freedom songs of the civil rights movement. Were any of these songs used to celebrate both?

The songs of the civil rights movement are referred to as freedom songs. Songs expressing freedom from slavery have been called hymns of deliverance.

"Oh, Freedom!"[24] is an example of a song that was first sung by the enslaved and sang again, one hundred years later, during the civil rights movement.

Oh, freedom! Oh, freedom!
Oh, freedom over me!
An' befo' I'd be a slave,
I'll be buried in my grave,
An' go home to my Lord an' be free.

But as songs come and go, "Slav'ry Chain"[25] is not remembered as a civil rights song:

(*Refrain*)
Slav'ry chain done broke at las',
Broke at las', broke at las',
Slav'ry chain done broke at las',
Goin' to praise God til I die.

(*Solo*)
'Way up in-a dat valley,
Prayin' on my knees;
Telling God about my troubles,
An' to he'p me if-a He please.

(*Repeat refrain.*)

I did tell Him how I suffer in de dungeon an' de chain;
An' de days I went wif head bowed down, an' my broken flesh an' pain.
   But brethren,

(*Repeat refrain.*)

I did know my Jesus heard me 'cause de spirit spoke to me
An' said "Rise my child, your chillum an' you too shall be free."

(*Repeat refrain.*)

Ironically, the Voting Rights Act of 1965 occurred exactly one hundred years after the Emancipation Proclamation. The enduring freedom song of the civil rights movement is "We Shall Overcome," by Zilphia Horton, Frank Hamilton, Guy Carawan, and Pete Seeger, from 1960. It began as a gospel hymn and union song, but was transformed by its four composers into the rallying cry of the black freedom movement for civil rights. The lyrics indicate that there was yet much work to be done:

   If in our hearts we do believe,
   We shall overcome someday.

SONG TRIVIA

The nation lost between 618,000 and 700,000 men during the Civil War. Of that number, 258,000 were from the South and 17,000 were from Texas. Few families went unscathed. Francis Abernethy wrote that "shadows cast by the Civil War still linger on the American landscape," and many "songs of sadness in eulogy for lost sons" were written. One of these begs to be mentioned here.[26]

ONE VACANT CHAIR

We shall meet but we shall miss him,
There will be one vacant chair;
We shall linger to caress him,
When we say our ev'ning pray'r.

When a year ago we gathered,
Joy was in his mild blue eye,
But a golden chord's been severed,
And our hopes in ruin lie.

We shall meet but we shall miss him,
There will be one vacant chair,
We shall linger to caress him,
When we say our ev'ning pray'r.

At our fireside, sad and lonely
Often will the bosom swell
At remembrance of the story,
How our noble brother fell;
How he strove to bear our banner
Through the thickest of the fight,
And uphold the Southland's honor
With the strength of manhood's might.

VOCABULARY

broke—forced apart; abruptly changed
broken—separated; torn open
camp meeting—outdoor religious gathering
camphor—medicine made from evergreen tree
Emancipation Proclamation—an order issued by President Abraham Lincoln to free the slaves
emancipation—setting free; liberation; delivering from slavery
enslaved—to make a slave of
freedom—unrestricted; state of being free; independent
hoe—tool used for gardening; long handled implement used for loosening the earth around plants

loosen his hide—whip; punish

overseer—supervisor; boss

praise grove—a secret place in the woods where meetings, religious
   or otherwise were held

promised land—heaven; a place where slavery would be no more

schooling—education

slav'ry chain—the state of being enslaved

years—over time

yonder—over there; somewhere distant

QUESTIONS

What freedoms did slavery prohibit?

What is the meaning of delayed gratification?

Why did the praise grove have to be a secret place? Why couldn't the
   enslaved worship out in the open?

Were worship services for the enslaved allowed?

CRAFT IDEA

Make paper chains. Place them around your neck, arms, and ankles. Connect
yourself to another person and practice walking.

WORD FIND

Create a word find using the vocabulary words. You may use this blank word
grid.

Porch Politics: Sam Houston Style

VOCABULARY

abstain—to refrain from an action or practice; to quit

coachman—man who drives a coach or carriage

Confederacy—the eleven southern states that seceded from the
   United States in 1860 and 1861

confederate—to unite in a confederacy

Blank Word Find

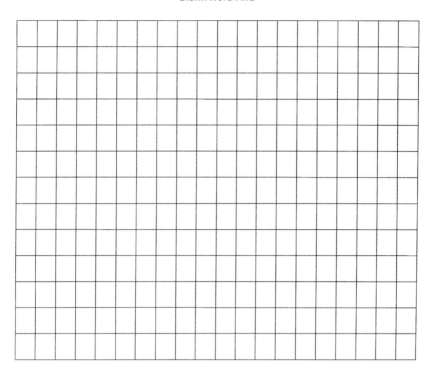

consumption—tuberculosis; a disease where the body progressively wastes away

designate—to appoint and set apart for a special purpose

free papers—documents declaring one to be emancipated

handkerchief—a small cloth used for personal purposes

impeccable—faultless; not capable of wrong doing

journal—a brief account of daily events

mulatto—a person of mixed white and black ancestry

negotiate—to confer with another to arrive at the settlement of some matter

preliminary—something that precedes or introduces the main business or event

promoter—one who advances or contributes to growth or prosperity

quill—pen made from a large, stiff feather

repress—to restrain; suppress or exclude from consciousness

CROSSWORD PUZZLE
Porch Politics

Across:

1. Man who drives a coach or carriage
3. Something that precedes or introduces the main business of event
5. One who advances or contributes to growth or prosperity of
8. To appoint and set apart for a special purpose
9. Payment for labor or services
10. A brief account of daily events
12. To restrain, suppress, or exclude from consciousness
13. To refrain from an action or practice; to quit
15. A native or inhabitant of northeastern United States
17. To unite in a confederacy
18. Faultless; not capable of wrong doing
19. A small cloth used for personal purposes

Down:

1. Progressive bodily wasting away; tuberculosis
2. Documents declaring one to be emancipated
4. Withdraw to form an organized body
6. A person of mixed white and black ancestry
7. To confer with another; to arrive at the settlement of some matter
11. Act of withdrawing from something dangerous or difficult
14. A horse-drawn coach that runs regularly between stations
16. Pen made from a large, stiff feather

retreat—to withdraw from something dangerous or difficult

secession—the act of withdrawing from an organized body

stagecoach—a horse-drawn coach that runs regularly between
stations

Union—adherence to the policy of a firm federal union before or during the Civil War; what the northern states were sometimes called

wages—payment for labor or services according to a contract

Yankee—a native or inhabitant of the northeastern United States

MAP QUEST

Locate these places known to Sam Houston on a United States
map: Alabama, Austin, Canada, Galveston, Houston, Huntsville,
Independence, Mexico, Tennessee, and Washington D.C.

Which of these places can be located on a Texas map?

Find these rivers: Rio Grande River, Mississippi River, Brazos River, and the
Colorado River.

Where did Stephen F. Austin settle his colony? Why?

North America consists of what three countries?

PART VII: RECONSTRUCTION

Social Politics in Victorian Texas: A Living History Interpretation of African Americans and Their Responsibilities

VOCABULARY

apron—a garment worn to protect the clothes

arthritis—inflammation of the joints

blacksmith—one who forges iron to make tools

boxcar—a roofed freight car; part of a train

churn—the process for making butter

confront—to challenge; oppose

deed—a document or contract for legal transfer

doilies—a small decorative mat

embroidery—decorative designs with needlework

herd—a group of animals

influence—to effect the condition or development of
kluckers—members of the Ku Klux Klan
Ku Klux Klan—a white supremacy organization
ledger—a book showing money collected and due
magistrate—an official administrator of laws
muse—to be absorbed in thought
parlor—a room for receiving guests
pester—to harass; to bother
plow—to break up and turn over soil
preoccupied—to have one's attention already absorbed
quadrille—a square dance
Reconstruction—historical period after the United States Civil War
sentimental—influenced by tender feelings
study—a room for reading and writing; office
supper—the evening meal

Juneteenth at the George Ranch

VOCABULARY
grave—a place in the earth for burial
handkerchief—a small piece of cloth used like a Kleenex
issue—a point of debate or controversy
jubilation—rejoicing
meditate—to think deeply about
shackles—something that confines the arms or legs to prevent free
    physical movement
youngster—a young person; child

GAMES
Drop the Handkerchief
All participants form a circle. One person, It, skips around the circle teasing everyone, while the others chant the rhyme printed below and clap. On the last "drop, handkerchief, drop" the It person finally drops the handkerchief behind his chosen one. The chosen one picks up the handkerchief and chases It, while It runs clockwise around the circle to get into the chosen one's place.

CROSSWORD PUZZLE
Social Politics in Victorian Texas

Across:

4. A square dance
6. Education
9. An official administrator of laws
11. A room for reading and writing; similar to an office
13. To be absorbed in thought
15. A group of animals
16. Decorative designs with needlework
18. The process for making butter
19. To break up and turn over soil
20. To have one's attention already absorbed
23. The evening meal
24. To challenge; oppose
25. Small decorative mat

Down:

1. A county officer charged with the execution of the law and the preservation of order
2. Members of the Ku Klux Klan
3. White supremacy organization
5. A roofed freight car; part of a train
7. A room for receiving guests
8. Influenced by tender feelings
10. To affect the condition or development of
12. Historical U.S. era from 1865 to 1877
14. To harass; to bother
17. Inflammation of the joints
21. A garment to protect the clothes
22. A document or contract for legal transfer

If caught and tagged, It goes to jail. Then the new It skips around the circle to choose behind whom It will drop the handkerchief.

I lost my handkerchief yesterday
I found it today
All full of rainwash
I dashed it away.
So, drop, handkerchief, drop
Drop, handkerchief, drop
Drop, handkerchief, drop

Guessing Game

Think of one of the vocabulary words. Tell your partner if you are thinking of a person, place, or thing. Give three clues. Whoever guesses what is being meditated about is the winner. Then it is the winner's turn to think of an object and give three clues.

Jump Rope Chants

The folk rhymes suggested here may or may not date back to slavery. However, the tradition of folk rhymes was quite prevalent during that time, as were simple games like hand-clapping and rope-jumping. The same rhymes could be used to accompany either. When I taught early childhood music classes, as well as classes with older students, these games never ceased to provide fun and laughter. Any of the following rhymes can be used for hand-clapping or rope-jumping games, and may have been enjoyed during early Juneteenth celebrations.

MISS MARY MACK, MACK, MACK

Miss Mary Mack, Mack, Mack
All dressed in black, black, black
With silver buttons, buttons, buttons
All down her back, back, back
She asked her mother, mother, mother
For fifteen cents, cents, cents
To see the elephant, elephant, elephant

Jump the fence, fence, fence
He jumped so high, high, high
He touched the sky, sky, sky
And he never came back, back, back
Til the fourth of July, July, July!

MISS LUCY HAD A BABY

Miss Lucy had a baby, his name was Tiny Tim,
She put him in the bathtub to see if he could swim.
He drank up all the water, he ate up all the soap,
He tried to eat the bathtub, but it wouldn't go down his throat.
Miss Lucy called the doctor, Miss Lucy called the nurse,
Miss Lucy called the lady with the alligator purse.
Mumps said the doctor, Measles said the nurse,
Nothing said the lady with the alligator purse.
Miss Lucy kicked the doctor, Miss Lucy hit the nurse,
And then she paid the lady with the alligator purse.

LAST NIGHT AND THE NIGHT BEFORE

Last night and the night before
Twenty-four robbers at my door.
I got up to let them in
Hit 'em on the head with a rollin pin.

RECIPES

Juneteenth is as much about food as any celebration. I hope you enjoy these soul food recipes and will share them with others.

Ham Hocks and Collard Greens[27]

The collard is a variety of kale native to the southeastern United States.

9 lbs. collard greens
salted cold water
6 medium smoked ham hocks
crushed red pepper

Slice the leaves off stalks of 9 lbs. of collard greens. Wash the leaves thoroughly in salted cold water to remove the sand. (Usually two or three such washings are required.) Rinse in unsalted water. Cut leaves across into three slices and soak for at least one hour.

Rinse 6 medium-sized smoked ham hocks. Place in three quarts of water. Sprinkle with crushed red pepper or two fresh hot peppers.

Cover and cook for 2½ hours. Mix lightly once or twice so that all cooks evenly.

Cornbread, Alabama Style[28]

2 c. white cornmeal

1 T. sugar

1 t. salt

2 t. baking powder

2 eggs

2½ c. milk or buttermilk

2 T. drippings or shortening

Put cornmeal, sugar, salt, and baking powder into mixing bowl. Add eggs and milk. Melt drippings or shortening in baking pan. Stir into batter. Pour batter into pan and bake 20–25 minutes at 450 degrees.

Sweet Potato Pie, Southern Style[29]

1½ lbs. sweet potatoes (or 2 large potatoes)

2 t. vanilla

1 t. cinnamon

2 c. sugar

½ t. nutmeg

¼ lb. butter

4 slightly beaten eggs

pie crust (prepare ahead; recipe follows)

Boil sweet potatoes in jackets until tender. Drain. Remove skin and mash with butter. Combine sugar, vanilla, cinnamon, nutmeg, and eggs. Beat for 5 minutes. Pour into pie crust. Bake in 350-degree oven for 45 minutes, or until knife inserted in center comes out clean. Makes one 9-inch pie.

Pie Crust

2 c. sifted flour

⅔ c. shortening

1 t. salt

½ t. sugar

1 t. vinegar

pinch baking powder

cold water

Sift flour, sugar, salt, and baking powder. Add shortening. Cut in with fork or use pastry blender. Pour the vinegar and water into the flour mixture a few drops at a time, mixing with a fork until it holds together. Chill. Roll out as quickly as possible. Makes a double crust for one 9-inch pie or two pie shells.

Crossword Puzzle Answer Keys

Christmas at Varner-Hogg

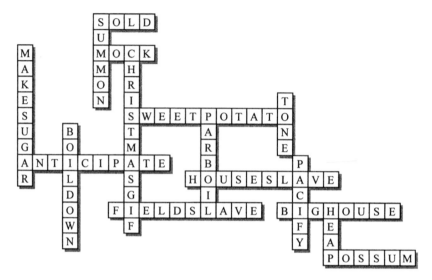

Arcy Makes Room for Judith Martin

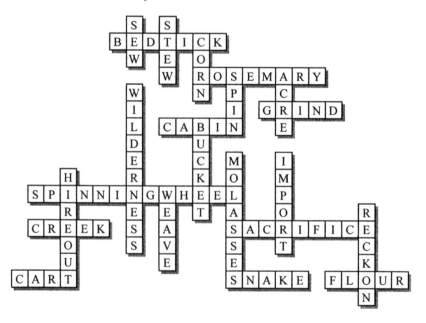

Fugitives of Passion

Hell or High Water

Still Am A'Risin'

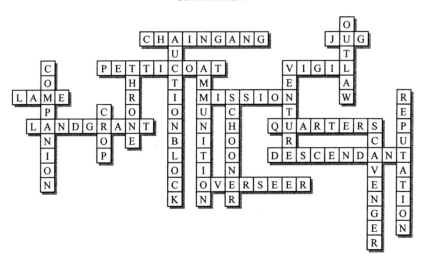

Plantation Liendo

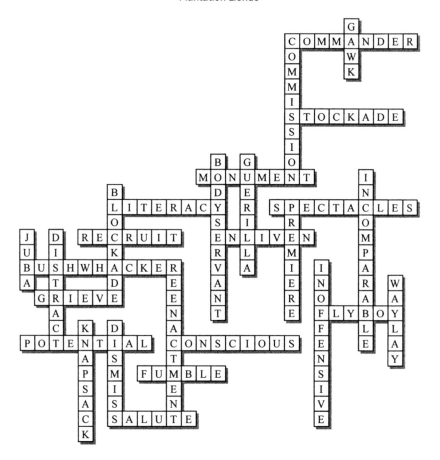

Cane Cutter Country No. 1

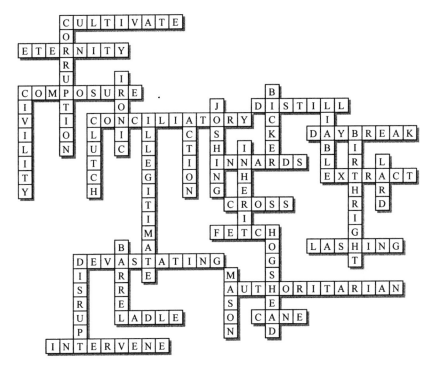

Cane Cutter Country No. 2

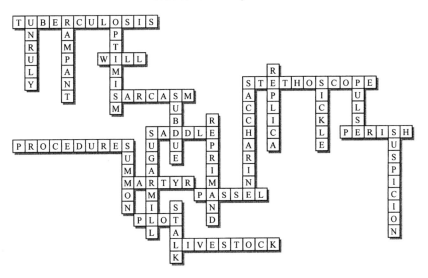

Social Politics in Victorian Texas

NOTES

PART I

1. Randolph B. Campbell, *An Empire for Slavery: The Peculiar Institution in Texas 1821–1865*. (Baton Rouge: Louisiana State University Press, 1989), 254.

2. Ibid., 121.

3. Eugene D. Genovese, *Roll, Jordan, Roll: The World the Slaves Made* (New York: Vintage Books, 1976), 315.

4. John W. Blassingame, *The Slave Community: Plantation Life in the Antebellum South* (New York: Oxford University Press, 1979), 117–118.

5. Genovese, *Roll, Jordan, Roll*, 316.

6. Ibid., 316.

7. Ibid., 320.

8. Kenneth M. Stampp, *The Peculiar Institution* (Toronto: Alfred A. Knopf, 1956), 368.

9. Blassingame, *The Slave Community*, 165.

10. Ron Tyler and Lawrence R. Murphy, eds., *The Slave Narratives of Texas* (Austin: State House Press, 1997), 113.

11. Ibid., 114.

12. Campbell, *An Empire for Slavery*, 158.

13. John Langstaff, *What a Morning! The Christmas Story in Black Spirituals* (New York: Margaret K. McElderry, 1987), 11.

14. Patricia C. and Fredrick L. McKissack, *Christmas in the Big House, Christmas in the Quarters* (New York: Scholastic, 1994), 30–31; Charlemae Hill Rollins, *Christmas Gif'* (New York: Morrow, 1993), xvii.

15. Ibid., 27

16. Ibid., 40

17. Ibid., 32; Langstaff, *What a Morning!*, 15.

PART II

1. John Hope Franklin and Alfred A. Moss, Jr., *From Slavery to Freedom: A History of African Americans*, 8th ed. (McGraw Hill, 2000), 133.

2. Ibid., 156.

3. Ibid., 157.

4. Deborah Gray White, *Ar'n't I a Woman?: Female Slaves in the Plantation South* (New York: W. W. Norton & Company, 1999), 145.

5. Franklin and Moss, *From Slavery to Freedom*, 132–133.

6. Michael Moore, "Peter Martin: A Stockraiser of the Republic Period," in *Black Cowboys of Texas*, ed. Sarah Massey (College Station: Texas A&M University Press, 2000), 40.

7. Ibid., 41.

8. Ibid.

9. Campbell, *An Empire for Slavery*, 111.

10. Michael Moore, "Settlers, Slaves, Sharecroppers and Stockhands: A Texas Plantation Ranch, 1824–1896" (master's thesis, University of Houston, 2001), 183.

11. Moore, "Peter Martin," 43.

12. Bryanna Leigh-Anne Marie O'Mara, "Museums and Controversy," (B.A. thesis, Baylor University, August 2007), 57.

13. Anson Jones valedictory speech, February 19, 1846. Archives and Information Services Division, Texas State Library and Archives Commission; Anson Jones papers, Archive Collections, Center for American History, University of Texas at Austin.

PART III

1. Aaron Mahr Yáñez, "The UGRR on the Rio Grande," CRM 4, 1998.

2. Patricia C. McKissack and Fredrick L. McKissack, *Black Hands, White Sails: The Story of African American Whalers* (New York: Scholastic Press, 1999), xvii.

3. Ibid., xviii.

4. Campbell, *An Empire for Slavery*, 218–219.

5. National Park Service, *Underground Railroad: Special Resource Study* (Washington D.C.: 1990).

6. "The National Underground Network to Freedom Program," National Parks Conservation Association, http://www.npca.org/cultural_diversity/black_history/NTF_facts.html (accessed March 25, 2009).

7. Ronnie C. Tyler, "The Callahan Expedition of 1855: Indians or Negroes?" *Southwestern Historical Quarterly* 70, no. 4 (April 1967); Ronnie C. Tyler, "Fugitive Slaves in Mexico," *Journal of Negro History* 57, no. 1 (January 1972).

8. Ibid.

9. Tyler, "The Callahan Expedition of 1855," 574–575.

10. Mahr, "The UGRR on the Rio Grande"; Tyler, "The Callahan Expedition of 1855," 579–582.

11. Herbert C. Aptheker, *American Negro Slave Revolts,* 5th ed. (New York: International Publishers, 1983).

12. "Born in Slavery: Slave Narratives from the Federal Writers' Project, 1936–1938," Manuscript Division, Library of Congress, http://memory.loc.gov/ammem/snhtml/snhome.html (accessed February 12, 2009).

13. Ibid.

14. Ibid.

PART IV

1. Peggy Smith, "Brit Bailey Talk," (lecture, January, 3, 1956); James Britton Bailey Papers, Brazoria County Historical Museum, Angleton, Texas.

2. Ibid.

3. Ibid.

4. J. Mason Brewer, *Dog Ghosts and Other Texas Negro Folk Tales* (Austin: University of Texas Press, 1958), 123.

5. Gregg Cantrell, *Stephen F. Austin: Empresario of Texas* (New Haven: Yale University Press, 1999), 9.

PART V

1. Rosa Groce Bertleth, "Jared Ellison Groce," *Southwestern Historical Quarterly Online* 20, no. 4, http://www.tsha.utexas.edu/publications/journals/shq/online/v020/n4/contrib_DIVL5212.html.

2. E. L. Blair, *Early History of Grimes County* (Austin: 1930), 84–85.

3. Ibid., 84–85.

4. Lester G. Bugbee, "The Old Three Hundred," *Texas Historical Association Quarterly,* I, 108–113.

5. Campbell, *An Empire for Slavery*, 14.

6. Eugene C. Barker, *The Life of Stephen F. Austin;* Eugene C. Barker, *Mexico and Texas, 1821–1835;* The *Handbook of Texas Online* (accessed March 8, 2008).

7. Bertleth, "Jared Ellison Groce."

8. "A History of Waller County, Texas," Waller County Historical Survey Committee, 1973.

9. Randolph B. Campbell, *An Empire for Slavery: The Peculiar Institution in Texas 1821–1865* (Baton Rouge: Louisiana State University Press, 1989), 274.

10. Barbara Karkabi, *Houston Chronicle*, June 30, 2002.

11. Joan Few, principal investigator, *Final Report of Research and Excavation at the Lake Jackson State Archeological Landmark, Lake Jackson, Texas, 41BO172, Between 1991 and 1996, Under Antiquities Permit 1072*, special report prepared for the Texas Historical Commission, Department of Antiquities Protection, December 1, 1996.

12. Abner J. Strobel, *The Old Plantations and Their Owners of Brazoria County* (Houston, 1926; rev. ed., Houston: Bowman and Ross, 1930; rpt., Austin: Shelby, 1980).

13. Few, *Final Report*.

14. Ibid.

15. Ibid.

16. Ibid.

17. Ibid.

18. Campbell, *An Empire for Slavery*.

PART VI

1. Clyde McQueen, *Black Churches of Texas* (College Station: Texas A&M University Press, 2000), 10–11.

2. Doris Hollis Pemberton, *Juneteenth at Comanche Crossing* (Austin: Eakin Publications, 1983), 54.

3. Ibid., 54.

4. Randolph B. Campbell, *An Empire for Slavery: The Peculiar Institution in Texas, 1821–1865* (Baton Rouge: Louisiana State University Press, 1989), 65–66.

5. Ibid., 219.

6. Jeff Hamilton and Lenoir Hunt, *My Master: The Inside Story of Sam Houston and His Times* (Dallas: Manfred Van Nort & Co., 1992), 99–100.

7. "Civil War Journal: The Conflict Begins," History Channel. http://americancivil war.com/tl/tl1862.html (accessed February 12, 2009).

8. Allen C. Guelzo, *Lincoln's Emancipation Proclamation: The End of Slavery in America* (New York: Simon & Schuster, 2004), 22.

9. Abraham Lincoln, "Emancipation Proclamation," September 22, 1862 (Washington, D.C.: National Archives and Records Administration).

10. Guelzo, *Lincoln's Emancipation Proclamation*, 184.

11. Isabel Boyd, *Slave Narratives Federal Writers' Project, 1936–1938, Texas Narratives*, Volume XVI, Part 1. Library of Congress, 115. http://memory.loc.gov/ammem/snhtml/snhome.html (accessed February 12, 2009).

12. Austin Grant, *Texas Narratives*, Volume XVI, Part 2, 85.

13. Dorothy Sterling, ed., *The Trouble They Seen: Black People Tell the Story of Reconstruction* (Garden City: Doubleday & Company, 1976), 29.

14. Ibid., 30.

15. Ibid., 30–34.

16. Ibid., 43–46.

17. James M. Smallwood, Barry A. Crouch, and Larry Peacock, *Murder and Mayhem: The War of Reconstruction in Texas* (College Station: Texas A&M University Press, 2003), 3.

18. William Watkins, *Texas Narratives*, Volume XVI, Part 4, 141–142. http://memory.loc.gov/ammem/snhtml/snhome.html.

19. Ibid., 103.

20. Abner J. Strobel, *The Old Plantations and Their Owners of Brazoria County* (Houston, 1926; rev. ed., Houston, Bowman and Ross, 1930; rpt., Austin: Shelby, 1980), 60–62.

21. Ibid., dedication page.

22. R. Nathaniel Dett, Mus.D, ed. *Religious Folk-Songs of the Negro as Sung at Hampton Institute.* (Hampton: Hampton Institute Press, 1927), 112.

23. Ibid., 27.

PART VII

1. Howard N. Meyer, *The Amendment that Refused to Die: Equality and Justice Deferred, A History of the Fourteenth Amendment* (Lanham: Madison Books, 2000), 46–47.

2. Guelzo, *Lincoln's Emancipation Proclamation*, 236.

3. Robert Perkinson, *Texas Tough: The Rise of a Prison Empire* (New York: Henry Holt and Company, forthcoming).

4. Thad Sitton and James H. Conrad, *Freedom Colonies: Independent Black Texans in the Time of Jim Crow* (Austin: University of Texas Press, 2005), 12; James Smallwood, *Time of Hope, Time of Despair: Black Texans during Reconstruction* (London: Kennikat, 1981), 55; *New Handbook of Texas,* "Black Codes," I: 562.

5. Barry A. Crouch, *The Freedmen's Bureau and Black Texans* (Austin: University of Texas Press, 1992), 65.

6. Sitton and Conrad, *Freedom Colonies,* 3.

7. Herman Wright, Jr., http://www.thelongblackline.org.

8. Ibid., 172; J. Mason Brewer, "Negro Legislators in Texas." (Dallas: Mathis Publishing Co., 1935), 110.

9. Pauline Yelderman, *The Jay Birds of Fort Bend County,* 48-49.

10. Ibid., 95-96.

11. Ibid., 100.

12. Ibid., 99-103.

13. Sitton and Conrad, *Freedom Colonies,* 1.

14. Ibid.

APPENDIX

1. Jacqueline L. Tobin and Raymond G. Dobard, *Hidden in Plain View: A Secret Story of Quilts and the Underground Railroad* (New York: Knopf Publishing Group, 2000).

2. Harold Courlander, *A Treasury of Afro-American Folklore* (New York: Marlowe and Company, 1996), 509.

3. "Slave Work Song," the Colonial Williamsburg Foundation, http://www.cwf.org/history/teaching/enewsletter/volume2/september03/primsource.cfm.

4. Moses Asch and Alan Lomax, eds., *The Leadbelly Songbook* (Oak Publications, 1962), 56.

5. Asch and Lomax, *The Leadbelly Songbook,* 50; Lomax, *The Folk Songs of North America,* 536-537.

6. "Down by the Riverside," Clarence C. Wright, arr., *Lift Every Voice and Sing II: An African American Hymnal* (New York: Church Pension Fund, 1993), 210.

7. Henry D. Spalding, ed., *Encyclopedia of Black Folklore and Humor* (Middle Village: Jonathan David Publishers, 1972), 242.

8. Ibid., 243.

9. Ibid., 235-236.

10. Ibid., 11.

11. Ibid., 7–8.

12. Rollins, *Christmas Gif'*.

13. "The African-American Mosaic: The Library of Congress Resource Guide for the Study of Black History and Culture," the Library of Congress, http://www.loc.gov/exhibits/african/afam015.html.

14. Bruce Fort, "American Slave Narratives: An Online Anthology," University of Virginia, http://xroads.virginia.edu/~HYPER/WPA/wpahome.html; George P. Rawick, ed., *The American Slave: A Composite Autobiography* (Westport, Conn.: Greenwood Press, 1972–1979).

15. Library of Congress, "Sarah Ford," *Born in Slavery: Slave Narratives from the Federal Writers' Project, 1936–1938*, vol. XVI, *Texas Narratives*.

16. Spalding, *Encyclopedia of Black Folklore and Humor*, 294.

17. Ibid., 114–116.

18. Frederick Douglass, *My Bondage and My Freedom*, 1853, 253

19. Asch and Lomax, *The Leadbelly Songbook*; Lomax, *The Folk Songs of North America*, 533.

20. Howard Thurman, *Deep River: Reflections of the Religious Insight of Certain of the Negro Spirituals* (New York: Harper & Brothers, 1955), 13.

21. Ibid., 12–13.

22. Ibid., 66–73.

23. Francis Edward Abernethy, *Singin' Texas* (Denton: University of North Texas Press, 1983), 166.

24. R. Nathaniel Dett, ed., *Religious Folk-Songs of the Negro as Sung at Hampton Institute* (Hampton: Hampton Institute Press, 1927), 110.

25. Ibid., 112.

26. Abernethy, *Singin' Texas*, 166–168.

27. Spalding, *Encyclopedia of Black Folklore and Humor*, 547.

28. Ibid., 560.

29. Ibid., 559.